The Land of Gold

Cornell University

Judith M. Bovensiepen

The Land of Gold

Post-Conflict Recovery and Cultural Revival

in Independent Timor-Leste

SOUTHEAST ASIA PROGRAM PUBLICATIONS
Southeast Asia Program
Cornell University
Ithaca, New York
2015

Cornell Southeast Asia Program Publications
640 Stewart Avenue, Ithaca, NY 14850-3857

Studies on Southeast Asia Series No. 67

Printed in the United States of America

ISBN: hc 978-0-87727-797-2
ISBN: pb 978-0-87727-767-5

Cover: designed by Kat Dalton

Cover image: Lulik site that is said to harbor gold. Photograph by Mathijs Pelkmans, 2015. Used with permission.

For Antje and Ana

TABLE OF CONTENTS

ACKNOWLEDGMENTS

This book would not have been possible without the hospitality and generosity of people in Funar, Laclubar, Dili, and other regions of Timor-Leste. My greatest obligation is to the couple whom I lived with and to the adults and children who were part of the household and looked after me during times that were not always easy.

It seems unjust that many of those who are the main contributors to anthropological monographs often remain unnamed. After careful deliberation and with a sense of unease, I nevertheless decided not to identify by their real names the people who feature in this book, apart from those who are no longer alive or who are public personalities. Regrettably, the use of pseudonyms has the unintended effect of preventing me from properly acknowledging those who contributed the most to this book. However, given that the book contains discussions of some sensitive issues, I decided that the protection of people's identities is more important. I am greatly indebted to all those who contributed to this study and thank each and every one of them for sharing with me some of their lives, their ideas, and their concerns.

During my preparations for this study and while living in Timor-Leste, a number of individuals gave me helpful advice, including Andreas Borgerhoff, Estêvão Cabral, Peter Carey, Phyllis Ferguson, Andrea Fleschenberg, Lusia Freitas, David Hicks, Tanja Hohe, Alexander Loch, Victoria Marwek-Smith, Andrew McWilliam, Andrea Molnar, Tracy Morgan, Monika Schlicher, the brothers of S. João de Deus, and the Maryknoll Sisters in Aileu. Jill Jolliffe put me in touch with Domingos de Oliveira, who helped me to find a home in the Laclubar subdistrict, and I am especially grateful to both of them. For their support and friendship while I lived in Timor-Leste and afterward, I offer my deep gratitude to Fidelis Magalhães, Cris Carrascalão, Seba Guterres, Selma Hayati, José and Lidia Hermenegildo, David Letishevsky, Lila, Hermenegildo Soares, Mica Barreto Soares, Fabia Tilman, Josh Trinidade, Sally Trobert, Maria Tschanz, and Eoghan Walsh. I also thank César Melito, from the National Institute of Statistics, for generously providing me with maps, and the staff members at the GIZ (Deutsche Gesellschaft für Internationale Zusammenarbeit), especially Heinz Heile, for their logistical assistance throughout my stay. Moreover, I am indebted to Catharina van Klinken for her invaluable help regarding language both during and after my fieldwork.

This book is based on my doctoral dissertation, at the London School of Economics and Political Science (LSE), and I thank those staff members who commented on various stages of my research in personal meetings or during writing-up seminars. These include Maurice Bloch, Stephan Feuchtwang, Michael Lambek, Gonçalo D. Santos, and Charles Stafford. I owe special thanks to those who supervised me at different points: Catherine Allerton, for her continuous support, and for her astute comments on countless chapters and drafts; Rita Astuti, for her analytical rigor, her dedication, and, most importantly, for not letting me get away with anything; and Matthew Engelke, for his empathy and his continuous encouragement to explore theoretically more imaginative lines of inquiry. Additionally, I am very grateful to my PhD examiners, Michael Scott and Janet Hoskins, whose careful and detailed feedback helped me to develop my ideas further in this book, and I am deeply indebted to Elizabeth Traube, whose critical comments on my work have been invaluable.

On the journey to complete this monograph, I received advice and feedback from a number of friends and colleagues, including assiduous proofreading, encouragement, detailed criticism, and comments. I am especially grateful to Indira Arumugam, Susana Barnes, Michaela Benson, Vicky Boydell, Gareth Dale, Ankur Datta, Katie Dow, Michael Goshgarian, Lizzy Hull, Gordon Lynch, Gwyneth Roberts, Dave Robinson, Ricardo Roque, Andrew Sanchez, Bob Smith, Hans Steinmüller, and Susana Viegas. For their support and feedback, I would also like to thank colleagues at the musée du quai Branly, where I did my postdoc between 2010–11, and at the University of Kent, where I have been working since. Special thanks go to the members of Kent's anthropology staff seminar, where some of my work was discussed, and especially to Roy Ellen and David Henig, who provided valuable written feedback on many of the chapters in this book.

The research on which this monograph is based was made possible through the financial support from a number of institutions, including the Economic and Social Research Council, the Wenner-Gren Foundation for Anthropological Research, the German National Academic Foundation, the British Foundation for Women Academics, the Association for Southeast Asian Studies of the UK, the Evans Fund of Cambridge University, and the musée du quai Branly. I also offer my thanks to the editors of the *Journal of the Royal Anthropological Institute, American Ethnologist,* and *The Asia Pacific Journal of Anthropology* for allowing me to reprint parts of articles already published in their journals. Large sections of Chapter 2 were published in the *Journal of the Royal Anthropological Institute* under the title "Words of the Ancestors: Disembodied Knowledge and Secrecy in East Timor."[1] An earlier version of Chapter 4 was published in *American Ethnologist,* "Installing the Insider 'Outside': House Reconstruction and the Transformation of Binary Ideologies in Independent Timor-Leste."[2] And a shorter version of Chapter 6 was published in *The Asia Pacific Journal of Anthropology* under the title "Paying for the Dead: On the Politics of Death in Independent Timor-Leste."[3]

Two people stand out particularly: Douglas Kammen and Janet Gunter. Their academic guidance, reading of chapter drafts, all-night discussions, fieldwork visits, and friendship has shaped this book in countless ways and they both know how much their input has meant to me. The same goes for members of my family who

---

[1] Judith Bovensiepen, "Words of the Ancestors: Disembodied Knowledge and Secrecy in East Timor," *Journal of the Royal Anthropological Institute* 20, no. 1 (2014): 56–73, http://onlinelibrary.wiley.com/doi/10.1111/1467-9655.12079/abstract, accessed June 30, 2015.

[2] Judith Bovensiepen, "Installing the Insider 'Outside': House Reconstruction and the Transformation of Binary Ideologies in Independent Timor-Leste," *American Ethnologist* 41, no. 2 (2014): 290–304,

http://onlinelibrary.wiley.com/doi/10.1111/amet.12076/abstract, accessed June 30, 2015.

[3] Judith Bovensiepen, "Paying for the Dead: On the Politics of Death in Independent Timor-Leste," *The Asia Pacific Journal of Anthropology* 15, no. 2 (2014): 103–22. http://www.tandfonline.com/doi/abs/10.1080/14442213.2014.892528#.VJVBucAiA, accessed June 30, 2015.

have been incredibly encouraging. I thank my father, Gustav Bovensiepen, and his partner, Christa Braun, for visiting me in Timor-Leste in 2006. Special thanks also go to Mathijs Pelkmans, for his love, feedback and gentle reassurance during the final stages of this project, and to our daughter, Sasha, for doing her best to distract me from completing it. Finally, I would not have been able to write this monograph without the strength and endless support of two exceptional women—Antje Winkelmann, my mother, and Ana do Rosário, who has been a mother to me—and it is to them that I dedicate this book.

NOTES ON
LANGUAGE AND TRANSCRIPTION

The language spoken in the Laclubar subdistrict is an Austronesian language called Idaté, which is closely related to Galoli, Lakalei, and Tetum.[1] In 2010, there were an estimated 13,500 Idaté speakers living in Timor-Leste.[2] During my fieldwork, I learned Idaté without access to any official guides to its grammar or vocabulary. There is one publication about Idaté in Indonesian, *Struktur Bahasa Idaté*, published in 1994 by the Indonesian government, but it contains only some basic phrases. I did, however, have access to personal word lists compiled by Idaté speakers that helped me to learn some basic expressions.

The lack of accessible published documentation of the Idaté language poses a problem for transcription. I have resolved the issue by modeling my spelling of Idaté words and sentences on the spelling of the national language, Tetum, the orthography of which has been standardized by the National Institute of Linguistics.[3] For sounds that are not found in Tetum, I have tried to be as consistent and systematic as possible, but the transcription of words still contains my own idiosyncrasies. A study by a trained linguist would be necessary for full documentation of Idaté and for deciding upon a more adequate writing system.

Timor-Leste is a linguistically complex country, and during my fieldwork I communicated not just in Idaté, but also in Tetum, which I learned first. As a result, some citations in the book are in both languages. Moreover, Idaté contains many loanwords from Tetum, Portuguese, and Indonesian. I have not marked these as being non-Idaté words unless the speaker specifically recognized them as such. Throughout the book, italicized words and phrases are in Idaté unless I note that they are in a different language, such as Tetum (T.), Portuguese (Pt.), or Indonesian (In.)

---

[1] Stephen A. Wurm and Shirô Hattori, *Language Atlas of the Pacific Area* (Canberra: Australian Academy of the Humanities in collaboration with the Japan Academy, 1981), 40.

[2] National Statistics Directorate (NSD) and United Nations Population Fund (UNFPA), *Population and Housing Census of Timor-Leste 2010* (Dili: NSD and UNFPA, 2011), 203. The number of Idaté speakers has increased significantly since 2004, when slightly more than 9,700 Idaté speakers were recorded, according to the NDS and UNFPA census: *Timor-Leste Census of Population and Housing 2004* (Dili: NDS and UNFPA, 2006), 80.

[3] As a reference, I used Geoffrey Hull, *Standard Tetum-English Dictionary*, 3rd ed. (Winston Hills, Australia: Sebastiao Aparicio da Silva Project in association with Instituto Nacional de Linguistica, Timor-Leste, 1999).

THE LAND OF GOLD

"Menina, are you not scared of the land?" Olívia asked me with surprise.[1]

It was late in the evening. The young teenager was sitting on her narrow iron bed in the room next to mine, with only a small candle on the floor to provide some light. From a neighbor's house in the distance, we could hear loud mortuary chanting, called *loli*. A man had died there that morning, so his relatives had gathered throughout the night to guard his body and keep him company. The melancholic mourning chants filled the night sky, making sleep impossible. Hearing whispers in the next room, I had gone to join Olívia and the other teenager, Helena, in their bed for company.

"Scared of the land?" I responded, wrapping a sarong over my head to protect me from the cold. "Why should I be scared of the land?"

"Oh, when a person dies and you sing the *loli*, the devils in the land start to dance," Olívia said, glancing shyly at Helena for reassurance. "They come out of the earth, and they can grab your leg and hurt you," she continued with greater determination.

"But you have to sing the *loli*," added Helena grandly, "to show that you remember the dead."

When I entered the room, Helena had been lying down and had just managed to convince Olívia to massage her legs. Now, the two of them were sitting bolt upright, huddled together under their thin blanket.

"This is what we do," Helena continued. "You need to follow the ancestors. To remember … to show respect."

"I am scared of the land," whispered Olívia—more to herself than to us—as the sound of the mourning chants grew in a crescendo.

"Scared of the land," repeated Helena, wrapping her blanket around me and poking Olívia to encourage her to continue the leg massage.

When Olívia refused, Helena, perhaps emboldened by my presence, started to tease Olívia with stories about land spirits, gruesome devils, and the dangers of the land. This went on until the head of the household, who slept in the next room, told us somewhat angrily to be quiet because he was trying to sleep.

• • •

How do people come to terms with experiences of systematic oppression and military occupation? What does it mean to leave your home behind, to be separated from the place where you and generations of your family once lived? How are these experiences expressed, and do such expressions facilitate healing? This book

---

[1] To protect the anonymity of research participants, I have used pseudonyms for all personal names, apart from those who are no longer alive or who are public personalities.

explores those questions by focusing on Funar, a village located in the mountainous interior of the central highlands of Timor-Leste, whose inhabitants rarely spoke about their experiences during the Indonesian occupation in the years immediately after Timor-Leste gained independence. Countering the assumption that the recounting of traumatic memories has by definition cathartic effects, this book explores other nonverbal forms of coming to terms with the past.

On December 7, 1975, Indonesian planes dropped paratroopers in the waterfront area of East Timor's capital city, Dili. The Indonesian military invaded the former Portuguese colony from air, land, and sea. During the years that followed, thousands of people fled to the mountains as Indonesian troops advanced farther into the countryside. Many spent months and years in hiding. It is estimated that at least a quarter of the entire population died as a consequence of the Indonesian occupation, either directly in fighting or as a result of military activity, or from famine and disease. The twenty-four years that Indonesia illegally occupied the territory (1975–99) included forced dislocation of the population, widespread arbitrary detention, torture, abuse, and sexual violence.[2]

Despite the systematic persecution of its political opponents, Indonesia's leaders and military faced continuous opposition. Timorese guerrillas sustained the armed resistance for twenty-four years, while figures in the East Timorese diaspora kept up diplomatic efforts to restore independence. The occupation ended as brutally as it began. When a large majority of the population voted in favor of independence in a UN-administered referendum in 1999, the Indonesian military and local militias launched a relentless campaign of persecution against suspected supporters.[3] During Indonesia's scorched-earth withdrawal, around fifteen hundred civilians were killed and several hundred thousand people displaced, and over 70 percent of the

---

[2] For a discussion of the death toll, see Ben Kiernan, "The Demography of Genocide in Southeast Asia: The Death Tolls in Cambodia, 1975–79, and East Timor, 1975–80," *Critical Asian Studies* 35, no. 4 (2003): 594. During the Indonesian occupation, it was often estimated that one-third of the population—over 200,000 people—died as a consequence of the occupation. The Timor-Leste Commission for Reception, Truth, and Reconciliation (CAVR, Comissão de Acolhimento, Verdade e Reconciliação de Timor-Leste), which conducted a detailed statistical analysis, found that there were 102,800–183,000 conflict-related deaths between 1974 and 1999, with 55.5 percent of surveyed households reporting one or more displacement events during this period; see CAVR, *Chega! Final Report of the Commission for Reception, Truth, and Reconciliation in Timor-Leste* (Dili, Timor-Leste: CAVR, 2006), part 6:2. For details on the human rights violations that took place during the twenty-four-year Indonesian occupation, see also: Amnesty International, *Timor-Leste Violations of Human Rights: Extrajudicial Executions, "Disappearances," Torture, and Political Imprisonment, 1975–1984* (London: Amnesty International Publications, 1985); James Dunn, *East Timor: A Rough Passage to Independence*, third ed. (Double Bay, Australia: Longueville Books, 2003); Geoffrey Gunn, *Timor Loro Sae: 500 Years* (Macau: Livros do Oriente, 1999); John Martinkus, *A Dirty Little War* (Sydney: Random House Australia, 2001); Joseph Nevins, *A Not-So-Distant Horror: Mass Violence in Timor-Leste* (Ithaca: Cornell University Press, 2005); and John G. Taylor, *East Timor: The Price of Freedom* (London: Zed Books, 1999).

[3] The referendum took place just after the collapse of Indonesia's authoritarian New Order regime, with 78.5 percent of those registered voting in favor of independence. Geoffrey Robinson has shown that the brutal campaign against suspected supporters of independence in the aftermath of the ballot was not, as official Indonesian sources propagated, the result of spontaneous "cultural" clashes, but, rather, was strategically planned and orchestrated by the Indonesian military and police. See Geoffrey Robinson, *"If You Leave Us Here, We Will Die": How Genocide Was Stopped in East Timor* (Princeton: Princeton University Press, 2009), 10ff.

country's infrastructure was destroyed.[4] The systematic violence was brought to an end by a UN-sanctioned military intervention. A UN mission (UNTAET, United Nations Transitional Administration in East Timor) then proceeded to administer the territory from late 1999 until May 2002, when independence was restored and Timor-Leste became a sovereign state.[5]

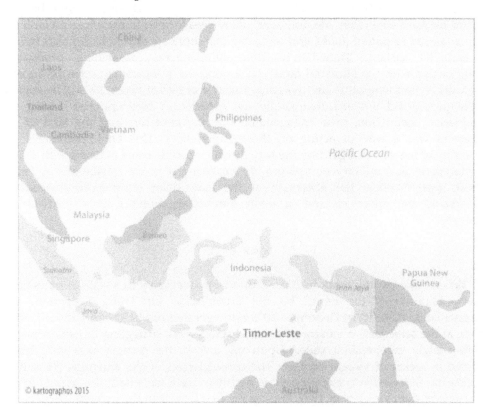

The island of Timor is situated at the easternmost tip of the Lesser Sunda Islands
(map by Julia Beer, used with permission)

---

[4] Figures for those internally displaced and for those forced to move to Indonesian West Timor vary. Robinson maintains that in 1999, an estimated 400,000 people were displaced. See Geoffrey Robinson, *East Timor 1999: Crimes against Humanity*, report commissioned by the United Nations Office of the High Commissioner for Human Rights (OHCHR), July 2003 (Jakarta, Indonesia, and Dili, Timor-Leste: HAK Association & Institute for Policy Research and Advocacy, 2006), 1. The CAVR report states that in the same year, 250,000–280,000 people were deported to Indonesian West Timor while 300,000 fled into the hills and forests near their homes. See *Chega!*, part 7.3: 123.

[5] Its official name is *República Democrática de Timor-Leste* (RDTL), Timor-Leste being Portuguese for "East Timor." The island of Timor is situated at the easternmost tip of the Lesser Sunda Islands, at the crossroads between Southeast Asia and the Pacific region (see map, this page). Its western half forms part of Indonesia, while the RDTL comprises the eastern half as well as the enclave of Oecussi and the island of Atáuro. Another common name for the country is *Timor Lorosa'e,* which is Tetum for East Timor (literally, "Timor of the Rising Sun"). In this book, I use "Timor-Leste" when referring to the period from 1999 to present, "East Timor" for the time of the Indonesian occupation (1975–99), and "Portuguese Timor" for the Portuguese colonial period.

Indonesia's occupation lasted for almost a quarter of a century and, for many, independence was a moment of radical transformation and relief. In Funar, however, the period directly following independence was not one during which people spoke openly about past suffering. Instead, villagers expressed an urgent concern for respecting the dead—as Helena explained—and for reconnecting with the ancestral land. In fact, those two concerns were intricately connected, since people become part of the land when they die. In Funar, many sites located in the ancestral land are seen as sacred or potent (*lulik*), and some say that there are vast gold deposits buried beneath its surface. Immediately after independence, sustaining productive relationships with the ancestral land was among the foremost concerns of Funar's residents, even though this land was also a source of fear at times. As will be shown, while people did not articulate orally the experiences they endured during the Indonesian occupation, their engagement with the ancestors and the land of the ancestors was a way of acting on those experiences. This book challenges the centrality of narratives regarding the way in which people come to terms with forced displacement and military occupation. By exploring how the inhabitants of Funar rebuilt their lives in the aftermath of the Indonesian occupation, it seeks to understand the unspoken and at times nonhuman dimensions of post-conflict recovery.

• • •

When I started fieldwork in 2005, Timor-Leste was truly in a state of transition.[6] The publication of the report by the Commission for Truth, Reception, and Reconciliation (CAVR) in December 2005 reinvigorated public debates about justice, while at the same time a variety of political actors were struggling to gain influence in the newly independent state.[7] Upon my arrival, the country was still clearly scarred by years of violent conflict. The consequences of the atrocities committed during the Indonesian occupation were highly evident, especially the effects of the post-referendum violence of 1999. During my first travels in the western districts, the physical reminders of this violent past were visible in many of the villages and towns I visited: empty, deserted, or burnt-out houses; destroyed roads; and, at times, a desolate and somber atmosphere. Throughout the course of the first conversations that I had during these excursions, I encountered a flood of painful narratives about the loss, separation, dislocation, and hardships caused by the Indonesian occupation and its ongoing repercussions.

In the village of Funar, where I ended up carrying out most of my fieldwork, the traces of the Indonesian occupation were less apparent. Funar is part of the Idaté-speaking Laclubar subdistrict, which lies approximately 120 kilometers from the

---

[6] This book is based on over twenty-two months of fieldwork carried out between 2005 and 2015. My doctoral fieldwork took place between November 2005 and August 2007, and several shorter postdoctoral field trips took place in 2010, 2012 and 2015.

[7] CAVR was an independent statutory authority established in 2001 to document and record information about violence and violent crimes committed between 1974–99. It was led by seven East Timorese commissioners and also undertook community reconciliation for less serious crimes. The commission was dissolved in December 2005 and published a report (*Chega!*) with its findings, which contained extensive policy recommendations.

capital city of Dili.[8] Situated on a mountain ridge in the central highlands, Funar could only be reached on foot or by horse when I first arrived. The verdant pastures, fields, and fruit trees stood out sharply against the charming red earth of the village center. There were no ruins or abandoned homes that characterized the post-conflict landscape in many other parts of Timor-Leste—neither smoke-stained and fire-gutted houses, nor piles of bricks or decaying walls covered with political graffiti. No destroyed roads led to the village, just a narrow footpath that cut through thick forest. Funar's houses and gardens were carefully tended. The pigs were tied up, dozing peacefully under houses built on long stilts to discourage rats from entering them. The school and the health center were the only buildings in the village with stone walls; most of the houses were made from woven bamboo and had hard-packed dirt floors and tin or thatched roofs, stained black by the smoke from the hearths.

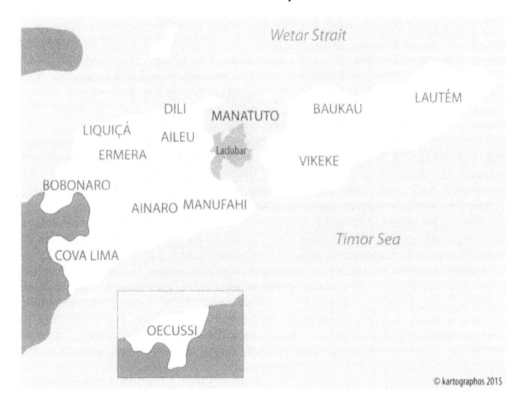

Laclubar is the second-most populous of Manatuto's six subdistricts
(map by Julia Beer, used with permission)

---

[8] Laclubar is one of six subdistricts within Manatuto district (see map, this page) and, with a population of 11,370 in 2010, is the second most populous of these; see National Statistics Directorate (NSD) and the United Nations Population Fund (UNFPA), *Population and Housing Census of Timor-Leste 2010*, 14. Laclubar is subdivided into six *suco* (administrative units or villages): Funar, Fatumakerek, Sananain, Batara, Manelima, and Orlalan. Laclubar Town is located in Orlalan. I carried out research both in Laclubar Town and Funar, spending about two-thirds of my time in the latter.

My original impression of Funar as an old, archetypical "traditional" village turned out to be inaccurate in many ways.[9] In fact, it had been rebuilt in the 1990s and its current location differed slightly from its original one. During the occupation, the Indonesian military had forcibly relocated the entire population to Laclubar Town. The goal of this resettlement program was to prevent villagers from supporting the armed resistance movement that was active in the central mountain range. The houses that had initially appeared to be longstanding had, in fact, been built only ten years earlier, when people were granted permission to start returning to their ancestral lands.

When I set out to conduct fieldwork in Timor-Leste, my initial objective had been to study the consequences and memories of the Indonesian occupation. However, unless prompted, the inhabitants of Funar rarely mentioned this period in their history. To an outsider, it seemed at times as if this place had been unaffected by the violent events of the occupation, which had come to an end six years before my arrival. Instead of focusing on the traumatic events of the recent past, the people of Funar nostalgically stressed their connections with the more distant past, emphasizing their ownership of long-established customary knowledge that had been inherited from the ancestors. To highlight the power and wealth of the ancestors, villagers told me that during ancestral times, golden discs (*ilis meran; belak mean* T.) would fly to Funar, and that specific sites in the landscape with an ancestral connection harbor vast gold deposits. The time of the ancestors was one of prosperity and well-being. To recreate such wealth in the present, some of the residents maintained, one had to revive ancient traditions to "follow the ways of the ancestors." This was done by rebuilding ancestral houses and reestablishing appropriate relations with the ancestral land through a series of ceremonies.

What is the significance of the ancestral connections that villagers are reviving in the independence period? And what does this tell us about the ways in which people come to terms with experiences of forced dislocation and military occupation? There is no doubt that the inhabitants of this region endured severe hardships during the Indonesian occupation, yet these experiences were rarely expressed in narratives of suffering, as is common in other parts of Timor-Leste.[10] Why was it, then, that people in Funar seemed to be so unconcerned by the recent occupation, yet so attached to their ancestral land and customs? The key to understanding this puzzle, I came to realize, lay in exploring the specific political history of this region, as well as the intricate interconnection of place and personhood.

This book focuses on the intense efforts Funar residents invested in reanimating the ancestral landscape and reinvigorating ancestral practices. The cultural revival is itself a form of post-conflict recovery—local residents distance themselves from certain aspects of the past while simultaneously feeling nostalgic for a long-lost time of prosperity, the timeless golden land of the ancestors. By engaging in this complex balancing act, the residents of Funar inadvertently modified the very cultural logics

---

[9] Compare with: James Ferguson, *Expectations of Modernity: Myths and Meanings of Urban Life on the Zambian Copperbelt* (Berkeley: University of California Press), 208; and Angie Bexley and Maj Nygaard-Christensen, introduction to "Engaging Processes of Sense-making and Negotiation in Contemporary Timor-Leste," *Asia Pacific Journal of Anthropology* 14, no. 5 (2013): 399.

[10] For an excellent analysis of local reworkings of national narratives of suffering in the Mambai-speaking region of Aileu, see Elizabeth G. Traube, "Unpaid Wages: Local Narratives and the Imagination of the Nation," *Asia Pacific Journal of Anthropology* 8, no. 1 (2007): 9–25.

they sought to revive. The cultural revival has hence challenged existing modes of sociality and has recalibrated modes of social engagement, engendering new conflicts over status and influence that have disrupted the social fabric. By focusing on the ways in which Funar residents reinvigorate their relationship with the ancestral past and the ancestral land, while at the same time describing how these relationships are altered by historical events, this book sets out to develop a dynamic interpretation of the ongoing processes of place and post-conflict recovery in Timor-Leste.

The monograph addresses three main themes that are crucial in making sense of the ways in which Funar's residents have reestablished themselves in place and history in the independence period. First, it explores how human subjectivity in this region is interwoven with the environment and how the affective relationship with the ancestral land shapes the recovery process. A second focus is the significance of ritual and customary practices to ways in which status and political influence are recognized and renegotiated. Finally, the collective amnesia of Funar's inhabitants is examined against the backdrop of their exclusion from current nation-building processes and the region's complex colonial history. The remainder of this introduction explores these three themes in more detail.

Recovering the Lost Land

In 1978, the Indonesian military imprisoned four-year-old Maria José Franco Pereira and her mother in Comarca jail. Situated in Balide, Dili, the prison was built in 1963, when the Portuguese colonial administration governed the eastern part of the island of Timor. By 1978, the Indonesian military, which had invaded the country three years earlier, was incarcerating political prisoners there.

Maria and her mother spent over a year in Comarca. During that time, the young girl followed her mother everywhere. She watched as her mother was forced to kneel under the red-and-white Indonesian flag for hours in the midday sun; she saw her mother being tortured. Twenty-five years later, at a public hearing organized by the Commission for Reception, Truth, and Reconciliation (CAVR) in February 2003, Maria Pereira gave testimony describing one of the days in Comarca prison:

> A Chinese man who owned a store in Santa Cruz had come to visit and brought food [...] such as cake, *tahu* [tofu], and red bean soup. Some guards called to me and ordered me to take the bean soup that was hot, and take it to the man who was torturing my mother under the Red White flag. I took it to the man [...], who ordered me to pour it over my mother's head. I was small and not tall enough, so they took a cement block and ordered me to stand on it [...] and by snapping at me and tweaking my eyebrows, they forced me to pour the hot soup over my mother's head while she was in the kneeling position. My mother was just quiet; her face was red, her body all wet and dirty with the soup. [...] That was when I realized that I had urinated in my pants.[11]

Today, Maria works as a police officer in what is now the independent country of Timor-Leste. The Commission for Reception, Truth, and Reconciliation in Timor-

---

[11] *Report of the Inauguration Ceremony and 2nd National Public Hearing* (Balide, Dili: CAVR, February 17–18, 2003; report February 19, 2003), 6.

Leste turned Comarca prison into its headquarters. The commission collected thousands of similar statements that document the atrocities committed during the twenty-four-year Indonesian occupation of East Timor.

In the village of Funar, I heard few narratives of the kind collected by CAVR.[12] The commission is itself based on the assumption that truth-telling, i.e., revisiting the past through narrative accounts, can lead to healing and reconciliation. However, instead of verbalizing memories of the past, residents of Funar concentrated their energies on reestablishing relations with the ancestral land and reviving ancestral traditions. How can we understand the absence of narratives of suffering in this region and the value people ascribe to the ancestral land? And what does this tell us about the different ways in which communities engage with traumatic events of the past?

Violence, suffering, and recovery have only gained real prominence in the anthropological literature over the past two decades. The growing scholarship includes examinations of the structural conditions that facilitate and promote violence, as well as the failure of international institutions and legal frameworks to prevent conflict and their role in promoting—or even producing—it.[13] There are studies of the subjective experience of violence and people's varied responses to violent conflict and war, as well as studies of reconciliation and recognition in post-conflict situations.[14] Yet these approaches all center on the human-human dimension

---

[12] One notable exception here were the statements given by political leaders from Laclubar, a number of whom testified in front of the commission (e.g., Domingo de Oliveira, who was a member of the party *União Democrática Timorense* (the Timorese Democratic Union, UDT), and José Estevão, who was a commissioner himself and former supporter of APODETI (*Associação Popular Democrática Timorense*, Timorese Popular Democratic Association, East Timor).

[13] See: Paul Farmer, *Pathologies of Power: Health, Human Rights, and the New War on the Poor* (Berkeley: University of California Press, 2003); and Arthur Kleinman, Veena Das, and Margaret Lock, *Social Suffering: Essays* (Berkeley: University of California Press, 1997).

[14] See: Veena Das et al., *Remaking a World: Violence, Social Suffering, and Recovery* (Berkeley: University of California Press, 2001); Veena Das et al., *Violence and Subjectivity* (Berkeley: University of California Press, 2000); Linda Green, *Fear as a Way of Life: Mayan Widows in Rural Guatemala* (New York: Columbia University Press, 1999); Nigel Eltringham, *Accounting for Horror: Post-Genocide Debates in Rwanda* (London: Pluto Press, 2004); Heonik Kwon, *Ghosts of War in Vietnam* (Cambridge: Cambridge University Press, 2008); Heonik Kwon, *After the Massacre: Commemoration and Consolation in Ha My and My Lai* (Berkeley: University of California Press, 2006); Mahmood Mamdani, *Colonialism, Nativism, and the Genocide in Rwanda* (Princeton: Princeton University Press, 2001); Elizabeth Povinelli, *The Cunning of Recognition: Indigenous Alterities in the Making of Multiculturalism* (Durham: Duke University Press, 2002); Fiona Ross, *Bearing Witness: Women and the Truth and Reconciliation Commission in South Africa* (London: Pluto Press, 2003); Richard A. Wilson, *The Politics of Truth and Reconciliation in South Africa: Legitimizing the Post-Apartheid State* (Cambridge: Cambridge University Press, 2001); and Judith Zur, *Violent Memories: Mayan War Widows in Guatemala* (Boulder: Westview Press, 1998).

In recent years, a large range of books and articles has been published about the Indonesian occupation of East Timor. Some of these studies have focused on the nature of the occupation and resistance; see, for example: CAVR, *Chega!*; Dunn, *East Timor: A Rough Passage*; Constancio Pinto and Matthew Jardine, *East Timor's Unfinished Struggle: Inside the Timorese Resistance* (Boston: South End Press, 1997); and Gunn, *Timor Loro Sae*. Others have focused on the participation of the Catholic church in the resistance, for example, Robert Archer, "The Catholic Church in East Timor," in *East Timor at the Crossroads: The Forging of a Nation*, ed. Peter Carey and G. Carter Bentley (Honolulu: University of Hawai'i Press, 1995), 120–33; and the role of women in the resistance, for example, Irena Cristalis and Catherine Scott, *Independent Women: The Story of Women's Activism in East Timor* (London: CIIR Catholic Institute for

of violence and recovery. What emerges in Funar is the significance of the nonhuman environment on the ways in which people remake their lives after a quarter of a century of military occupation. Focusing on the nonhuman and nonverbal dimensions of post-conflict recovery allows me to interrogate the commonly held psychological assumption that recounting traumatic events leads—by definition—to healing and has cathartic effects. Instead, I examine the repercussions of conflict and displacement by focusing on people's engagement with the lived environment.[15]

Most residents of the Laclubar subdistrict are engaged in slash-and-burn farming and shifting cultivation, mostly at the subsistence level. Due to the steep and rugged terrain, the staple crops are maize and various tubers, such as cassava, taro, and sweet potatoes.[16] Coffee is one of the major cash crops, and there is also an active trade in palm wine and liquor. The land is thus the main guarantor of people's livelihoods. Yet the land is not solely of economic significance; it is also considered a source of life and prosperity. Funar's residents described their relationship with the ancestral land through the common Austronesian botanical metaphor of a banyan tree. For them, the land of the ancestors is the "trunk of life" (*mori ni uun*) and the descendants are the "tip"—that is, the flowers (*hunan*) and fruits (*huan*). This metaphor is, in fact, key to understanding how people locate themselves geographically and historically.

When people die, they are considered to "go back to the land"—they become part of the land as ancestors. Burial is perceived as a return because human beings are considered to have emerged from the land when they came into being. A number of cosmogonic myths in this region recount how human beings were born from a particular site in the landscape. Before life and after death, humans and the land are thus composed of the same substance. The unity of land and people is temporarily relinquished during life, when humans are separated from the land. This relationship with the land is crucial to the way people perceive themselves as subjects. Human subjectivity emerges through a process of separation from the land. The ancestral land is not just an object to be acted upon through agricultural labor; it is part of the process by which humans come into being.

International Relations, 2005). Others feature the role of the international community; see, for example: James Cotton, *East Timor, Australia, and the Regional Order: Intervention and Its Aftermath in Southeast Asia* (London and New York: Routledge Curzon, 2004); Nevins, *A Not-So-Distant Horror*; and Samuel Pietsch, *The Deputy-Sheriff Warns his Apurs: Australia's Military Intervention in East Timor, 1999* (PhD thesis, Australian National University, 2009). Especially with regard to the contested oil resources of the Timor Sea, see Paul Cleary, *Shakedown: Australia's Grab for Timor Oil* (Crows Nest, Australia: Allen & Unwin, 2007). Research has also been undertaken regarding the role of the UN in the reconstruction process and the country's entry into the market economy; see Damien Kingsbury and Michael Leach, *East Timor: Beyond Independence* (Melbourne, Australia: Monash University Press, 2007).

[15] Compare with: Jens Meierhenrich, "The Transformation of Lieux de Mémoire: The Nyabarongo River in Rwanda, 1992–2009," *Anthropology Today* 25, no. 5 (2009): 13–19; Katharina Schramm, "Introduction: Landscapes of Violence: Memory and Sacred Space," ed. Katharina Schramm, special issue, *History & Memory* 23, no. 1 (2011): 5–22; and Christopher C. Taylor, *Sacrifice as Terror: The Rwandan Genocide of 1994* (Oxford: Berg, 2001), 128.

[16] Other agricultural produce includes beans, peanuts, various leafy vegetables, pumpkins, bananas, citrus fruits, avocados, mangos, and chilies; some people also collect wild honey. In contrast to the large rice paddies in some of the lowland areas, only relatively small patches of dry-rice fields are found in this mountainous subdistrict.

In many areas of eastern Indonesia and Timor-Leste, place is an essential dimension of the way in which people relate to the past and to each other.[17] The pertinence of place for ways of being in the world resonates with theories of phenomenologists like Edward Casey, who argues that there is a primordial dimension to place; dwelling exists prior to any other form of human experience.[18] Or as Timothy Ingold argues, the landscape becomes meaningful through people's constant practical engagement with it; meaning is not "attached to the world," but rather "gathered from it."[19] If place is an essential dimension of human ways of being in the world, surely it must also play a key role in the way in which people recover from occupation and conflict.

While reunification with the ancestral land is part of how Funar's residents come to terms with the past, this place is also a source of anxiety, respect, and awe. As the opening vignette illustrates, villagers repeatedly expressed a fear of the land. Such fear was experienced particularly intensely after a person had died. Hence, the fear of the land is also a fear of the deceased, who will become part of the land as ancestors. The Catholic influence in this region adds another twist to this affective expression, such that the dangers of the land are identified with devils that can "grab your leg."

To understand how the land is at once a source of prosperity and anxiety, this book explores the intersection of recent political events and biblical and cosmological ideas about human origins. To recover from the forced dislocation they experienced under the Indonesian occupation, the highlanders seek to reestablish a mythical primordial unity with the land. However, this unity also has a dark side. The villagers' reengagement with the land is accompanied by a powerful fear: a fear of being swallowed up by the land during life, as one is upon death.

---

[17] See: Peter Bellwood, "Hierarchy, Founder Ideology, and Austronesian Expansion," in *Origins, Ancestry and Alliance: Explorations in Austronesian Ethnography*, eds. James J. Fox and Clifford Sather (Canberra: The Australian National University, 1996), 18–40; James J. Fox, ed., *The Poetic Power of Place: Comparative Perspectives on Austronesian Ideas of Locality* (Canberra: Australian National University, 1997); Andrew McWilliam and Elizabeth G. Traube, eds., *Land and Life in Timor-Leste: Ethnographic Essays* (Canberra: ANU E-Press, 2011); and Thomas Reuter, ed., *Sharing the Earth, Dividing the Land: Land and Territory in the Austronesian World* (Canberra: ANU E-Press, 2006).

[18] Edward S. Casey, *Getting Back into Place: Toward a Renewed Understanding of the Place-World* (Bloomington: Indiana University Press, 1993).

[19] Timothy Ingold, "The Temporality of the Landscape," *World Archaeology* 25, no. 2 (1993): 155. Ingold criticizes the common distinction between the physical features of the "natural landscape" and the "cultural landscape" of representation and symbols; see also Ingold, *The Perception of the Environment: Essays in Livelihood, Dwelling, and Skill* (London: Routledge, 2000), 189. His phenomenological critique is part of a broader shift in anthropology regarding the ways in which relations between human and nonhuman domains are conceptualized; see also: Philippe Descola, "Human Natures," *Social Anthropology/Anthropologie Sociale* 17, no. 2 (2009): 145–57; Philippe Descola, *Par-delà Nature et Culture* (Paris: Gallimard, 2005); Morten A. Pedersen, "Totemism, Animism, and North Asian Indigenous Ontologies," *Journal of the Royal Anthropological Institute* 7, no. 3 (2001): 411–27; Stuart Kirsch, *Reverse Anthropology: Indigenous Analysis of Social and Environmental Relations in New Guinea* (Stanford: Stanford University Press, 2006); Eduardo Viveiros de Castro, "Cosmological Deixis and Amerindian Perspectivism," *Journal of the Royal Anthropological Institute* 4 (1998): 469–88; and Rane Willerslev, *Soul Hunters: Hunting, Animism, and Personhood among the Siberian Yukaghirs* (Berkeley: University of California Press, 2007).

The ancestral land is not just part of the way in which subjects are constituted; it is also a crucial medium in people's relationship with the past. As James Fox has noted, Austronesian populations frequently recount their history through the recitation of place names, a practice he calls "topogeny." Topogenies reflect ancestral journeys through the landscape and therefore relate the entire history of a large group in a semantically condensed form.[20] Thus, the past is not evoked through the recollection of momentous events, but rather by tracing movements across the land. Based on her fieldwork among the Kodi of Sumba, Janet Hoskins has argued that the Kodinese rarely spoke about their past through autobiographical narratives, and thus she suggests focusing on "things" rather than narratives to understand Kodinese life histories.[21] Similarly, Jennifer Cole has examined the absence of memories of the colonial war in Madagascar, focusing instead on the way in which the past emerges in rituals of cattle sacrifice.[22] These cases can help us to understand the situation in Funar, where people likewise engaged with the memories of the colonial and neocolonial past by reinvigorating their relationships with the land and the ancestors, rather than by recounting narratives of suffering.[23]

By showing how people deal with the past nonverbally through their engagement with the lived environment and customary practices, this book moves beyond social constructivist approaches that perpetuate a distinction between the subjective world of humans and the objective domain of the nonhuman environment.[24] Therefore, it speaks to the emergent body of materialist approaches focused on developing object-centered analyses that emphasize the agency of nonhuman objects.[25] Funar offers an opportunity to explore the relationship between human and nonhuman domains in a post-conflict context, and of the tensions engendered by attempts to reanimate the landscape. People's forced dislocation resulting from the Indonesian occupation has both disrupted and reinforced their relationship with the landscape, making visible some of the challenges and tensions inherent in dwelling in an animated environment.

---

[20] James J. Fox, "Place and Landscape in Comparative Austronesian Perspective," in *The Poetic Power of Place*, 9.

[21] Janet Hoskins, *The Play of Time: Kodi Perspectives on Calendars, History, and Exchange* (Berkeley: University of California Press, 1993), 137. See also: Janet Hoskins, *Biographical Objects: How Things Tell the Stories of People's Lives* (New York: Routledge, 1998).

[22] Jennifer Cole, *Forget Colonialism? Sacrifice and the Art of Memory in Madagascar* (Berkeley: University of California Press, 2001).

[23] Studies of memory and history have of course made related arguments about the significance of embodied memory, about the transformation of individual into collective memory, and about the difference between representations of the past and actual presentation. The large philosophical and anthropological literature on memory cannot be discussed here in detail, but these issues have been examined, for example, in: Maurice Bloch, *How We Think They Think: Anthropological Approaches to Cognition, Memory and Literacy* (Oxford: Westview, 1998); Michel de Certeau, *The Practice of Everyday Life* (Berkeley: University of California Press, 1988); Maurice Halbwachs, *On Collective Memory* (Chicago: University of Chicago press, 1992); and Paul Ricoeur, *Histoire et Vérité* (Paris: Le Seuil, 1955).

[24] See: Timothy Ingold, "Rethinking the Animate, Re-animating Thought," *Ethnos* 71, no. 1 (2006): 9–20; Ingold, "The Temporality of the Landscape"; and Willerslev, *Soul Hunters*.

[25] See, for example, Bruno Latour, *We Have Never Been Modern* (London: Harvester Wheatsheaf, 1993). See also Yael Navaro-Yashin, *The Make-Believe Space: Affective Geography in a Postwar Polity* (Durham: Duke University Press, 2012), 5.

By concentrating on people's relationship with the lived environment, my approach seeks to go beyond an emphasis on suffering that evokes the language of trauma.[26] As Fassin and Rechtman have pointed out, "over the last twenty-five years, trauma has become established as a unique way of appropriating the traces of history and one of the dominant modes of representing our relationship with the past."[27] The focus on psychological and moral dimensions of conflict seems to have replaced an interest in the political and global inequalities that enable wars to take place. Fassin maintains that where once activists would denounce imperialist domination, defend the revolution of oppressed people, and glorify their resistance, they now favor a psychological vocabulary and "scrutinize the resilience of individuals."[28] This is true not only for scholarship, but also for the self-descriptions mobilized by those who find themselves in situations of oppression, violence, or marginalization.

The case of Timor-Leste illustrates Fassin's argument in many ways: the activist discourse has shifted from mere glorification of resistance movements to focus on their humanitarian and psychological impacts. Whereas once the East Timorese people were venerated for their impressive resistance in the face of brutal oppression, they are now subject to speculation about the impact of trauma and the possibility of psychological reconstruction. It appears that cultural and psychological representations are now more salient than political and economic arguments about equality and redistribution. This psychological perspective is not just an external discourse; it is also one that is readily adopted by many of those who are subject to human rights abuses. As Fassin notes, "humanitarian psychiatry is itself another instance of power that, in war zones particularly, prescribes a certain discourse: its compassion for trauma produces a particular form of subjectification that is imposed on individuals, but through which they can also exist politically."[29] It may be argued that the national narratives about suffering experienced during the Indonesian occupation produced a form of subjectification that allowed Timor-Leste to exist politically as a nation.

Due to peculiar historical circumstances, as I will discuss later, Funar's residents were largely excluded from the national collective imagination that shaped political processes after the restoration of independence. For many residents, there was also a desire for self-determination and for autonomy from those seeking to monopolize power. Yet, the way of achieving this was by reviving the "golden" ancestral past and by looking after the ancestral land. However, reconnecting with the land was not the only way in which Funar residents dealt with the past; there was also a widespread reinvigoration of customary practices.

---

[26] This is not to say that large portions of the East Timorese population were not severely affected by the events of the Indonesian occupation. A report found that in 2000, 7 percent of patients at the Bairo-Pite clinic in Dili had symptoms that matched the criteria for post-traumatic stress disorder (PTSD); see Bahar F. Firoz et al., "Psychiatric Morbidity Associated with Human Rights Abuses in East Timor" (report, Yale Genocide Studies Program, Yale East Timor Project, 2001), http://elsinore.cis.yale.edu/gsp/east_timor/index.html, accessed 12 June 2015.

[27] Didier Fassin and Richard Rechtman, *The Empire of Trauma: An Inquiry into the Condition of Victimhood*, trans. Rachel Gomme (Princeton and Oxford: Princeton University Press, 2009), 15.

[28] Didier Fassin, "The Humanitarian Politics of Testimony: Subjectification through Trauma in the Israeli-Palestinian Conflict," *Cultural Anthropology* 23, no. 3 (2008): 532.

[29] Fassin, "The Humanitarian Politics of Testimony," 534.

RITUAL EFFERVESCENCE

While I was preparing for my first visit to Funar, I met a Catholic priest who was originally from that region. He expressed some surprise at the fact that I wanted to live in the countryside away from the comforts of Dili, but agreed that Funar was an appropriate place for anthropological investigation. Then he added that the inhabitants of Funar had a very strong belief in the ancestors, but that, regrettably, their belief in God was not so fervent. There was some truth to the priest's statement. Apart from some notable exceptions, few of Funar's residents regularly attended church, even though most described themselves as Catholic. Nonetheless, everyone was strongly invested in practices that involved maintaining their relationship with the ancestors.

All Souls' Day (2006; author's photo)

This does not mean that Catholicism did not matter, but residents carefully picked those Catholic-influenced practices and events that appealed to them. One such occasion was All Souls' Day (*Loron Matebian*), which involved paying respect to the ancestors. Compared to the generally low turnout during other Catholic holidays in Funar, this event was well attended, and villagers from every background visited the cemetery in order to remember the dead. Everyone put on their most beautiful clothes, assembled in the village center, and walked to the cemetery in a tight-knit group. Once they arrived at the cemetery, people spread out to go to the graves of their ancestors and put flowers and candles on them (see photo, above). Then, after the candles had been lit, the villagers hurried home. The aim of this communal occasion was to remember the dead appropriately, to keep them satisfied, and to show them that they were not forgotten.

This All Souls' Day celebration was one of a number of ceremonies I witnessed that were aimed at revitalizing relations with the ancestors. Since the restoration of independence in 2002, there has been an astonishing proliferation of ritual activities and customary practices across the country, a phenomenon that has been referred to as "cultural revival."[30] Many of these activities, such as the rebuilding and inauguration of ancestral houses, focus on remembering the ancestors and reinvigorating ancestral practices. While large sums of foreign donor money have been spent on the reconstruction of basic infrastructure and state institutions in the aftermath of the Indonesian occupation, a considerable amount of local resources have been devoted to reviving relations with the ancestors.

In the growing scholarly literature on Timor-Leste, we find two main ways of conceptualizing the post-occupation years, especially regarding the revival of ancestral customs. On the one hand, there are scholars who highlight the resilience and continuity of traditional practices and focus on the restorative dimensions of people's engagement with the ancestral past. On the other hand, there is an emphasis on the rapid transformations that have been taking place in the post-occupation years, the heterogeneity of people's experiences, and the paradoxes evoked by traditional practices and exchange negotiations.

The emphasis on continuity can be found, for example, in Annette Field's study of post-conflict Bidau, an area of Dili, where she describes the revival of ritual practices in the aftermath of the occupation as part of a healing process that followed extreme suffering. She maintains that the proliferation of ritual and exchange enhanced social cohesion and contributed to the remaking of the social order.[31] In a similar vein, Alexander Loch's research in the Baukau region focuses on the different dimensions of psychological and social reconstruction in the years after independence. He argues that people's engagement with "tradition" presented a mode of psychosocial healing, while also acknowledging the influence of the Catholic church and discourses of modernity on this very process.[32]

Andrew McWilliam has equally emphasized the restorative aspects of the post-occupation revival of customary practices. Focusing on Fataluku-speaking communities in the east of the country, he has argued that exchange practices

---

[30] Lisa Palmer and Demetrio do Amaral de Carvalho, "Nation Building and Resource Management: The Politics of 'Nature' in Timor-Leste," *Geoforum* 39 (2008): 1321. For literature on the role and revival on *adat* in Indonesia, see, for example, Greg Acciaioli, "Culture as Art: From Practice to Spectacle in Indonesia," *Canberra Anthropology* 8, no. 1–2 (1985): 148–72; David Bourchier, "The Romance of Adat in the Indonesian Political Imagination and the Current Revival," in *The Revival of Tradition in Indonesian Politics: The Deployment of Adat from Colonialism to Indigenism*, ed. Jamie S. Davidson and David Henley (London: Routledge, 2007), 113–29; David Henley and Jamie S. Davidson, "In the Name of Adat: Regional Perspectives on Reform, Tradition, and Democracy in Indonesia," *Modern Asian Studies* 42, no. 4 (2008): 815–52; Joel S. Kahn, *Southeast Asian Identities: Culture and Politics of Representation in Indonesia, Malaysia, Singapore, and Thailand* (Singapore: Institute of Southeast Asian Studies, 1995); Patricia Spyer, "Diversity with a Difference: Adat and the New Order in Aru (Eastern Indonesia)," *Cultural Anthropology* 11 no. 1, (1996): 25–50; and Adam D. Tyson, *Decentralization and Adat Revivalism in Indonesia: The Politics of Becoming Indigenous* (Abingdon: Routledge, 2010).

[31] Annette M. Field, *Places of Suffering and Pathways to Healing: Post-Conflict Life in Bidau, East Timor* (PhD thesis, James Cook University, 2004).

[32] Alexander Loch, *Haus, Handy & Halleluja: Psychosoziale Rekonstruktion in Osttimor. Eine Ethnopsychologische Studie zur Postkonfliktuösen Dynamik im Spannungsfeld von Identität, Trauma, Kultur und Entwicklung* (Frankfurt: IKO, Verlag für Interkulturelle Kommunikation, 2007).

express Fataluku "cultural resilience" and their ability to reconstitute their lives after periods of social adversity.[33] He develops this argument further in his analysis of the reconstruction of sacred houses, stating that this practice also demonstrates people's resilience and capacity to recover from the hardships of the Indonesian occupation. In "Houses of Resistance in East Timor," McWilliam stresses people's "cultural capacity to endure," arguing that "indigenous economic, social, and cultural systems were able to reproduce themselves intact" despite the foreign interventions and historical conditions of colonialism.[34] What these diverse studies have in common is the interpretation of the proliferation of customary practices as a way of recovering from violent conflict, addressing unresolved problems from the past, and expressing the resilience of pre-Indonesian forms of sociality.

By comparison, other studies put an emphasis on contestation, renegotiation of social relations, and on the paradoxes of post-occupation political imaginaries. This approach is most explicitly outlined in Angie Bexley and Maj Nygaard-Christensen's introduction to a special issue of the *Asia Pacific Journal of Anthropology*, entitled "Engaging Processes of Sense-Making and Negotiation in Contemporary Timor-Leste," in which the authors emphasize the importance of taking into account "the heterogeneity and unpredictability of contemporary Timor-Leste."[35] With reference to some of the articles in the special issue, they conclude that "'tradition' and exchange practices ... are constantly redefined through negotiation and contestation in shifting historical contexts."[36]

The need to take into account contemporary transformations is succinctly illustrated in Kelly da Silva's contribution to the same special issue, which examines the diverse attitudes of Dili's emergent and Christianized middle-class elites toward the gift exchanges that traditionally take place upon marriage. Interestingly, da Silva concludes that the enduring significance of Catholicism does not undermine existing marriage practices; instead, Christian values of solidarity and fraternity end up reinforcing local institutions that center on exchanges between wife-givers and wife-takers.[37]

In the same volume, Victoria Kumala Sakti examines the aftermath of the Passabe massacre in Oecussi, arguing that the abundance of "bad deaths" has led to "blockages" that need to be removed before any kind of life-giving rituals, such as marriage exchanges, can take place. Customary practices are important to the continuity of life, yet the accumulation of distressing events can lead to the breakdown of existing kinship alliances and the "closing of doors," i.e., the obstruction of potential future marriage alliances.[38] What these studies have in

---

[33] Andrew McWilliam, "Exchange and Resilience in Timor-Leste," *Journal of the Royal Anthropological Institute* 17, no. 4 (2011): 746.

[34] Andrew McWilliam, "Houses of Resistance in East Timor: Structuring Sociality in the New Nation 1," *Anthropological Forum* 15, no. 1 (2005): 28, 34, 38. McWilliam further develops this argument in McWilliam, "Fataluku Healing and Cultural Resilience in East Timor," *Ethnos* 73, no. 2 (2008): 217–40.

[35] Bexley and Nygaard-Christensen, introduction to "Engaging Processes," 399.

[36] Ibid., 401.

[37] Kelly da Silva, "Negotiating Tradition and Nation: Mediations and Mediators in the Making of Urban Timor-Leste," *Asia Pacific Journal of Anthropology* 14, no. 5 (2013): 467.

[38] Victoria K. Sakti, "'Thinking Too Much': Tracing Local Patterns of Emotional Distress after Mass Violence in Timor-Leste," *Asia Pacific Journal of Anthropology* 14, no. 5 (2013): 449–50.

common is that they emphasize the tensions, transformations, and contradictions that accompany the post-occupation cultural revival.[39]

The difference of these two approaches—one focusing on the restorative and resilient aspects of customary practices, the other stressing their transformation and ambiguity—may partly stem from the fact that many of the former focus on rural areas, whereas the latter tend to center on more urban contexts.[40] It may also be due to the fact, as Bexley and Nygaard-Christensen argue, that scholars bring different assumptions and expectations with them to the field; hence, they are more likely to find something that more closely resembles their initial vision of what the country may look like.[41] Most of the studies mentioned do make an effort of taking into account both continuities with the past (including the continuities of customary practices as well as the legacies of the Indonesian occupation and the Portuguese colonial heritage) *and* some of the contemporary transformations. However, they seem to set the emphasis somewhat differently.[42]

Both approaches—those emphasizing the resilience of customary practices and those stressing their transformation—are significant when considering the post-conflict cultural changes in Funar. It is through the continued evocation of a mythic ideal of unchanging ancestral customs (what I refer to as "the land of gold") that people seek to accommodate change, conflict, and ambiguity. On the one hand, I was struck by the remarkable emphasis on the continuity of ancestral practices in Funar and on the importance, as people put it, of "following the ancestors." On the other hand, I was confronted with conflicting accounts and with the transformation and ambiguity of these very practices. Attempts to restore ancestral ways of life were often tense and prone to disputes and contestation. The peaceful impression I had of Funar when I first visited was undermined as I became aware of the disagreements and tensions existing among different factions in the village—tensions that lingered beneath the surface, but that were, on occasion, expressed in public. After the All Souls' Day celebrations, for example, when I had already left the cemetery, a fight broke out between a woman and her husband's sister. Several villagers remarked how awful and even dangerous it was to fight so near the graves of the ancestors.

---

[39] See also: Alex Grainger, "Alternative Forms of Power in East Timor 1999–2009: A Historical Perspective" (PhD thesis, London School of Economics and Political Science, 2014); Laura S. Meitzner Yoder, "Tensions of Tradition: Making and Remaking Claims to Land in the Oecusse Enclave," in McWilliam and Traube, *Land and Life in Timor-Leste*, 187–216; Maj Nygaard-Christensen, "Chapter Ten: The Rebel and the Diplomat: Revolutionary Spirits, Sacred Legitimation, and Democracy in Timor-Leste," in *Varieties of Secularism in Southeast Asia: Anthropological Explorations of Religion, Politics, and the Spiritual*, ed. Nils Bubandt and Martin van Beek (London: Routledge, 2012), 209–29; and Sandra Pannell, "Welcome to the Hotel Tutuala: Fataluku Accounts of Going Places in an Immobile World," *Asia Pacific Journal of Anthropology* 7, no. 3 (2006): 203–19.

[40] Compare with Bexley and Nygaard-Christensen, "Engaging Processes," 399.

[41] Maj Nygaard-Christensen and Angie Bexley, introduction to *Doing Fieldwork in Timor-Leste* (Copenhagen: NIAS Press, forthcoming).

[42] For examinations of how traditional narratives or practices are mobilized to accommodate changing historical events, see, for example: Andrew McWilliam, "Diasporas: New Fataluku Diasporas and Landscapes of Remittance and Return," *Local-Global: Identity, Security, Community* 11 (2012): 72; da Silva, "Negotiating Tradition and Nation"; Traube, "Unpaid Wages"; and Elizabeth G. Traube, "Planting the Flag," in McWilliam and Traube, *Land and Life in Timor-Leste*, 117–40.

Tensions between different social groups are not unique to Funar, but were found elsewhere in the country. In 2006, this led to an intense civil conflict at the national level, referred to as the "crisis" (*krise*), which eventually required an international peacekeeping force for the reestablishment of peace. In the early 2000s, Timor-Leste had been hailed within the global community as a success story for international intervention and UN-sponsored peace-building. Hence, many international observers were taken by surprise when, in April 2006, conflict broke out following the dismissal from the country's fourteen-hundred-member army of nearly six-hundred soldiers, who had gone on strike to protest alleged discrimination. This internal conflict intensified, leading to violent clashes involving sections of the civilian population in Dili, and eventually resulting in the collapse of key state institutions, which prompted an official request for international military intervention.[43] While the 2006–07 conflicts centered on Dili, other parts of the country were also affected by violence, especially during the 2007 elections. There was no open violence in the Laclubar subdistrict, although it was subject to an influx of people fleeing from conflicts elsewhere and there was widespread fear that violence would break out in the region.

It has been argued that the *krise* erupted partly because of unresolved conflicts from the Indonesian occupation, such as tensions that had developed within the resistance movement.[44] Unresolved problems from the past also came to the surface during my fieldwork in Funar. In most cases, they were not expressed openly but instead emerged indirectly in seemingly unrelated events, including rituals of reconstruction and the fear people felt toward the land. Hence, in this book I show how the cultural revival was a way of addressing problems from the past, while also focusing on the conflicts and dilemmas that the revival of ancestral relations evoked. My observations from Funar show that the cultural revival did not just bring unresolved issues to the fore, but also engendered new conflicts.

Although it appeared at first as if the people of Funar were not concerned about the Indonesian occupation and subsequent dislocation, it turned out that they were re-engaging with the recent past by reinvigorating ancestral practices. This reinvigoration was a process fraught with uncertainties, and three main tensions characterized the cultural revival. First, the disagreements that surfaced during this revival made inherent tensions within people's social and ritual practices more visible. Second, this process not only produced further conflict, but also led to the transformation of the very dynamics underlying social and ritual interactions. Third, while people were rebuilding their village and their ancestral houses, they were also

---

[43] The *krise* was fueled by power struggles within the political elite, by regional tensions between "Easterners" (*lorosa'e*) and "Westerners" (*loromonu*), and by long-standing disagreements stemming from rifts that had developed within the resistance movement during the Indonesian occupation. During the 2006 conflict, more than thirty people were killed and over 140,000 people were once again internally displaced. See International Crisis Group (ICG), "Resolving Timor-Leste's Crisis," *Asia Report* 120 (2006): 21; Edward Rees, *Under Pressure: FALINTIL—Forças de Defesa de Timor Leste: Three Decades of Defence Force Development in Timor Leste, 1975–2004* (Geneva: Geneva Centre for the Democratic Control of Armed Forces, 2004).

Despite the presence of international peacekeeping forces, these tensions did not subside until early 2008. They included the shooting of President José Ramos-Horta and the failed assassination attempt on Prime Minister Xanana Gusmão in February 2008.

[44] Rees, *Under Pressure*.

faced with the possibility of recalibrating power relations that had existed in the past. Thus, the cultural revival involved renegotiating the status of different social groups and the way these groups related to one another.

I am, of course, not the first to point out that ritual practices, and the evocation of mythic origins, can be used to justify and reproduce domination and status differences. Maurice Bloch has made this argument in a range of different studies, discussing, for example, whether ritual speech presents an extreme form of traditional authority, and how ritual communication enables ideological mystification, creating a transcendental order by devaluing human experience and action.[45] In his examination of representational practices, Webb Keane has developed the idea that the staging of ancestral signs that takes place during "scenes of encounter" centers on making these signs look "natural," therefore negating the notion that their authority is a product of social convention.[46] This argument is implicit in my claim that the revival of customary practices in Timor-Leste involves an appeal to the unchanging ancestral sphere by negating recent transformations or foreign influences. I develop this idea by highlighting that the negation of historical change not only fosters the reproduction of relations of inequality, but that, in the post-occupation context, the denial of historical change can also be used to modify and contest rank and status differences.

By focusing on the hazards of social existence and the role of ritual in reproducing power relations, the works of Bloch and Keane are implicit influences that shape the argument of this book. Another less explicitly examined influence is the work of John Pemberton, whose fine study of Javanese texts and ethnography focuses on the colonial and post-colonial constructions of what was considered to be authentically Javanese. I would not say that the customary practices that are currently being revived in Timor-Leste have their origins in colonial practices in the same way, but Pemberton's study nevertheless draws attention to how appeals to cultural authenticity can be connected to articulations of power—in his case, to the repressive practices and needs of totalizing state power.[47]

This book examines how status and authority are renegotiated during the revival of ancestral tradition in the post-occupation years.[48] By doing so, it seeks to capture how people are transforming the very traditions they seek to revive and thus reveals one of the underlying mechanisms at the heart of the recovery process, namely, how social relations in the present are reconstituted and actively modified precisely by

---

[45] See, for example, Maurice Bloch, "The Past and the Present in the Present," *Man* 12 no. 2 (1977): 278–92; "Symbols, Song, Dance and Features of Articulation: Or Is Religion an Extreme Form of Traditional Authority?" *Archives Européennes de Sociologie* 15 (1974): 497–514; and Maurice Bloch, *From Blessing to Violence: History and Ideology in the Circumcision Ritual of the Merina of Madagascar* (Cambridge: Cambridge University Press, 1986).

[46] Webb Keane, *Signs of Recognition: Powers and Hazards of Representation in an Indonesian Society* (Berkeley: University of California Press, 1997), 19.

[47] John Pemberton, *On the Subject of "Java"* (Ithaca: Cornell University Press, 1994), 543.

[48] Compare with: Susana Barnes, "Gift Giving and Gift Obligations: Strategies of Incorporation and Accommodation in the Customary Domain," paper presented at the seventh Euroseas Conference, Lisbon, July 2–5, 2013; Daniel Fitzpatrick, Andrew McWilliam, and Susana Barnes, *Property and Social Resilience in Times of Conflict: Land, Custom, and Law in East Timor* (Farnham and Burlington: Ashgate Publishing Company, 2012); and Enrique Alonso Población and Alberto Fidalgo Castro, "Webs of Legitimacy and Discredit: Narrative Capital and Politics of Ritual in a Timor-Leste Community," *Anthropological Forum* 24, no. 3 (2014): 245–66.

way of reference to the unchanging nature of the ancestral past. This book shows how such logic is at work in different social and ritual contexts, allowing me to tease out the fragility of the process of recovery and illustrating how attempts to manage the past can fail, as well as how new conflicts and tensions are generated.

This brings me to the third main theme of this book, which explores the ways in which being at the margins of a nation whose strong identity is based on narratives of suffering has affected the ways in which Funar villagers relate to each other.

WITHOUT A PLACE

In 2007, the international peacekeeping forces that had been called in during the 2006 *krise* were searching for the so-called "rebels" who had defected from the military. The rebels were suspected to be hiding in the highlands, so for weeks military helicopters flew low over the Laclubar subdistrict as part of their search. The interminable drone of the helicopters circling over Funar put everyone on edge, and the wind that they produced blew through the houses as though it would blast their roofs off. One evening, I sat with some friends in the kitchen, where fire provided warmth and comfort. There were murmurs that war was once again imminent, and those present were clearly scared.

It was on this occasion that I made another attempt to ask what life was like during the Indonesian occupation and whether they were also scared at that time. In response, Lisa—an educated woman now in her late fifties—told me of an encounter she had with Indonesian soldiers in the late 1990s. Members of the armed resistance (FALINTIL, Forças Armadas da Libertação Nacional de Timor-Leste, The Armed Forces for the National Liberation of East Timor) had passed through the area.[49] Everyone knew about them, but no one said anything. Early one morning, Lisa heard her brother walking around the house calling her name. He was very upset. When he found her, he told her that a number of Indonesian troops were searching houses for FALINTIL members suspected of hiding in the area and that the soldiers were on their way to her house. Lisa got up immediately, but she did not panic; instead, she started cooking. When the Indonesian soldiers burst into the house a little later, they found Lisa sitting in front of a large pot of soup, which she proceeded to offer them.

During my fieldwork, I often asked the family I lived with and other friends what life was like during the Indonesian occupation. I posed this question to almost everyone I knew well. The most common answer was simply that it was the time when they "ran away" (*halai* in Tetum; *alari* in Idaté). This was primarily a reference to the first years of the Indonesian occupation, when Funar's residents spent months—and sometimes years—hiding in the forests surrounding the village before turning themselves in or being captured by the Indonesian troops. It was difficult to find details about the time after that.[50] I was aware that everyone had been resettled in Laclubar Town, but knew little about how they made a living. Although there was a military post in Laclubar Town, I hardly ever heard anyone talk about their

[49] FALINTIL was originally the armed wing of the independence party, FRETILIN (Frente Revolucionária de Timor-Leste Independente, Revolutionary Front for an Independent East Timor). In 1988, the commander-in-chief and later president, Xanana Gusmão, turned FALINTIL into a nonpartisan arm of the unified resistance.

[50] An exception to this was the testimony given by members from Funar's political elite (not living in Funar), a number of whom gave detailed interviews about the political events of the 1970s (see footnote 12).

interactions with Indonesian soldiers, aside from the occasional comment about how it was easier to sell vegetables in the past because the soldiers would buy them, or how the road leading to Laclubar from Manatuto was much better at the time.

The Laclubar subdistrict has an ambiguous status in relation to the independent government, and it was largely excluded from state-sponsored memorialization of the past. In Timor-Leste, especially in the capital city, people living in the Laclubar subdistrict are widely believed to have favored integration with Indonesia, and residents of this region are sometimes considered to have collaborated with the occupying regime. This is partly due to the fact that the last governor of Indonesian-occupied Timor, Abílio Osório Soares, was from Laclubar. Yet this representation hardly captures the complex ways in which inhabitants of the Laclubar subdistrict related to the Indonesians. The story Lisa told exemplifies the complicated and often pragmatic ways of engaging with the various outsiders who sought control over the region. This engagement lies behind the ambiguous position that Funar and Laclubar occupy today within the independent nation-state of Timor-Leste, a position whose history extends back to the time of European colonial expansion. As will be seen in more detail later, the ways in which the highlanders position themselves toward powerful outsiders today have been shaped by Timor-Leste's turbulent colonial and national history.

• • •

The current geographical boundaries of Timor-Leste are a direct result of colonial politics. During the colonial period, the island of Timor became inexorably caught up in the political and economic rivalries of the Dutch and the Portuguese. This led ultimately to the island's division, with the Dutch controlling the western half and the Portuguese claiming enclaves in the eastern regions.[51] The Portuguese first reached Timor in the early sixteenth century, although trade and missionary

---

[51] See: Charles R. Boxer, *The Portuguese Seaborne Empire 1415–1825* (London: Hutchinson & Co, 1969), 143; and Dunn, *East Timor: A Rough Passage*, 13.

Although administrative control was not fully consolidated until the mid-nineteenth century, European trading companies had been involved in the regional trade network from the sixteenth century onwards. See: Shepard Forman, "East Timor: Exchange and Political Hierarchy at the Time of the European Discoveries," in *Economic Exchange and Social Interaction in Southeast Asia*, ed. Karl L. Hutterer (Ann Arbor: Center for South and Southeast Studies, University of Michigan, 1978), 99; and Hans Hägerdal, "Colonial Rivalry and the Partition of Timor," *IIAS Newsletter, International Institute for Asian Studies* 40 (2006): 16.

Historical sources suggest that the island had been a trade destination for Chinese navigators from at least the fourteenth century, if not before; see Frédéric Durand, *East Timor: A Country at the Crossroads of Asia and the Pacific: A Geo–Historical Atlas* (Bangkok: IRASEC, 2006), 161. There is also some evidence that before the Portuguese arrived, Timor had been included in the trade networks of the east Javanese principalities and kingdom on Makassar; see Forman, "Exchange and Political Hierarchy," 99. There is little information available on the precolonial political and social structure of Timor, and that which was gathered by the colonial powers is of questionable reliability. Portuguese historical sources suggest that when the Europeans arrived, Timor was divided into two unified political kingdoms: Servião in the west and Belu in the east. Forman, however, points out that this division corresponds suspiciously neatly with the Portuguese and Dutch zones of control and suggests that these neat divisions of kingdoms may well be a Portuguese invention (Forman, "Exchange and Political Hierarchy," 100). The question of whether the unified kingdoms of Belu and Servião ever actually existed in precolonial Timor has generated much debate and cannot be discussed in detail here.

activities were initially conducted from Solor and, later, from Larantuka in Flores.[52] Despite the multiple disputes and negotiations involving the Dutch and the Portuguese, neither of the two powers actually exercised direct rule or controlled any territory beyond the coastlines and their various trading posts until the mid-nineteenth century.[53]

Funar, then an independent "kingdom" (*reino*) in the highlands, was subject to the "pacification" campaigns of the Portuguese governor Celestino da Silva as well as to two brutal military operations—one in 1905 and another in 1907—that led to the division of Funar between the neighboring domains.[54] The year 1975 was thus not the first time Funar was entirely demolished. As part of a policy of indirect rule early in the twentieth century, the Portuguese appointed rulers in Funar and Laclubar who were willing to collaborate with the colonial administration, whereas previous rulers had been imprisoned or killed. The appointment of specific rulers (*liurai*) by the Portuguese is absolutely crucial for understanding the political choices that the region's elite made in later years, since many of them relate their actions to the Portuguese intervention in local politics.

The "pacification" campaigns attested to a dramatic shift in Portuguese strategy at the turn of the twentieth century toward an attempt to establish effective control over the colony. This shift entailed not only the introduction of cash crops and a head tax, but also the restructuring of the overall political and administrative system in an effort to undermine existing alliances and instigate rivalries among different domains. Portuguese rule in Timor was interrupted by the Japanese invasion and occupation of the island during World War II, an event that was accompanied by dislocation, forced labor, starvation, and violence that left an estimated sixty thousand Timorese dead. After the Japanese finally left, the Portuguese reestablished

---

[52] In 1566, Dominican friars built a fortress on the island of Solor with the aim of converting the local population to Christianity. These settlements gave rise to a group called "Topasses," or "Black Portuguese," by the Dutch. Topasses were the offspring of Portuguese sailors, soldiers, and traders who had intermarried with women from Solor; see: Charles R. Boxer, *The Topasses of Timor* (Amsterdam: Koninklijk Vereeniging Indisch Instituut, 1947); and Hans Hägerdal, *Lords of the Land, Lords of the Sea: Conflict and Adaptation in Early Colonial Timor, 1600–1800* (Leiden: KITLV Press, 2012). The Topasses later played a vital role in the sandalwood trade with Timor, where they established settlements in the mid-seventeenth century. The seventeenth and eighteenth centuries were marked by power struggles between the Dutch, Portuguese, Topasses, and Dominican missionaries, which continued into the nineteenth century and were finally settled through treaties at the turn of the twentieth century.

[53] When the Portuguese started to penetrate the interior, they came up against resistance and indigenous uprisings; these were brutally put down by the colonial military, which was heavily dependent on Timorese "second line" troops. See: René Pélissier, *Timor en Guerre: Le Crocodile et les Portugais, 1847–1913* (Orgeval: René Pélissier, 1996); Monika Schlicher, *Portugal in Ost-Timor: Eine Kritische Untersuchung zur Portugiesischen Kolonialgeschichte in Ost-Timor: 1850 bis 1912* (Hamburg: Abera-Verlag Meyer, 1996), 268.

Due to the financial difficulties that it faced, Portugal became increasingly dependent on the economic exploitation of its colonial territories. At the turn of the century, Celestino da Silva, the governor of Portuguese Timor (1894–1908), intensified the creation of large-scale coffee plantations, which relied on forced labor. Schlicher, *Portugal in Ost-Timor*, 230, 250.

[54] See: Pélissier, *Timor en Guerre*, 224–25; Zola [Antonio Pádua Correia], *Quatorze Annos de Timor*, 1ª Série (Dili, 1909), 27–29; and Judith Bovensiepen, "Diferentes Perspectivas Sobre o Passado: os Portugueses e a Destruição e Vitória de Funar," in *Timor-Leste: Colonialismo, Descolonização, Lusotopia*, ed. Rui Feijó (Porto, Portugal: Afrontamento, forthcoming March, 2016).

control over the eastern part of the island. The former Dutch colony in the western part, however, was integrated into Indonesia in 1950. From the 1950s onwards, Timor was a low priority for the Portuguese government. Many Timorese today joke about the inability of the Portuguese to develop the country. Nonetheless, the need to train Timorese for administrative positions during this period led to the expansion of state schools. The small, educated elite later played an important role in the independence movement that gained momentum in the 1970s.[55]

To summarize the complex events that followed, immediately after the military coup in Portugal to overthrow the Caetano regime in 1974, political parties began to form in Portuguese Timor.[56] There were three main parties and several minor ones; the former included the União Democrática Timorense (UDT), a party that initially stood for self-determination following an intermediate period of federation with Portugal, but that then became associated with a pro-Portuguese position. The second main party, FRETILIN (Frente Revolucionária de Timor-Leste Independente), developed out of the Associação Social Democrática Timorense (ASDT) and stood for independence, initially with a socialist agenda. A third party, Associação Popular e Democrática Timorense (APODETI), favored integration with Indonesia, with eastern Timor to be designated as an autonomous province.

Growing tensions among the political parties, exacerbated by the interference of the Indonesian intelligence services, eventually led to an armed conflict between UDT and FRETILIN, Portugal's withdrawal from the island, and, on November 28, 1975, FRETILIN's unilateral declaration of independence.[57] On December 7, 1975, Indonesian forces launched a full-scale invasion and declared East Timor a province of Indonesia the following year.

In the Laclubar region, political affiliations were varied; the three main parties (UDT, FRETILIN, and APODETI) all enjoyed some support. Funar's ruling house (*liurai*) largely supported UDT, even though some joined FRETILIN.[58] The ruling house was allied through marriage with members of *suco* Manelima's political elite, who supported the pro-Indonesian APODETI. Those in Laclubar who supported APODETI during the turbulent years of the 1970s were mostly members of the original ruling family, which had lost power when the Portuguese put a man from a

---

[55] See: Dunn, *East Timor: A Rough Passage*, 30; and Taylor, *The Price of Freedom*, 10–17.

[56] Taylor, *The Price of Freedom*, 26–28.

[57] Ibid., 50–65. See also: Dunn, *East Timor: A Rough Passage*, 139–74; Helen Hill, *Stirrings of Nationalism in East Timor: FRETILIN 1974–1978—The Origins, Ideologies, and Strategies of a Nationalist Movement* (Otford: The Contemporary Otford Press, 2002), 140–44; and Jill Jolliffe, *East Timor: Nationalism and Colonialism* (Queensland: University of Queensland Press, 1978), 92–143.

[58] The term *liurai* has been translated as "king," "Timorese native chief," and "active ruler," as opposed to a passive ritual authority; see: Geoffrey Hull, *Standard Tetum-English Dictionary*, 3rd ed. (Winston Hills, Australia: Sebastiao Aparicio da Silva Project in association with Instituto Nacional de Linguistica, Timor-Leste, 1999), 221; Herman G. Schulte Nordholt, *The Political System of the Atoni of Timor*, trans. Maria J. L. van Yperen (Verhandelingen van het Koninklijk Instituut voor Taal-, Land- en Volkenkunde, No. 60, The Hague: Martinus Nijhoff, 1971), 236; and Elizabeth G. Traube, *Cosmology and Social Life: Ritual Exchange among the Mambai of East Timor* (Chicago: University of Chicago Press, 1986), 259. In Funar/Laclubar, *liurai* is used to refer to a single person, as well as to all those who are members of the *liurai*'s social group (named house of origin). The translation "ruler" is somewhat inadequate, since not all of these people actually "rule" (even though the village chief tends to be from that group), but for lack of a better term, I will translate *liurai* as "ruler" throughout this book.

different region in charge as *liurai*. The ruling family's frustration at having lost power when the Portuguese conspired to undermine its rule had a profound impact on political events in the years to come, since losing power was one of the reasons why Manelima's *liurai* decided to support APODETI.[59] Political affiliations and choices of the elite in this region cannot be understood through the prism of national and international politics alone. These choices are deeply entrenched in local power struggles, which were intensified by Portuguese colonial policies.

There are conflicting accounts of what exactly happened in Funar and the neighboring *suco* Fatumakerek in 1975. In Funar, the most commonly told version of events is that members of FRETILIN from Aileu and Turiscai attacked Funar and Fatumakerek, where they burned houses and killed members of the *liurai*. During a visit to Turiscai, I was told by local residents that villagers from Funar attacked them first. In 1975, when these fights took place, the Indonesian occupation was imminent and preceded by conflicts between UDT and FRETILIN all over the country as these parties disagreed over the nature of the desired decolonization process.[60] Faced with the Indonesian onslaught, many of the residents of Laclubar subdistrict were forced to flee, spending months or even years hiding in the remote and inaccessible forests and mountains of the region. After this period of running away, Funar's residents and many people from other remote areas of the subdistrict were forcibly resettled in Laclubar Town by the Indonesian military. These internal refugees stayed there until their return home in the 1990s, when a few villagers asked the Indonesian military for permission to return to their ancestral land. The large majority of Funar residents only returned after the end of the Indonesian occupation.[61]

After Timor-Leste regained independence in 2002 and the Indonesian occupation ended in 1999, the country experienced an influx of foreign-aid workers, consultants, and personnel working with UN agencies and NGOs. All were involved in projects of post-conflict reconstruction and state-building, into which billions of US dollars were invested.[62] Supporters of the resistance, many of whom had been in exile during the Indonesian occupation or had been part of the armed resistance, took up important government positions. It was striking that in the midst of this development and reconstruction boom, the Laclubar subdistrict received little attention. When I carried out fieldwork, there were hardly any NGOs active in the region.

It seems likely that the relative exclusion of the Laclubar subdistrict from national politics immediately after independence is related to the political history of the region. Inhabitants were not recognized as having participated fully in the resistance, and only a few adopted a nationalist language of sacrifice that allowed them to claim a stake in the nation-building process and the post-conflict

---

[59] For a more detailed analysis of this issue, see Judith Bovensiepen, "Entanglements of Power, Kinship, and Time in Laclubar," in Nygaard-Christensen and Bexley, *Doing Fieldwork in Timor-Leste.*

[60] *Chega!*, part 7.2: 11.

[61] During the 1999 post-referendum violence, Funar was spared; however, Indonesian troops and militias did reach Laclubar Town. There, they went on a rampage, burning houses and forcing large parts of the population into Indonesian West Timor, where some of them still live today.

[62] Guteriano N. S. Neves, "The Paradox of Aid in Timor-Leste" (paper presented at Cooperação Internacional e a Construção do Estado no Timor-Leste, University of Brasilia, Brazil, July 25–28, 2006).

development boom. Immediately after independence, political discourse in the capital revolved around the dichotomy of opportunists and oppressed—that is, those who collaborated with the Indonesians as opposed to those who suffered.[63] Political participation in the nation was largely premised on the degree to which one had resisted the Indonesian regime. In the collective national imagination, there was no place for people who did not fit into these categories.

From the story that Lisa told me about handing out soup to Indonesian soldiers, it becomes clear that the dichotomy of opportunists and oppressed does not adequately capture the true experiences of people in the Laclubar subdistrict during the Indonesian occupation.[64] While it can be seen that Lisa did not openly resist the incoming soldiers, making soup for the Indonesian troops seemed the most pragmatic means to guarantee security for herself and her family.[65] Whereas some of the members of the political elite in the Laclubar subdistrict sided with Indonesia, many ordinary people in this region were trying to survive and therefore did not frame their actions solely in nationalist or pro-Indonesian terms. In fact, they frequently explained their actions in terms of local politics, especially in relation to the ousting of specific rulers by the Portuguese.[66]

In 2009, Timorese state officials initiated the inauguration of the Hero Cemetery of Metinaro, commemorating the tenth anniversary of the independence referendum in 1999. This national symbol became the resting place for resistance fighters who had participated in the struggle for independence. The Hero Cemetery is a place for those who openly resisted the occupation—not for those who had a more ambiguous role. As Heonik Kwon has pointed out, state-sponsored projects of commemoration do not always capture the complex ways in which people have experienced violence and war.[67] In his study of how the Vietnamese state centralized and unified commemorative practices, he shows how the institution of war heroes tends to exclude more ambiguous victims of war. In Vietnam, Kwon argues, this exclusion led to the reinvigoration of ancestor worship and a proliferation of ghosts many decades after the end of the American War. Similarly, the cultural revival that took place in Funar must be understood as the background of the region's exclusion from national commemorative practices and projects of nation-building. Unable to come together around national memorials, people focused all of their attention on their ancestral origins. It is no coincidence that Funar's inhabitants emphasized the potent value of their ancestral place precisely at a time when their place within the nation was unrecognized.

---

[63] Douglas Kammen, "Master–Slave, Traitor–Nationalist, Opportunist–Oppressed: Political Metaphors in East Timor," *Indonesia* 76 (October 2003): 69–85.

[64] For other studies of East Timorese negotiating their relationship with the Indonesian legacy, see: Angie Bexley and Nuno Rodrigues Tchailoro, "Consuming Youth: Timorese in the Resistance against Indonesian Occupation," *Asia Pacific Journal of Anthropology* 14, no. 5 (2013): 405–22; and Maj Nygaard-Christensen, "Negotiating Indonesia: Political Genealogies of Timorese Democracy," *Asia Pacific Journal of Anthropology* 14, no. 5 (2013): 423–37.

[65] In his excellent study of life under Indonesian rule in West Papua, Eben Kirksey has shown that collaboration, rather than resistance, is frequently a strategy of political movements. See Eben Kirksey, *Freedom in Entangled Worlds: West Papua and the Architecture of Global Power* (Durham: Duke University Press, 2012).

[66] See also David Hicks, *Rhetoric and the Decolonization and Recolonization of East Timor* (London: Routledge, 2014).

[67] Kwon, After the Massacre.

• • •

The Land of Gold explores how the inhabitants of Funar have responded to the uprooting and suffering caused by the Indonesian occupation, and their marginalization from national politics, by negating recent historical events and connecting themselves instead to a mythic ancestral past. It does so by linking people's understanding of how humans are constituted as subjects to broader political events in both the past and the present. The impact of colonialism and military occupation emerges not in explicit narrative accounts, but in interactive relations with the ancestral land and in emotional, moral, and political dilemmas. Accordingly, the objective is to go beyond human-centered approaches to post-conflict reconstruction, which largely neglect the ways in which people's relationships with their lived environments are reified or transformed by conflict.

The revival of ancestral practices in Timor-Leste since its independence has not simply produced social cohesion and stability—it has engendered conflicts, dilemmas, and tensions. These tensions derive in part from conflicts of the past, but they are also inherent in the logics upon which the cultural revival is based. This book, therefore, shows how conflict and displacement can make inherent contradictions in people's ideological frames particularly visible while transforming them in the very process. It is for this reason that every chapter starts with an ethnographic puzzle that establishes an analytical framework for the empirical discussion. In the framing of the chapters, I do not prioritize theoretical concerns in the literature, but instead focus on dilemmas, problems, or paradoxes that emerge directly from the ethnographic context. The insights gained are then used to discuss aspects of the relevant literature.

This approach is part of a more general attempt to develop arguments using ethnography and focus on the significance of the everyday lived experiences of those people concerned.[68] The focal point is not so much on the rules and regulations governing social and ritual life. Rather, emphasis is placed on the subjective experiences of the events discussed.[69] Moreover, rather than concentrating on information provided by key "experts," the monograph describes how many different kinds of people, including children, women, and ordinary folks, experience and relate to the ancestral practices in which they are reinvesting. Even when it focuses on information provided by ritual authorities, it does so not simply by describing generic ideals of desired behavior but by paying attention to the doubts, worries, and uncertainties that have emerged during the post-occupation years. I adopted this particular ethnographic style not only to bring out more vividly what life was like in the highlands of Timor-Leste during the post-occupation years, but also to highlight the amount of effort that goes into the production and reproduction of specific ideological representations and to underline how much this process is characterized by contradictions and fraught with conflict.

Throughout my stay in Timor-Leste, I found myself asking a range of questions that have come to frame the different chapters. Why is it, for example, that residents claimed that there is a lot of gold in Funar, when there is little evidence that this

---

[68] See, for example, Catherine L. Allerton, *Potent Landscapes: Place and Mobility in Eastern Indonesia* (Honolulu: University of Hawai'i Press, 2013).

[69] Catherine L. Allerton, "The Path of Marriage: Journeys and Transformation in Manggarai, Eastern Indonesia," *Bijdragen tot de Taal-, Land- en Volkenkunde* 160, no. 2/3 (2004): 339–62.

region is particularly rich in gold? What happened to people's customary knowledge during the Indonesian occupation, when public gatherings during which such knowledge is performed were restricted? Why were Funar villagers in such a rush to reconstruct their origin houses, and why is the transfer of a person from one origin house to another experienced as a painful event? How come there was a proliferation of death rituals in the years after independence was restored? And what do people mean when they say that they are "scared of the land"?

To find responses to those and other questions, I had to delve deep into the people's relationships with the lived environment, with the ancestors, and with one another, and I examined how those various relations were being reinvigorated and sustained. I realized, however, that I also needed to consider the region's comparative exclusion from nation-building processes that were taking place across the country—the absence of relations with the national center—as well as explore how the interventions of previous colonial governments left an imprint on local power relations. In trying to find responses to such questions, this book brings together the political and cosmological dimensions of post-conflict recovery, and explores how the revival of ancestral traditions has engendered new modes of being in place and history.

CHAPTER ONE

SACRED ORIGINS OF LIFE

In the early stages of my fieldwork, I lived in Laclubar Town. Because my language skills were still rather limited, Eliana, a young woman from the western district of Baukau, accompanied me on my first forays into town. One day, Eliana called me into the bedroom that we shared; she was clearly very agitated. Sitting down on the bed beside me and gently holding my hand, she whispered, "The men in the house next door say you have come to Laclubar in order to steal gold from the *lulik* houses!" These men, she continued, had consulted a person whose "eyes reach far" (*matan dook*, T.) to find out whether their suspicions were true. In the course of my fieldwork, no one else ever expressed suspicions of this kind to me directly, but I heard similar rumors about other foreigners who lived in the region and had supposedly come to steal gold. People said the gold deposits were contained in the ancestral *lulik* houses or else in the ground, located at specific sites in the landscape, which were usually demarcated by a small fence (*lalutuk*).

Residents in Funar and Laclubar recurrently made claims about possessing gold resources or at least being the potential guardians of gold. A man in his sixties described how, in the past, golden discs would fly to Funar, bringing wealth and prosperity to its inhabitants. Apparently, however, the villagers no longer had the ability (i.e., ritual knowledge) to receive these golden discs, and this shortcoming had prompted the discs to move elsewhere. Similar allusions were made when the priest from Laclubar Town came to visit Funar. We were having coffee together with a number of prominent elders when the priest suddenly said to me in a conspiratorial tone, "There is a lot of gold in Funar! All the information about the gold is inside the book I gave you." The men sitting beside us nodded in agreement and flashed me knowing grins. The priest had, indeed, given me a book, but its subject was the history of the Catholic Church in Timor-Leste and it made no special mention of any gold.

The mistrust directed toward me and other foreigners is hardly surprising when one considers the history of colonialism in Timor-Leste, during which foreigners have repeatedly tried to exploit local people and their natural resources. I found no evidence to suggest that this region was ever particularly rich in gold, even though there are known to be gold deposits in other areas of Timor-Leste. Nevertheless, references to gold were made on countless occasions during my fieldwork, and I learned that gold made an appearance in a variety of oral traditions. Yet I never came across any gold objects in the *lulik* houses or anywhere else.[1]

---

[1] As is common in Timor-Leste, Funar residents did possess metal discs that served a ritual function, but as far as I could tell they were not made of gold. According to Durand (*East Timor: A Country at the Crossroads*, 33), there are some gold and silver deposits in Timor-Leste, for example, around Same and Fatuberliu. It is also entirely possible, of course, that people in the Laclubar subdistrict did possess some golden objects, but simply did not want to show them to me. See also Boxer, *The Portuguese Seaborne Empire*, 164, on the role of the desire for gold in motivating the Portuguese colonial expansion.

In spite of their claims to be the potential owners of great riches, the residents of Funar and Laclubar were living in what many would consider extremely poor living conditions. Though little regionally specific data is available, the UN Human Development Report from 2006 states that Timor-Leste was one of the poorest countries in Southeast Asia, with the lowest levels of human development in Asia.[2] When I carried out my doctoral fieldwork, Funar was cut off from the public transport network, and access to healthcare, electricity, and water was severely limited. Apart from a small number of teachers, nurses, and government employees, people had few means of earning money and subsisted mostly on what they made from farming. Yet because of their long absence due to their forced displacement, many of Funar's residents struggled to make a living even from the land: their fields did not yield sufficient produce, and some had become accustomed to rice donations from the Indonesian government. In light of such manifest poverty, how can we make sense of the claims that this region is rich in gold?

After living in Funar for a considerable length of time, I became aware that the term "gold" (*osa meran*) was always used in connection with *lulik*.[3] *Lulik* has been translated from Tetum as "prohibited" or "taboo," as well as "holy" or "sacred,"[4] and Josh Trinidade has described it as the "core of Timorese values."[5] In Funar, *lulik* was connected to particular sites in the landscape that had a special ancestral connection, but it was also sometimes associated with Catholic understandings of the sacred. In several of the origin narratives recounted in Funar and Laclubar, ancestral objects, which are *lulik*, are described as golden (e.g., golden scepters, golden discs).[6] The sites in the landscape that were said to contain gold were also considered *lulik*, as were the ancestral houses that supposedly sheltered gold.

According to Trinidade, *lulik* refers "to the spiritual cosmos that contains the divine creator, the spirits of the ancestors, and the spiritual root of life including sacred rules and regulations that dictate relationships between people and people and nature."[7] He notes that *lulik* can be a source of morality and social obligation, and that it sits at the very core of Timorese society. For the Mambai, claims Elizabeth

---

[2] United Nations Development Programme (UNDP), *Timor-Leste Human Development Report 2006: The Path out of Poverty, Integrated Rural Development* (Darwin and Dili: United Nations Development Programme, 2006), 2.

[3] I have based my translation of the Idaté term for "gold" (*osa meran*) on the Tetum term *osan mean*, which is frequently, but not necessarily literally, translated as "gold." There are some indications that people refer to any metal as *osa meran*, with *osa* meaning "coin" or "money" and *meran* meaning "red." I am less interested in establishing whether people actually possessed gold than in understanding the way people use references to gold to make claims about the potency of the land. There might also be a connection between the "heat" of spiritual potency and the "red" color of gold.

[4] Hull, *Standard Tetum-English Dictionary*, 227. Hull also notes that *lulik* can mean "totem," "ancestral spirit," and "sacred object," although these translations are less commonly used in the anthropological literature.

[5] José "Josh" Trinidade, "*Lulik*: The Core of Timorese Values," paper presented at the Third Timor-Leste Study Association (TLSA) Conference (Dili, Timor-Leste: June 30, 2011), 16.

[6] Claudine Friedberg has similarly examined how golden objects are passed down through generations among the Bunaq of Central Timor. See Claudine Friedberg, "Boiled Woman and Broiled Man: Myths and Agricultural Rituals of the Bunaq of Central Timor," in *The Flow of Life: Essays on Eastern Indonesia*, ed. James J. Fox (Cambridge: Harvard University Press, 1980), 289.

[7] Trinidade, "*Lulik*," 16.

Traube, *luli* is a relational category; it "signifies a *relation of distance,* a boundary between things."[8] Meanwhile, David Hicks, borrowing directly from Durkheim, states that among the Tetum, *lulik* means "sacred" and that it is opposed to the category for the profane, *sau.*[9]

In the Laclubar subdistrict, *lulik* is clearly associated with prohibition—the term *luli* also means "forbidden." In Funar, people forbid their children from doing certain things by saying "*luli, luli.*"[10] Moreover, all *lulik* places, houses, and objects are clearly separate or removed from everyday life, as well as being proscribed in certain ways.[11] I will translate *lulik* here as "potent" or "potency," since *lulik* is considered to be an energy that can give life and that animates specific sites in the landscape, objects, or houses—and is frequently associated with ancestral activities.

The notion of potency is, of course, well known in the anthropological literature on Southeast Asia, at least since Benedict Anderson's distinction between the Javanese notion of potency and European notions of power.[12] He describes the latter as abstract relations between people and the former as a concrete substance that exists independent of its users and suffuses the entire cosmos. Shelly Errington has developed the notion further by describing Southeast Asian spiritual potency as a creative energy that can take a variety of different forms across the region.[13] *Lulik* may be considered one such form, as it is external to living human beings and has a life-giving, creative potential.

This chapter examines the significance of *lulik* in the lives of Funar's inhabitants, specifically in relation to narratives about ancestral origins from the land. Furthermore, it explores practices designed to reinvigorate the ancestral land, through which villagers hoped to achieve the wealth and prosperity that they associated with the past—the "golden" time of the ancestors. Yet this reinvigoration of the ancestral land was not a straightforward process. To revive the prosperity of the ancestral past, residents of Funar faced the burden of having to recreate the earlier union between people and the land. Their dilemma, then, was how to negate their separation from the land while at the same time integrating historical changes into their everyday lives.

---

[8] Traube, *Cosmology and Social Life,* 143, italics in the original.

[9] David Hicks, *Tetum Ghosts and Kin: Fertility and Gender in East Timor,* 2nd ed. (Long Grove: Waveland, 2004), 25.

[10] *Lulik* or *luli* (both terms were common) is used as an adjective (potent/sacred), a noun (potency/creative energy), and as a verb (don't; to be prohibited/proscribed). When used as an adjective, *lulik* is frequently adapted to the noun, such as *ada lulin,* although not everyone does this.

[11] Elsewhere I have discussed in detail whether *lulik* is best understood through a Durkheimian framework (as a sacred power opposed to the profane) or as a form of animism. Judith Bovensiepen, "Lulik: Taboo, Animism, or Transgressive Sacred? An Exploration of Identity, Morality, and Power in Timor-Leste," *Oceania* 84, no. 2 (2014): 121–37.

[12] Benedict R. O'G. Anderson, *Language and Power: Exploring Political Cultures in Indonesia* (Ithaca: Cornell University Press, 1990), 1–19.

[13] Shelly Errington, "Recasting Sex, Gender, and Power: A Theoretical and Regional Overview," in *Power and Difference: Gender in Island Southeast Asia,* eds. Jane M. Atkinson and Shelly Errington (Stanford: Stanford University Press, 1990), 42. More recently, Catherine Allerton has also developed the notion of potency as residing in the landscape; see Allerton, *Potent Landscapes.*

ORIGINS FROM THE LAND

"For everyone, their own land!" (*Ida idak nia rai!*, T.)

Funar residents evoked the phrase "For everyone, their own land!" to highlight their need to live close to the land of their ancestors, which was the main reason they gave for returning to their land in the 1990s following their forced displacement to Laclubar Town during the Indonesian occupation. They said that they wanted to live on their own land rather than "sitting," as they put it, on other people's land, saying that they "missed" their land when they were away from it and that they tended to "think" and "worry" about it. Although some returnees complained about the lack of public amenities in Funar, they never failed to stress how the powerful and creative qualities of their connection with the landscape more than compensated for this. According to them, their ancestral land was "the trunk of life, the center of life" (*mori ni uun* in Idaté or *moris nia hun, moris nia sentru* in Tetum). The ancestors had built their houses in Funar, and these sites were now *lulik*. Because Funar was the place of the ancestors, it was the "true place" (*hatin loloos*). People asserted, half in jest and half seriously, that if they worked long enough close to the land associated with their ancestors, they might suddenly strike it rich. Ancestral land was considered to be a source of life, morality, wealth, and prosperity, hence villagers' desire to return to Funar and thereby reconnect the tip (the descendants) to its trunk. Those villagers who lived far away from Funar—in Laclubar Town, Dili, or abroad—were said to "just live inside the field" (*diuk he namo lalak saek*), a phrase that implies a temporary arrangement since "the true house is in Funar" (*ada loloos he Hunar*).

When the former pro-Indonesian governor of Timor, Abilío Osório Soares, who fled to West Timor after independence, died of cancer in 2007, several residents claimed that he had died because he had abandoned his land by moving away. A number of the resettled villagers who were still living in Laclubar Town emphasized that they were planning to return to their ancestral land in the future, even though this would mean forsaking their easy access to markets, schools, and healthcare and water facilities. Residents of Funar stressed that they had returned to their land because of its connection with their ancestors and its *lulik* potency.

The anthropological literature concerning Timor-Leste frequently divides the population into a number of ethno-linguistic groups. In many cases, such as those of the Mambai or the Tetum, this seems to coincide with the self-identification of the given group. However, even though they share a common language (Idaté), the people in the Laclubar subdistrict did not use their language as a self-selected identifying label. They did not, therefore, call themselves the "Idaté" or "Idaté people."

When I visited some of the more remote areas in the Laclubar subdistrict, the highlanders who met me for the first time frequently commented to my companions, "Ai, she speaks ours" (*ai, ni nadaté amik*). Hence, Idaté simply means "to speak" and is not the basis for identification of a clearly defined ethnic group. Of course, residents of Funar were aware that those from other sucos of the Laclubar subdistrict shared their language, yet there was a sense that Funar was a separate political unit and had once been a powerful and independent "kingdom" (*reino*), governed by a ruling house (*liurai*) called Lawadu.

Instead of identifying as Idaté, Funar villagers stressed that people were divided into named houses on the basis of shared ancestry and a common place of origin. Every house that traces its origin to a common ancestor has a separate narrative recounting how its ancestors came into being, their settlement, journeys, and their interaction with the landscape. Members of the house Fahelihun, for example, say that their ancestors were born from a stone called "Hato Lolo'aak." During the time of the ancestors, this stone had been split into two parts and two brothers had been born out of it. These brothers, who later married the sisters of other autochthonous brothers from Funar, were the founders of the Fahelihun hamlet, which is why the people of Fahelihun are today said to be "owners/people of the land" (larek-nain).[14]

According to this origin narrative, a site in the landscape gave birth to human beings. During this process, the stone was cleaved into two, thus separating the primordial human ancestors from the landscape and bestowing entitlement to the nearby land upon these humans and their descendants. Before emerging from the stone, the ancestors had been, by implication, part of the landscape. The ancestral landscape is thus seen not simply as the place where the ancestors used to live; rather, humans are considered to belong to the landscape, for they emerged from it.

Members of other origin houses in Funar also asserted that they were "people of the land," meaning that they represented the autochthonous population. A ritual expert told me that his ancestors had "grown from the land like grass" in a place called Ai Salor. They sprouted out of the earth and brought with them a potent drum and a flag (*baba nora bandeira*); they then built a house in which to store these objects. Today, this ancestral house, called Bubai, is a unit of social organization, and its members are considered to be the descendants of the indigenous ancestors. Bubai's ancestors were thus also part of the land, shooting up from it "like grass." As the direct extensions of the piece of land from which they emerged, Bubai's descendants are also autochthonous "people of the land." In the two origin narratives of Bubai and Fahelihun, the landscape and the primordial ancestors are consubstantial. Human ancestors are extensions or offspring of the landscape; they are part of the landscape, yet they have been separated from it.[15]

In Funar, three groups trace their ancestors to the landscape: Berlibu, Fahelihun, and Bubai. These autochthonous groups are thought to have separate origins, having descended from different ancestral siblings at different sites in the landscape. According to James Fox, there is something "distinctively Austronesian" about this understanding of ancestral origins and settlement, as it brings together notions of ancestry with ideas of place.[16] In Funar, these origin narratives also recount the founding of named ancestral houses, which are called "potent/sacred houses" (*ada lulin*), "head houses" (*ada ulun*), or "customary houses" (*ada lisan*). These houses still exist today as physical buildings, although to an outsider they are not necessarily distinguishable from regular houses. The members of a named house are said to be descended from the ancestral siblings who founded the house at some point in the distant past. The male members of a single named house, who are considered to be brothers, are said to share the same origin or trunk (*uun*). As Fox has noted with regard to origin discourses, these houses combine particular places with the notion of ancestry, which is why I use the term "origin house" to describe them.[17]

---

[14] The word *nain* in Idaté can mean "owner" or "master," but also just "person."

[15] This original state of nondifferentiation between humans and the land is reminiscent of Amerindian notions of an original state of "undifferentiation between humans and animals" in mythology and the subsequent processes of differentiation that take place, whereby animals loose their human qualities. See, for example, Viveiros de Castro, "Cosmological Deixis and Amerindian Perspectivism," 471–72.

[16] James J. Fox, introduction, in *Origins, Ancestry, and Alliance*, 5.

[17] Ibid.

The members of an origin house are directly identified with plots of land or features in the landscape such as prominent rocks or hilltops. Origin houses refer to the dead ancestors, their descendants, and the actual buildings; and their names sometimes derive from sites in the landscape associated with ancestral origins and ancestral settlements. When a child is born, the placenta, or "younger sibling" (*walin*), is buried along with some food beneath the house of the parents. For the newborn to gain a separate identity, its "younger sibling" is returned to the land, thereby unifying the land, people, and house. Origin houses likewise embody the unity between persons, dwellings, and potent sites in the landscape. This unity is expressed by comparing the origin houses to a banyan tree; as mentioned previously, the ancestors are the trunk (*uun*), while the descendants are the flowers (*hunan*) or fruits (*huan*). Reviving the link with the ancestral land was thus an attempt by the mobile tip (i.e., the ancestors' descendants) to be reconnected with the immobile trunk, thereby reestablishing the original unity between trunk and tip.

This relationship between people and the land is not only expressed through botanical metaphors, but also by identifying the land with certain parts of the body. In Laclubar Town, for example, there is a site called "Balulin" (literally translated as "*lulik* place/settlement"). Balulin is considered to be "the land of the navel, the land of the liver" (*larek usar, larek nau*), meaning that the land is central and represents the origin or trunk (*uun*) of humanity.[18] The metaphors of the trunk and the navel refer both to people's geographical position and to their location in human history. Several adults in Laclubar Town told me that all humankind originated from this navel land, a place marked by a hole in the ground closed by a stone. I was never allowed to go near this particular *lulik* site, but I was told that the sound of human voices and cockcrows could be heard emanating from the hole, and that, in actual fact, an entire separate world was located there, underground. The first ancestors, those who founded the Balulin origin house, are buried at this site, which is why the place is considered to be exceptionally potent and why people are forbidden to go there. Consubstantiality with the land is achieved not just by being born from it or by settling thereon, but also through unification with the earth upon death.

These varied accounts illustrate that there is a close connection between *lulik* and ancestral interactions with the landscape. Ancestors are mostly referred to using the Portuguese-derived term for grandparent, *avô*, although another term for ancestors is *luliwai*, which contains the term *luli*.[19] Houses that were founded by ancestors are called *ada lulin*, and objects that have been handed down from the ancestors are also *lulik*. *Lulik* places must be avoided, and trees near *lulik* sites cannot be cut down since the ancestors retain a presence therein. Sites out of which ancestors were born, or at which they settled or died, are also *lulik*, which suggests that *lulik* is specifically associated with the ancestors.

Ancestors are not the only beings present at potent sites, however. On one occasion I was out walking with two teenage girls past a *lulik* place near Fahelihun. The girls had distanced themselves from me to secretly smoke a cigarette behind a nearby tree when one of them saw a snake; she screamed loudly and both girls ran

---

[18] See Traube, *Cosmology and Social Life*, 39, 162, and 265, for comparable suggestions about the burial ground Raimaus, described as the "navel of the earth" by the Mambai of Timor.

[19] I was told that in the past, people differentiated between generations of ancestors, using terms such as *luliwai, dorowai,* and *nanuwai*. Today, however, people simply use the term *luliwai* to refer collectively to the various generations of ancestors.

away. When I caught up with them, they told me that they should never have come near this *lulik* place, because what they had just encountered was the *larek-nain*, the owner of the land. The term *larek-nain* (or *namo-nain*) has a variety of different meanings. As Fahelihun and Bubai's origin narratives illustrated, the first people to inhabit a specific region, along with their descendants, are referred to as *larek-nain*.[20] Hence, the term denotes autochthonous people whose ancestors emerged from the land. However, I was also told on numerous occasions that *larek-nain* refers to spirits (*espiritu*) of the land, which can appear in the form of snakes or beautiful women, soldiers, or strangers.[21]

These land spirits are liable to appear in uninhabited places and are considered to be the owners or guardians of *lulik* land. A place is rendered *lulik* when a human or spiritual presence resides therein. When I asked people specifically, most of my respondents contended that land spirits and ancestors are not the same, even though there seemed to be some uncertainty and ambiguity concerning the precise relationship between the two. When holding rituals at *lulik* sites, for example, participants frequently used the terms *lulik* land, larek-nain, and avô interchangeably. They addressed these entities, for example, to ask permission to plant corn. On one such occasion, a participant also said that *larek-nain* were the ancestors residing within the land.

The life-giving and creative potential of *lulik* was made clear during a journey I undertook to a mountain called Maubere, situated between Laclubar Town and Funar. Walking up the mountain slope, Gilberto, who was accompanying me, told me that *lulik* land near the mountain had created the first inhabitants, bestowing golden objects upon the earlier humans who then built houses to store them in. He concluded his explanation by asserting that "everything comes from the land." From the way that he talked about *lulik*, it became clear that *lulik* referred to a creative and generative potency of the land. In this cosmogonic account of the genesis of human beings, *lulik* has the ability to generate objects and create humans, who are the direct extensions of the land by virtue of having emerged from it. *Lulik* is what animates the land, arising where humans become part of the land or where they are separated from it.

In many Southeast Asian societies, the inhabited environment, including certain sites in the landscape (rivers, trees, rocks, or hilltops) are "intersected by a spiritual or invisible realm."[22] This is also the case in Funar, where people have a personal and moral relationship with the landscape, which is closely identified with the ancestors and a number of spiritual entities. Place and landscape are key themes in the anthropological literature of eastern Indonesia and Timor, and are important topics

---

[20] Comparative discussions of spirit owners of the land in Southeast Asia can be found, for example, in Catherine Allerton, "Introduction: Spiritual Landscapes of Southeast Asia— Changing Geographies of Potency and the Sacred," ed. Catherine L. Allerton, special issue, *Anthropological Forum* 19, no. 3 (2009): 240; Hicks, *Tetum Ghosts and Kin*, 35; and Andrew McWilliam, "Fataluku Living Landscapes," in McWilliam and Traube, *Land and Life in Timor-Leste*, 61–82.

[21] See Hicks, *Tetum Ghosts and Kin*, 37, on Tetum narratives about nature spirits appearing as an attractive Timorese woman or an African soldier.

[22] Allerton, "Introduction: Spiritual Landscapes," 235. See also Errington, "Recasting Sex, Gender, and Power," 42.

of comparison among scholars of the Comparative Austronesian Project.[23] In the edited volume *The Poetic Power of Place*, Fox promotes the comparative study of place and landscape among Austronesian-speaking populations with the aim of investigating ways in which the landscape provides "the underpinnings of a diverse array of social knowledge."[24] According to this approach, place in Austronesian societies is vested with social knowledge that is projected onto the landscape.

In the Laclubar subdistrict, people gather knowledge from the landscape in order to categorize, rank, and divide people into social groups. People make status claims in different ways: one is to make claims to autochthony; another is to claim to have received power from an outside source. The various origin narratives are in competition with one another, yet they are all versions of a foundation myth based on interactions between autochthonous original inhabitants and immigrants or late arrivals who are connected to an outside realm.

One way of describing this opposition between autochthones and immigrants is through James Fox's notion of "precedence." This idea refers to a discourse of origins that is mobilized by individuals or groups to establish position, rank, or status by valuing priority in time. As Fox explains, precedence is "an oppositional notion based on the assertion of a relational asymmetry"[25] in which the first-comers retain an element of superiority, even if they pass political power over to outsiders.

Accounts of autochthones emerging from the land are complemented by another variety of origin narrative about ancestors who gain political power through their connection with an outside realm. These oppositional origin narratives produce a diarchic division of power whose elements simultaneously complement and compete with one another. These elements are identified with a series of analogous oppositions, such as inside/outside, female/male, spiritual/political, and female/male.[26] The diarchic ideology encoded in the narrative representations of interactions between landed authorities (human and spiritual) and newcomers who bring in other forms of power (embodied in spears and scepters) could also be seen as versions of the paradigm Sahlins called the "stranger king." Stranger king narratives describe how the indigenous population retains ritual responsibilities while the "outsiders" gain political office.[27]

In the Laclubar subdistrict, *lulik* objects or *lulik* places are used as evidence for competing narratives, providing support for the status claims of individual groups. As people of Funar returned to their land, the reinvigoration of the ancestral landscape also involved the renewal of these status differences, while inhabitants

---

[23] See, for example, Bellwood, "Hierarchy, Founder Ideology, and Austronesian Expansion"; Fox, ed., *The Poetic Power of Place*; and Reuter, ed., *Sharing the Earth, Dividing the Land*.

[24] Fox, *The Poetic Power of Place*, 3.

[25] James J. Fox, "The Transformation of Progenitor Lines of Origin: Patterns of Precedence in Eastern Indonesia," in Fox and Sather, *Origins, Ancestry, and Alliance*, 131.

[26] David Hicks, similarly, argues that Tetum distinguish between the spiritual world that is associated with femininity (based on references to an Earth Mother) and the political, secular sphere that is associated with men; see Hicks, *Tetum Ghosts and Kin*; and David Hicks, *A Maternal Religion: The Role of Women in Tetum Myth and Ritual*, special report, Monograph Series on Southeast Asia, no. 22 (DeKalb: Northern Illinois University Center for Southeast Asian Studies, 1984). Also see Chapter 3, this volume.

[27] Marshall Sahlins, "The Stranger-King or, Elementary Forms of the Politics of Life," in "Stranger Kings in Indonesia and Beyond," ed. Ian Caldwell and David Henley, *Indonesia and the Malay World* 36, no. 105 (2008), special issue: 177–99.

attempted to strengthen and mobilize the life-giving properties of the land. Moreover, the return to Funar strengthened variants of a foundational stranger-king paradigm with its implicit division between locals and immigrants.

REINVIGORATING THE ANCESTRAL LANDSCAPE

Status and Precedence

One day I was walking with a man in his sixties to his field on the edge of the village, accompanied by a number of children and teenagers. As we passed along a narrow ridge, we spotted Mount Lawadu in the distance. The man paused and pointed toward the mountain, telling me that this was where he and the other members of his origin house had lived before the Indonesian invasion. He then proceeded to tell me the origin narrative of his house group, Lawadu (Manekaoli).

His ancestors were originally part of the origin house Fahelihun and had lived near the river Lo Alohowiri. They "were lucky" (*hetan sorti*), because they encountered a golden star that showed them the way to a place called Wehali, an event heralding their high status. The star told the ancestors, "You are the *liurai,* you will become the *Dom*" (*o liurai, o sai Dom*)—*Dom* being one of various titles adopted from the Portuguese to refer to local rulers. In Wehali, the ancestral siblings Na'i Koli and Na'i Nahak ("the older" and "the younger") received a potent spear. When they arrived back in Funar, they went to the hamlet of Fahelihun and thrust the spear into the ground. The spear was so "hot" and potent (*lulik*) that the nearby pond dried out.[28] Wehali refers to a Tetum domain located in West Timor, a place that figures widely in a variety of narratives from across Timor-Leste. Inhabitants of Wehali represent their domain as the ultimate center of the land—the epitome of the inner, indigenous, female realm of spiritual authority.[29] Yet Wehali also "exports" men and masculine objects associated with the power of rule (such as spears, drums, and flags), as can be seen in the Funar account of how the journey to Wehali bestowed political power upon the ancestors that is opposed to the indigenous ritual or spiritual power of the autochthones.

In some origin accounts of Funar's named houses, political rulers are represented as having originated in Wehali, and hence are seen as indigenous "stranger kings" whose legitimacy is derived from their connection with a domain other than Funar. For example, a member of the origin house Bamatak, which traces its origins to Wehali, once let me in on "a big secret"—namely, that Mount Sinai is actually located in Wehali. Tapping into biblical accounts was a way of stressing his special status, since, according to him, this secret was evidence that members of his house were "God's chosen people." Bamatak is the only house group that does not claim original descent in Funar. In the accounts of other groups, autochthonous brothers from Funar travel to Wehali and return as political chiefs by bringing objects of rule from Wehali. The status of a specific house group depends on how effectively it can

---

[28] The narrative illustrates another way of becoming "one" with the land: in addition to being born from it, one may penetrate it with a spear.

[29] See: Tom Therik, *Wehali: The Female Land: Traditions of a Timorese Ritual Centre* (Canberra: Australian National University—Pandanus Books, 2004); and Gérard Francillon, "Incursions upon Wehali: A Modern History of an Ancient Empire," in Fox, *The Flow of Life*, 248–65.

make claims to different sources of authority, as can be seen from the ways in which Lawadu's origin narrative proceeds.

Once they returned from Wehali, Lawadu's ancestral siblings moved on to a place called Mount Aihahi, where they encountered members of the Bamatak origin house (the latter claim to have originated in Wehali, as will be discussed in the next chapter). The ancestors of both houses organized a contest that included various competitions, such as shooting mangos off branches and climbing palm trees. Bamatak's ancestors won all of the different games, which should have meant they won the right to settle there. However, Lawadu's ancestors were "owners" of a specific "custom" (*lisan*), that of burying the dead in the ground. Since Bamatak's ancestors, who were not autochthonous, used to hang their dead from trees (because, they said, the earth had started shaking when they had buried them in the ground), Lawadu's ancestors had something to bargain with: the exchange of their customary knowledge (*lisan*) for land. As a result, they settled at Mount Lawadu, which is today part of Funar, while Bamatak's ancestors stayed in Aihahi. Due to their customary knowledge—that of burying the dead in the ground—and the great strength of their *lulik* objects, the ancestors of Lawadu became the rulers (*liurai*) of Funar.

There are a variety of other narratives that recount how and why members of the Lawadu origin house became the *liurai*, including an account in which their ancestors received a scepter (*ua*) from the Portuguese with which to rule over the people of Funar. These accounts appear as variants of the "stranger king" paradigm that has been described in a variety of Southeast Asian and Melanesian contexts.[30] In Funar, the most common way of mobilizing this paradigm was by representing political rulers not as total outsiders, but as returning younger brothers. Similar dynamics have also been described by Traube, who has examined how Mambai absorbed the Portuguese colonial rulers into their "cultural order" by presenting them not just as outside rulers, but also as returning younger brothers opposed to their Mambai older brothers who had stayed and guarded the ritual sphere. It is for that reason that some Mambai saw the process of decolonization that started in 1974 as a violation of the proper order.[31]

In Funar and the Laclubar subdistrict more generally, narratives of "outside rulers" are similarly used to accommodate historical events, such as the appointment of rulers by colonial powers. Through these origin accounts, hierarchies imposed by the Portuguese colonial administration, which included the appointment of loyal rulers and the ousting of those who did not cooperate, are integrated into the indigenous hierarchy and thereby naturalized. This is the case in Lawadu's origin narrative, for example, as it recounts how an ancestor called José do Espirito Santo received a scepter from the Portuguese, bestowing him with legitimacy to "rule" (*ukun*) over Funar.

---

[30] For examinations of "stranger king" narratives in Southeast Asia and the Pacific, see Ian Caldwell and David Henley, eds., "Stranger Kings in Indonesia and Beyond," especially James J. Fox, "Installing the 'Outsider' Inside: The Exploration of an Epistemic Austronesian Cultural Theme and Its Social Significance," 201–18. See also: David Henley, "Conflict, Justice, and the Stranger-King Indigenous Roots of Colonial Rule in Indonesia and Elsewhere," *Modern Asian Studies* 38, no. 1 (2004): 85–144; Michael W. Scott, "Proto-People and Precedence: Encompassing Euroamericans through Narratives of 'First Contact' in Solomon Islands," in *Exchange and Sacrifice*, eds. Pamela J. Stewart and Andrew Strathern (Durham, NC: Carolina Academic Press, 2008), 141–76; and Traube, *Cosmology and Social Life*, 51–65.

[31] Traube, *Cosmology and Social Life*, 54; see also Scott, "Proto-People and Precedence."

Although Lawadu's account mentions that the Portuguese appointed José do Espirito Santo, those who recount this narrative generally maintain that the ruling status of Lawadu's ancestors had been predetermined due to their possession of customary knowledge and the strong potency of their ancestral objects.[32] The representation of the foreign political domain as originating inside Funar (including the representation of foreign rulers as returning autochthones or as younger brothers who had been on a journey) collapses the established diarchy, since the political outside is described as having its ultimate origins on the inside.

The opposition between the spiritual female inside, and the political male outside, is one that is recursively collapsed and re-instantiated. The male invader dries up the earth with his spear and hence captures the reproductive powers of the female land and underground springs. This instance of the stranger-king paradigm, whereby powerful outsiders replace original rulers, evolves around a range of analogous oppositions (indigenous/immigrant, female/male, immobility/mobility, hot/cold), which together produce and reproduce a dual sovereignty that can be realized in a variety of forms.[33]

These origin accounts of Funar's named houses are not detached from material processes; narratives of ancestral interactions with the landscape were frequently related while walking past these sites. Hence, it is important to live near the ancestral land, since the landscape itself is used to support the claims to land ownership and status that are derived from these accounts.

When I spoke to members of the origin house Fahelihun, they confirmed that the ancestors of Lawadu did, indeed, originate from their land, yet they emphasized a different aspect of the narrative. A ritual specialist from Fahelihun said that the ancestors of his origin house, who emerged from beneath the ground (*larek ruan*), had invited members of Lawadu to become the *liurai*. Hence today, whenever the latter want something, they have to ask Fahelihun first, since it provides the "door" (*lalamatak*) to the inside—the door to the *liurai*. This role of Fahelihun as the gateway was also acknowledged by members of Lawadu and was invoked when talking about present-day relations between the houses. During the national elections of 2007, for example, the ASDT (Associação Social Democrática Timorense) party, which had a strong base in Fahelihun, received the highest number of votes in Funar. Shortly after the results had been announced, I was standing at Funar's kiosk with members of Lawadu when one of the women present told me that even though the ASDT had won the elections, the inhabitants of Fahelihun would pass the rule (*ukun*) back to them (i.e., Lawadu) because Fahelihun was just the "door" and did not have the right to rule.

Political status and right to land may be claimed on the basis of autochthony as well as acquired through exchange, as occurred between Lawadu and Bamatak. Moreover, the status of a house group is justified with reference to certain aspects of the origin narratives, such as Lawadu's ownership of valuable customs and potent objects. Ancestors of the other origin houses are also said to have owned potent objects. Some of these are thought to have been in the possession of the ancestors

---

[32] For a more detailed account of how José do Espirito Santo became *liurai*, see Chapter 3, this volume; and Bovensiepen, "Diferentes Perspectivas Sobre o Passado."

[33] We will come across this recursively reconstituting diarchic ideology again in Chapters 3 and 6. The latter chapter recounts how the land was "opened" and its potency enlisted to expel the Indonesian military, thereby "heating" the land, which subsequently had to be cooled again.

since they came into being, while others were acquired as gifts, in exchange, or were given to the ancestors by *lulik* land.

Today, claims to land ownership, status, and economic access to land are based on ancestral connections. However, narratives that recount the journeys of the ancestors and their interactions with the landscape are not in themselves sufficient to secure such claims—they must be accompanied by material proof of this ancestral presence in the form of stones, a dried-up pond, or potent objects (e.g., golden discs or spears). Funar's inhabitants say that sites in the landscape, ancestral houses, and ancestral objects are "signs" (*signal*) of their ancestors' presence and power. Since the landscape and ancestral objects provide the material basis for the narratives and claims to status of different origin houses, it is vital for people to live close to their ancestral land in order for their narratives to be convincing and their entitlements to land to be ensured.

During the Indonesian occupation, people were effectively disconnected from their ancestors when they were evicted from their land, their houses were destroyed, and many of their possessions were lost. By moving back to their land and reviving ancestral relationships, they were not just reinvigorating past customs; rather, they were also rebuilding claims to status and land ownership. The existence of tangible sites, which are signs of the ancestors' continued potency, makes these claims more authoritative. Thus, hierarchical relations between different human groups are produced and renegotiated in interaction with the landscape. Via the land, the highlanders were naturalizing status differences—even those that were evidently a result of Portuguese colonial intervention, such as the appointment of certain people as "Dom."

INTERLUDE: GOLD

In the origin narratives discussed above, a golden star showed the ancestors of Lawadu the way to Wehali, where they obtained a potent spear. A similar narrative is told in Laclubar, according to which a golden star—the embodiment of the *lulik* land—gave a scepter to the ruling house. In several of the origin narratives recounted in Funar and Laclubar Town, ancestral objects, which are *lulik*, are described as golden.[34]

There were several other narratives that made a mention of gold. While traveling through territory belonging to the *liurai* of Funar, my neighbor Ronaldo told me that, in the past, gold had flown between two mountain peaks in an area known as Hatu Kasola. In the mornings, he explained, gold would hover above the mountains; then, when night fell, it would return to the land. Here, *lulik* is associated with subterranean wealth in the form of gold. Because of this gold, the ruling family was able to breed a large herd of goats, for which the mountains served as pasture. In effect, the goats were "given" to the *liurai* by the *lulik* land. Ronaldo said that because

---

[34] Narratives containing a guiding star that helps people to achieve prosperity, autonomy, or power are easily recast through a biblical lens. Similar accounts can also be found in West Papua, where the narrative of the Morning Star has gained political significance in the Papuan independence movement. See: Kirksey, *Freedom in Entangled Worlds*, 29; and Danilyn Rutherford, *Raiding the Land of the Foreigners: The Limits of the Nation on an Indonesian Frontier* (Princeton: Princeton University Press, 2003), 24.

this place was *lulik*, the water that ran out of the spring nearby was very hot (just as *lulik* objects are thought to be hot).

On another occasion, Ronaldo told me how in the past he had found a small piece of gold, the size of a peanut, in his pocket. Following this discovery, he started traveling in his dreams. During his travels, he would fly around the mountains near Laclubar Town, and in the morning he would wake up near the *lulik* site of Susuk at the bottom of Mount Maubere. With the piece of gold in his pocket, he could travel through the earth and emerge at the openings found at *lulik* sites. He was frightened by these unwanted journeys, and so tried to throw the gold away, but it kept reappearing in his pocket.

In a similar vein, a member of the ruling house in Laclubar Town told me that when his origin house was re-inaugurated after Timor-Leste's independence, golden stars had fallen from the sky. He also claimed that the British monarchy had financed the construction of his origin house. Similar claims have been made by political leaders in Dili: the leader of the Timor's People's Party (Partido do Povo de Timor, PPT), Jacob Xavier, who is from Ainaro, contended that his *lulik* house was Buckingham Palace and that gold from Timor's *lulik* houses was stolen to establish the World Bank.[35] The day after Jacob Xavier claimed publicly on television that he was the owner of the World Bank and that East Timorese citizens could get money there, a crowd gathered in front of the World Bank building in Dili to collect "their" money. In this narrative, too, gold is associated with the *lulik* houses.

In Funar and Laclubar, potential riches are thought to be located underground, since gold is associated with specific sites in the landscape. In the various accounts detailed above, gold is used as a metonym of *lulik*. When the priest told me that there was a lot of gold in Funar, the villagers present were quick to agree with him. His statement affirmed the widespread claim that origin houses in Funar are particularly strong and that the land there is especially potent. However, the priest might have been conflating Catholic activities with *lulik*, since the book he gave me concerned the history of the Catholic Church; Catholicism is seen by many to be equivalent to *lulik*. The fear of losing gold expressed by some villagers when I arrived in the area might have reflected people's concerns about outside interference in their control over local resources. Nevertheless, people's claims to possess gold also illustrated the pride they took in the land that they inhabited. Rather than presenting themselves as victims of historical events, the people I encountered during my fieldwork were quietly confident that affluence would come their way in the future.

Signe Howell, who has examined the equation of women and gold amongst Lio in Flores, maintains that "gold to the Lio represents an extreme example of the fused identity of humans and things."[36] Similarly, in Funar, sacred sites in the landscape are considered to contain gold when the ancestors retain a presence therein. As Strathern and Steward have argued, gold is life-giving, just as women, the land, or the ancestors are.[37]

---

[35] Douglas Kammen, "Fragments of Utopia: Popular Yearnings in East Timor," *Journal of Southeast Asian Studies* 40, no. 2 (2009): 397–98.

[36] Signe Howell, "Of Persons and Things: Exchange and Valuables among the Lio of Eastern Indonesia," *Man* 24, no. 3 (1989): 422.

[37] Andrew Strathern and Pamela Stewart, *The Python's Back: Pathways of Comparison between Indonesia and Melanesia* (Westport, CT: Greenwood Publishing Group, 2000), 17.

Agricultural Productivity, Health, and Fertility

The ancestral objects owned by a house group all have their own names, as well as their own histories recounting how the ancestors obtained them. The members of the Ada Lulin origin house (of Bamatak), for example, claim to own a golden disc (*ilis*) known as *Ilis Urier*. The members of this house told me that their ancestors had obtained the disc in Wehali and that it could be used in a ceremony to ensure that the fields were fertile and would provide ample food—indeed, the name *urier* refers to a high-quality and plentiful harvest. They also told me that they owned a pair of earrings (*mamulik*) known as *Mamulik Ter Aas* (the "earrings of shooting mangos"), which their ancestors acquired during their contest with Lawadu when they shot mangos from the trees. Another object obtained by Bamatak's ancestors in Motain/Motael came in the form of a scepter called *Ua Parlemento Arnat Arnai* (a name possibly derived from the mestizo Hornay family, which played a key role in the early Portuguese colonial expansion in Timor). There are additional narratives about a variety of other objects that, according to the members of Bamatak, possess unusually hot *lulik*—so hot, indeed, that at some point in the past their *lulik* destroyed the objects and the house of another group by setting them alight.

The ancestors of the Ada Virtudi house, who also form part of Bamatak, are said to have found a stone in the river while washing potatoes. The stone was given to them by the *lulik* land, and it brought them luck (*sorti*) in the form of high yields for their crops and fertility for their livestock.[38] When a member of the Bamatak origin house decided to go abroad to study, he brought a pig and some money to the house to seek good luck.

The members of Manekaoli (part of the *liurai* house Lawadu) told me that they used to own a multicolored stone in the shape of a buffalo head with horns that made buffalo noises. This *lulik* stone, which stood near the cemetery in a place called Hia Uuk, was so potent that the owners were able to raise a large herd of buffalo. At some point in the past, however, the ruler of the *suco* of Fatumakerek had stolen the stone, which led to a long-standing conflict between the two ruling houses.

Rituals carried out to ensure the fertility of livestock are called *lanur*. In 2006, a member of the *liurai* house of Fatumakerek wanted to initiate a *lanur* ceremony to increase the fertility of his buffalo.[39] When we went to Fatumakerek, the ritual speaker there told us that it was impossible to carry out the ceremony before the scepter house of Manekaoli (in Funar) had been rebuilt. Moreover, it was necessary to "clean" the house that the *liurai* of Fatumakerek used to live in, since it had been destroyed during the conflict between FRETILIN (Frente Revolucionária de Timor-Leste Independente) and UDT (União Democrática Timorense) in 1975. To do this, a special ritual had to be carried out in the ruins of the house to get rid of the blood that had once been spilled there. This involved ritual speeches and an offering of a goat, betel nuts, and palm liquor to the ancestors (see photo, next page). Furthermore, I was told that before rebuilding everyday houses in Funar, the returnees always had to ask the ancestors and the *lulik* land for permission. There

[38] The significance of notions of fertility in the region has been widely discussed in the regional literature, including by Hicks in *Tetum Ghosts and Kin* (esp. pp. 1–4, 93–112), and in Fox's edited volume, *The Flow of Life*.

[39] The *liurai* of Funar and Fatumakerek are connected, since Fatumakerek is said to have been part of Funar until it was separated into two by the Portuguese administration. Today they are two separate *suco*.

were certain sites where only the "people of the land" could live, since anyone else would inevitably become ill there.

In the ruins of the *liurai's* house (2006; author's photo)

When the people of Funar moved back to their ancestral land, they had to restore their relationship with the landscape in order to ensure human wellbeing and the fertility of their crops and livestock. The positive and life-giving properties of the land were mobilized by means of a number of important rituals, during which small offerings were made. One of these rituals, called *wer matan*, which was carried out before I started my fieldwork, was aimed at reinvigorating the springs and wells. I was told that all the different origin houses from Funar had participated in this ceremony, in which the ancestors had been asked to give their permission to plant crops in this area and to ensure their productivity and plentiful supply of water.

When people returned to Funar, they had to clear new fields; this necessarily involved a ritual to appease the spiritual landowners. During this type of ritual, people have to kill an animal (usually a pig or a chicken) to "feed" the land, as well as pour coconut juice (seen as cooling) over a stone and offer betel nuts and money to the *larek-nain*. When I took part in one of these rituals in 2006, an elder explained to me that they were asking the *lulik* land for permission to plant crops there, adding that they had to ask the *larek-nain* for permission and show respect toward the ancestors (*avô*). The elder's successive use of *lulik* land, landowners (*larek–nain*), and *avô* in this instance underlines how these different agents are closely connected through the landscape.[40]

Lulik site by Fahelihun (2006; author's photo)

I mentioned earlier that some of the residents who had not yet returned to their ancestral land complained of poor health. People say that by living on and making offerings to their ancestral land, they can alleviate their health problems. In addition, it is believed that rain can be produced by making offerings to the land. Near Fahelihun, there is a small fenced-off mound of stones (*lalutuk*) on a hill that is *lulik* (see photo, above). Some villagers told me that gold is to be found beneath the stones. The elders of the nearby hamlet are responsible for ensuring that the rains start after the dry season. They do this by making a small offering of money and palm liquor to the *lulik* land. This offering is accompanied by ritual speech uttered by a local expert who can predict whether there will be rain: if the cup of palm wine remains full, the rains will come (*kopu nabenu, wari nama*); if it is empty, the rains will be delayed (*kopu mau, wari bi nama hei*).

Ensuring crop fertility requires similar rituals. When corn is harvested, for example, some food is first offered to the *lulik* land near the fields. Subsequently, the harvest is brought to the *lulik* houses to prompt the ancestors' permission to eat the

---

[40] Compare this with Gregory Forth's study of Nage spirits, *Beneath the Volcano: Religion, Cosmology, and Spirit Classification among the Nage of Eastern Indonesia* (Leiden: KITLV Press, 1998). First of all, Nage "earth spirits" called *nitu* need to be expelled in order to cultivate land, but they are "chased" away rather than being appeased through offerings. Moreover, unlike *larek-nain* in Funar, *nitu* in Flores are not addressed directly in agricultural ritual. Even though *nitu* are not equated with human landowners (*moi tana*), they are nonetheless considered to be in possession of the land. Similar to Timorese *larek-nain*, *nitu* also appear as eels, beautiful women, or snakes, and inhabit land that is restricted or prohibited (*pie*) (Forth, *Beneath the Volcano*, 67). They are also associated with gold (ibid., 82).

produce. An offering of corn is made to the ancestors as a way of showing respect toward them and "removing the ban" (*kore bandu*) from the new corn, thereby making the corn edible for human consumption. During this ceremony, called *asauk,* the ancestors are asked to eat first, after which the living descendants consume their produce, thereby transforming the agricultural fruits of the land into an edible resource.[41]

Inhabitants of Funar would tell me that with the right knowledge of ritual speech, they could get anything from the ancestral land, including fertility, good health, and even political power, as well as wealth in the form of buffalo or large sums of money. When a road-building project was inaugurated near the village, a goat was killed to ask the land for permission to proceed with the work, since no roads had existed at the time of the ancestors. During the course of this ritual, one of the participants stated that the tractor that was to be used to build the road would no longer need any diesel to run, since blood from the goat had been poured over its wheels.

These examples show that the land is thought to have desires and preferences and that it needs to be looked after and cared for. Yet in addition to revitalizing the unity and reciprocal relations with the land, these rituals were also a way of establishing a separation between *lulik* land and human beings, creating, as Traube says, "a boundary between things."[42] This boundary differentiates humans from the land during life, much as the small fences separate *lulik* sites from the everyday concerns of the living. In the ways in which Funar residents relate to the landscape, we find both unity between human and nonhuman categories (especially on ritual occasions) and separation through boundary-marking.

Moving back to the ancestral land after their forced dislocation necessitated the reunification of people and place. Yet *lulik* can nevertheless provoke disorder and death if not kept separate from everyday life by a clear boundary. The rituals discussed in this section all involve the creation of a boundary between the world of the living and the world of the dead. The life-giving qualities of the potent land can be mobilized when differentiation is established between nonhuman and human categories. This process of differentiation always involves making a small sacrifice to the land, such as burying the placenta when a baby is born or giving food to the ancestors when the harvest is taken into the house. This process strengthens the boundary between the living and the ancestral landscape, thereby reproducing life by generating wealth, fertility, health, and agricultural productivity.

THE CATHOLIC LANDSCAPE

The resettlement of Funar involved an attempt to recreate and reinvigorate past relations with the ancestral land. Villagers stressed that the status of each origin house was determined during ancestral times. There are, however, some indications that the current landscape is not what it was during the time of the ancestors. So how, exactly, did it change while its inhabitants were away? One important transformation was the mass conversion to Catholicism that took place while the residents were living in Laclubar Town during the Indonesian occupation. This final

---

[41] Compare with: Hicks, *Tetum Ghosts and Kin,* 62; and Traube, *Cosmology and Social Life,* 142.

[42] Traube, *Cosmology and Social Life,* 143.

section examines how people reconcile their insistence on the potency of the ancestral landscape with their conversion to Catholicism.

During the Indonesian occupation of East Timor, the percentage of people who professed Catholicism grew rapidly from nearly 30 percent in the 1970s to 80 percent in 1980 and over 90 percent in 1990.[43] There were many different reasons for this sharp increase in the number of converts, among them the Indonesian regulation, based on the *pancasila*, that obliged people to adopt one of five officially recognized religions, and the major part played by the Catholic Church in the resistance struggle. The increasing popularity of Catholicism was also apparent in Laclubar and Funar, where many of the older residents converted to Catholicism as adults during the time of the occupation.

In a small booklet celebrating the one hundredth anniversary of the Catholic Church in Soibada, Jorge da Cruz da Silva represents the establishment of the Catholic mission in the region as an "alliance" between Catholicism and *lulik*.[44] He argues that this alliance shows how the Timorese already had a relationship with God (*Nai Maromak*) before the Portuguese introduced the Catholic religion to the country, and concludes that this connection brought with it many advantages, such as education.[45] He admits, however, that at times the conversion entered into conflict with the spirit of the alliance, since priests obliged people to abandon their beliefs in *lulik* by burning *lulik* houses, imprisoning ritual experts, and erecting crosses on *lulik* land.

Right up to the present day, the landscape has been repeatedly marked with Catholic structures and relics, and today it is still easy to find such signs at important *lulik* sites. One example is the chapel (*capela*) dedicated to *Nossa Senhora de Aitara* ("Our Lady of the Thorns"), situated in Soibada Town. It was built on a small hill above a large tree that in the past—and even today, according to some people—was considered to be *lulik*. The Virgin Mary is reputed to have once appeared on the hill and therefore the site annually attracts hundreds of pilgrims from all over Timor-Leste.

In the Laclubar subdistrict, too, Catholic symbols have been "planted" in the landscape, even though Catholicism here does not have such a long history as in Soibada.[46] It was only after Timor-Leste's independence that a priest took up permanent residence in Laclubar Town, where a large and conspicuously white-colored church had been built just before the end of the Indonesian occupation. Since this time, crosses have been planted at numerous *lulik* sites, such as the grave of one of Laclubar's most important ancestors, Dom Geraldo. Crosses can also be found alongside the main road in Laclubar Town, forming part of the Catholic "Stations of

[43] Frédéric Durand, *Catholicisme et Protestantisme dans l'Ile de Timor 1556–2003: Construction d'une Identité Chrétienne et Engagement Politique Contemporain* (Toulouse: Editions Arkuiris; Bangkok: IRASEC, 2004), 94.

[44] Jorge da Cruz da Silva, *Hanessan Hatohar (Aliança) Maklouk entre Lulik no Religião Católica. Comemoração Igreja Soibada Halo Tinan Atus Ida, 1904–2004* (Baucau, Timor-Leste: Diocese of Baucau, 2004).

[45] Compare with: James J. Fox, "Adam and Eve on the Island of Roti: A Conflation of Oral and Written Traditions," *Indonesia* 36 (1983): 15–23; and Trinidade, *Lulik*, 25.

[46] In the past, Catholics from Laclubar traveled to Soibada for important Catholic ceremonies. Some of Funar's residents told me how their parents or grandparents received their religious education or baptism in Manatuto Town (on the north coast), which was the first permanent religious settlement in the eastern part of Portuguese Timor.

the Cross" procession route. Nowadays, however, the erection of these crosses is not interpreted as a hostile act directed at traditional practices. Instead, people tend to regard Catholic markers as signs or symbols that testify to the potency and strength of their *lulik* land.

Several ritual specialists in Laclubar linked their origin narratives to the Catholic faith, arguing that the region's most important founding ancestors were actually called Adam and Eve (*Adão e Eva*) and that the names in the narratives were simply their equivalent "heathen names" (*naran gentio*). Some people also claimed that the Virgin Mary was born in Laclubar, where she was transformed from a civet cat (*laku*) into a human being. The Catholic-inspired equation of the ancestors with Adam and Eve is analogous to the statement that Laclubar is the land of the liver and the navel. Both assertions emphasize the significance of Laclubar's landscape, in the sense that both maintain that Laclubar is the place where humankind originated.[47] The fact that Laclubar's inhabitants claim a common origin for all humanity might also reflect the increasing influence of Catholicism in Laclubar Town, since people from Funar, where Catholicism has been less prevalent, claim separate origins. It is possible, therefore, that ritual experts in Laclubar Town tried to recast their origin narratives in a way that would better fit with Catholic narratives about human genesis.

The landscape in Funar also contains some traces of Catholicism, and its influence has been growing. There is a small chapel in Funar and a little shrine (*gruta*) to the Virgin Mary on a hill near the school. Some of the villagers I spoke with said that the Virgin Mary had actually appeared in Funar before she arrived in Soibada, but that she had moved on because there were not enough stones in Funar. Stones are frequently seen in places where *lulik* is encapsulated or can become visible. Interestingly, the qualities attributed to the Virgin Mary were similar to those ascribed to *lulik*. We can deduce this by analogy: Mary did not establish a permanent presence in Funar because of the lack of stones, which is why she was unable to become visible and why she moved on to Soibada. Thus, Mary needed stones in the same way *lulik* needs stones. The claim that the Virgin Mary arrived in Funar "first" (*uluk*)—that is, before Soibada—is also a claim to precedence. Inherent in this statement is the idea that Funar was her favored destination because the land there was particularly worthy and potent. When I returned to Funar in April 2015, the path up to the small shrine had been improved and crosses had been planted alongside it. With the improvement of the physical signs marking the Catholic presence, there was also an increase in attendance at Catholic ceremonies.

The inhabitants of Funar say that the hill beside the school is *lulik* in the sense that it is spiritually charged. At the same time, they maintain that it is associated with the apparition of the Virgin Mary. A further commonly held view was that God (*Maromak*) lived on the hill. *Maromak* is not just the missionaries' term for "God," but is also the name of a precolonial deity, whose existence allows people to claim that they already "knew God" before the Portuguese arrived. Even though people in Funar did not always distinguish between Mary and God,[48] they did insist on a

---

[47] This is a way of "centering" which, according to Feuchtwang, is an intricate part of place-making; see Stephan Feuchtwang, "Theorising Place," in *Making Place: State Projects, Globalisation, and Social Responses in China*, ed. Stephan Feuchtwang (London: UCL Press, 2004), 4.

[48] People in this region frequently treated the Virgin Mary and God as one and the same being. Several villagers told me that God was a woman with a white face, just like the statue of the Virgin Mary.

conceptual difference between God, *lulik*, and ancestors, whose importance they ranked in that order. In practice, these different agents are not clearly demarcated, and the potency of particular sites is a consequence of these agents working in tandem. The idea of an alliance between the Catholic Church and *lulik*, the contention that Adam and Eve (and thus humankind), as well as Mary, originate in Laclubar, and the assertions about Marian apparitions are all seen as evidence that the land in this region is particularly potent. Catholicism does not replace the existing potency; rather, it is integrated into the landscape.

Another case of the incorporation of Catholicism into existing practices takes place during Easter, when people take a portion of their harvest to the church to be blessed, mirroring the practice of taking the harvest to the named houses in order to ask the ancestors to "eat first." In both cases, the relationship between human and nonhuman domains was symbolically constituted in the form of an act of offering food to the ancestral realm, carried out with the expectation of blessings to follow.

It is not clear whether the integration of Catholicism into the spiritual landscape was part of a deliberate strategy of "inculturation" instigated by Catholic missionaries. As Fenella Cannell notes, the Catholic Church (in contrast with many Protestant missions) has been rather tolerant when it comes to accommodating local customs, especially since Vatican II.[49] In Timor-Leste, this stance has been specifically shaped by the way in which the Catholic Church opted to classify certain practices as part of traditional rather than religious custom. This deliberate separation of religion (*agama*, In.) and culture (*adat*, In.) that took place in Indonesia can also be observed in Laclubar.[50] The priest, for example, repeatedly stressed that although he was not originally from Laclubar, he was nonetheless Timorese and thus shared the "Timorese culture" of his parishioners. It was for this reason that he actively encouraged certain practices that he considered to be "cultural"—as evidenced, for instance, by his eagerness to invite ritual speakers to important public events. These practices were not seen as antagonistic toward Catholicism.

Although there is some evidence to suggest that the attitudes expressed toward Catholic missionaries in Timor-Leste have not always been positive, today the Catholic Church is highly influential and well-respected. People have embraced the ways in which their landscape has been marked out as particularly potent through the placement of Catholic signs. The idea of an "alliance" between the Church and *lulik* captures the perceived nature of the relationship quite clearly.

Despite their general integration, the potency of Catholicism and that of the landscape were on occasion seen as direct competitors. This was apparent in discussions with the landowners of Bahareduk village, who told me that they did not want the priest to baptize their children for fear of the holy water touching the land and causing the *lulik* to "jump away." They were worried that if this happened, the land would no longer be fertile. Some people also argued, more explicitly, that the power of *lulik* had declined in recent years because of the growing importance of Catholicism. Others, however, denied that any such change was taking place. What is striking, though, is that despite these different evaluations, Catholic potency and *lulik* are not considered to be fundamentally different in nature—people relate to both via the landscape.

---

[49] Fenella Cannell, *The Anthropology of Christianity* (Durham: Duke University Press, 2006), 26.

[50] On the tension between *adat* and *agama*, see, for example, Rita Smith Kipp and Susan Rodgers, eds., *Indonesian Religions in Transition* (Tucson: University of Arizona Press, 1987).

According to the majority of villagers I spoke to, the land of Funar has not lost its potency due to the influence of Catholicism. Instead, local residents actively and creatively integrate outside influences with their belief in the potency of the land. By combining Catholic beliefs, practices, and signs, the villagers have superimposed another layer of meaning onto existing semiotic terrain, which has ultimately resulted in a strengthening, rather than weakening, of the potency of the landscape. In this region, then, one cannot clearly distinguish between the Catholic and the ancestral landscape, since the two are not fundamentally opposed but rather creatively combined in a process that reinforces the power of the land at large.

The Return to Ancestral Land

In the years after Timor-Leste regained national independence, Funar remained relatively cut off from the financial and logistic support provided elsewhere by governmental and nongovernmental institutions that had invested heavily in state building and post-conflict reconstruction during the years of transition. Facing severe poverty and agricultural insecurity, a major concern for Funar villagers was to reconnect with and reinvigorate the ancestral land from which they were separated for over two decades during their forced dislocation.

Whereas accounts about the hardships of the Indonesian occupation accompanied the revival of ancestral practices in other regions of Timor-Leste, such accounts were comparatively rare in Funar. Instead, a strong emphasis was put on the potency of the ancestral land, described as the location of potentially vast gold deposits. This chapter has shown that when invoking gold, Funar residents were usually speaking about *lulik*. When mentioning gold or golden objects, they mostly referred to *lulik* objects, *lulik* houses, or *lulik* sites in the landscape. The inhabitants of Funar were thus in agreement with the priest's suggestion that there was a lot of gold in Funar, and I take this consensus to mean that the landscape in this area is particularly potent. Saying that there was a lot of gold in Funar meant that the *lulik* of this ancestral place was exceptionally strong. By speaking about *lulik* as a permanent material (i.e., gold), the enduring nature of this potency was candidly expressed and its value as a source of wealth was highlighted as well.

At the beginning of this chapter, I raised the question of how the landscape and its *lulik* potency are significant for local inhabitants. As I have tried to show, this significance consists of the life-giving properties of the landscape; it is the "trunk of life." The residents of Funar talked about the ancestral land in much the same way that they spoke about people who had died, saying that they "missed" and "worried" about their land when they were living in Laclubar Town. The return to Funar was itself part of the "revival" of ancestral practices that has been witnessed across Timor-Leste in recent years, especially since independence. What is being "revived" are the relations with the ancestors themselves, as they are located in the land. In this respect, the return to the ancestral land is a way of responding to the experience of dislocation, as it involves reestablishing an original unity between the ancestral trunk and its human tip.

There are several reasons why the ancestral land is so important to the inhabitants of the region. For one thing, potent sites are not only a source of life, they are also signs of status and sources of fertility, morality, health, and nourishment—in other words, all forms of wealth and well-being. However, the landscape is not immune to changes and transformations, both during ancestral times (such as when the planting of a *lulik* spear caused a pond to dry out) and more recently (e.g., through the influences of Catholicism). In contrast to other contexts where ancestral and world religions came to be seen as incompatible,[51] Catholicism in the Laclubar subdistrict was generally not viewed as a threat to the potency of the landscape. Instead, it was taken as evidence of the land's existing potency, a fact that the Catholic Church appears to have recognized.

Origin narratives of Funar's house groups center on a primordial consubstantial unity between the autochthonous ancestors and the land from which they emerged, as well as on the journeys of political authorities. The land bestows wealth upon those who look after and are close to it. The return to Funar throughout the late 1990s and early 2000s and the ongoing reinvigoration of the ancestral land did not just reenact variants of the stranger-king paradigm and its diarchic ideology, but it also involved the reestablishment of the primordial unity between people and place. This process of reunification necessarily involved the negation of historical experiences that set people apart from their ancestral trunk.

There is another dimension to the process of reconnecting with the land, namely the need to distance and separate current residents from places that contain ancestral *lulik* potency. Small fences surrounded *lulik* sites, since they were off-limits and had to be avoided. The life-giving qualities of the potent land are mobilized at the precise moment when place and people become differentiated, as was clear in the narrative about Fahelihun's ancestors who emerged from a split stone. Life-giving properties were usually motivated by making small sacrifices to the land, such as burying the placenta under the house when a baby is born or giving food to the ancestors before eating harvested corn.

From the agricultural rituals discussed, it becomes clear that wealth is derived from a reciprocal relationship between people and the land. However, such a reciprocal relationship requires separation. Strathern has analyzed in depth how in Papua New Guinea, separation is the basis of social relations: reproduction is achieved through detachment by momentarily distinguishing the product from its source.[52] Applying this insight to Funar, it becomes clear that if humans and the nonhuman environment were of the same substance during life, no such exchanges could take place. Exchanging entities need to be distinguished from one another in order to enter into a reciprocal relationship.

While the return to Funar involved the unification of people with the ancestral place of origin, this unification itself necessitated small acts of differentiation through boundary-marking. Humans have to be, at least temporarily, separated from their source (the land) to benefit from its life-giving properties. It is only through this detachment from the source of life that the benefits of the ancestral land emerge. Therefore, while emphasizing their close connection with the ancestral land, the returnees also had to invest efforts into maintaining a distance from it. Dynamic processes of unification and differentiation underpin all aspects of people's relationship with the land in Funar.

---

[51] See, for example, Allerton, "Introduction: Spiritual Landscapes of Southeast Asia"; Webb Keane, *Christian Moderns: Freedom and Fetish in the Mission Encounter* (Berkeley: University of California Press, 2007).

[52] Marilyn Strathern, *The Gender of the Gift: Problems with Women and Problems with Society in Melanesia* (Los Angeles: University of California Press, 1988), 124, 199.

CHAPTER TWO

CONCEALING TRUNK KNOWLEDGE

Just before leaving Funar at the end of my fieldwork in 2007, I visited a number of villagers to invite them to my farewell event. Elísio, a hamlet chief (*chefe de aldeia*), expressed both surprise and discontent at my impending departure. This thin man with his walking stick, dressed as usual in a shirt, sarong, and hat, told me, assertively, "You cannot leave yet. Your research is not yet complete!" He continued, "You only know the tip. There are many more words that we have not yet given to you."[1] I tried to smile confidently as I told him that I knew that there was still much more for me to learn, but that I needed to return to England. This answer did not seem to satisfy him, however, and he proudly declared that it would take seven days and seven nights for him to tell me everything that I needed to know. I asked whether he could share his knowledge with me before I left, to which he responded that this would not be feasible, because "the time was not right."

The idea that it would be possible to tell me everything I needed to know through the revelation of certain truthful words at a particular moment in time was by this point familiar to me. Several villagers had already told me that all I needed for my research was to speak to the right person at the right time and, in some cases, to bring along some "right gifts," such as chicken, betel nuts, money, or palm wine. However, during the course of my fieldwork I never received a complete account of the secret truths alluded to and occasionally promised. Several times I spent hours recording and writing down the words of a particular ritual expert, only for this person to stop at some point and inform me that he had not yet told me everything and that now was not the right time. Typically, a follow-up meeting never took place.

In this region of Timor-Leste, certain kinds of knowledge and types of words can only be revealed on specific occasions, and not everyone is thought to be able to disclose them. The words that people talked about usually concerned ancestral times. They are thought to have been passed down directly from the ancestors, and relate to the latter's origins and journeys, ritual speech, knowledge about medicinal plants, and other secrets—the nature of which is never explicitly described. Sometimes the people with whom I spoke referred to this as "culture" (*kultura*) or "custom" (*lisan*, or *adat* in Indonesian), but mostly such things were described as "words/speech" (*haha* in Idaté and *lia* in Tetum). These potent words are not only connected to particular individuals who are able to reveal them, but are also associated with specific places where they can be disclosed or places to which the ancestors have traveled. The interconnection between language and the landscape is pertinently expressed in the description of these "truth words" as the "trunk" (*uun*), like the trunk of a tree, which is the same word used to refer to the ancestral land.

It was assumed that I was in Timor-Leste to learn about these potent "cultural" words in order that I might document them. Some tried to facilitate this process,

---

[1] He used the Tetum term *rohan* for "tip," which is *iras* in Idaté.

while others used it as a reason to refuse to talk to me. Despite revealing some aspects of this knowledge to me—for example, by recounting origin myths and letting me participate in a number of important rituals—people always maintained that there was much more to know beyond what they had already disclosed. From their point of view, I had only learned the "tip" of their knowledge and never really got to the "trunk." Nonetheless, they remained ambiguous about what these undisclosed words were actually about. It is this ambiguity that makes these words both so appealing and so potentially powerful.

The tension between the emphasis on discovering the most truthful "trunk knowledge" and the simultaneous and persistent concealment of precisely what this "trunk" comprised contributed to a strained rivalry between different house groups.[2] Concealing and revealing cultural knowledge was an intricate aspect of negotiations surrounding hierarchical relations. There were high levels of contestation over who was a legitimate guardian of customary knowledge and who knew how to speak "truthfully." The dilemma that people faced was how to maintain this notion of unchanging and truthful "trunk" knowledge while confronting conflicting and competing accounts and challenges to the legitimacy of individual speakers.

The suggestion that specific kinds of words are handed down directly from the ancestors is common in Southeast Asia.[3] Nevertheless, ideas about the essentialized and unchanging nature of knowledge sit at odds with a range of recent anthropological approaches to the topic, which emphasize the ways in which knowledge is embodied or shaped and transmitted through practice,[4] which view knowledge as "relational positioning,"[5] or present knowledge as constituting personhood. In his criticism of Barth's model of Melanesian knowledge practices (which suggests that such practices are based on secrecy), for example, Tony Crook argues that in Bolivip "knowledge" is not a distinct domain but is "constitutive of persons," since knowledge-making practices are described as an "exchange of skin."[6] Ethnographic analyses of Melanesian knowledge, he argues, have been shaped by the anthropological practice of isolating knowledge domains from one another. Crook instead emphasizes the relational aspect of knowledge using the metaphor of a tree—which, like Bolivip stories, unfolds from the base to the crown—to structure his book.[7]

---

[2] Similar to the experiences of Traube, I was also told on a number of occasions that I must look for the "true words" or the "trunk." Traube notes that despite people agreeing about the importance of this trunk knowledge, there was a level of ambiguity about what it entailed (Traube, *Cosmology and Social Life*, 32).

[3] See James J. Fox, introduction, in *To Speak in Pairs: Essays on the Ritual Languages of Eastern Indonesia*, ed. James J. Fox (Cambridge: Cambridge University Press, 1988), 12.

[4] See, for example, Pierre Bourdieu, *The Logic of Practice* (London: Polity Press, 1990), 52–65; Trevor H. J. Marchand, preface and introduction, in "Making Knowledge," ed. Trevor H. J. Marchand, special issue, *The Journal of the Royal Anthropological Institute* 16, no. 1 (2010): iii–v, 1–21; and Marcel Mauss, "Body Techniques," in *Sociology and Psychology*, ed. Marcel Mauss (London: Routledge and Kegan Paul, 1979), 79–123.

[5] James Leach, "Leaving the Magic Out: Knowledge and Effect in Different Places," in "Recognising and Translating Knowledge," eds. James Leach and Richard Davis, special issue, *Anthropological Forum* 22, no. 3 (2012): 251–70.

[6] Tony Crook, *Anthropological Knowledge, Secrecy and Bolivip, Papua New Guinea: Exchanging Skin* (Oxford: Oxford University Press, 2007), 11.

[7] Crook, *Exchanging Skin*, 219. For additional discussion of approaches to the anthropology of knowledge, see: Malcolm R. Crick, "Anthropology of Knowledge," *Annual Review of*

For Idaté speakers, knowledge is similarly understood through the botanic metaphor of the tree trunk, which points to its connection to the ancestral realm. Yet unlike Crook's example, the language ideology in Funar does not suggest a relational understanding of knowledge. Instead, knowledge is considered to exist as an isolated domain, separate from the world of the living. This chapter focuses on the difficulties of upholding this ideology, which negates the relational, embodied, and subjective dimensions of knowledge. The goal is thus to explore the way people handle the differences among narrative accounts while seeking to maintain the notion that ancestral words are unique and unchanging.

MASTERS OF WORDS

The term *haha* in Idaté refers not only to words or speech, but also to the rituals that are led by certain male elders who fulfill the official function of ritual speakers. Only those individuals who are recognized as "masters of the mouth" (*ibar-nain*) or "masters of words/speech" (*haha-nain*) are entitled to speak publicly on these occasions.[8] Each origin house in Laclubar and Funar has one or, at most, a few ritual speakers who represent it during ritual events. The "masters of words" are responsible for performing ritual speech during marriage negotiations, as well as during the inauguration of origin houses (*ada wer*) and at rituals to ensure rain, the fertility of livestock (*lanur*), and a prosperous harvest (*asauk*). Through their communication with ancestors, ritual speakers can foretell the outcome of wars, anticipate conflict, or ask for fertility, protection, and wealth. A "master of the mouth" also performs ritual speech on more somber occasions, such as prior to a battle or during death rituals (*haha metan*). "Masters of words" are experts on subjects relating to the ancestors, their past journeys, and the relationships between origin houses. During land disputes, ritual speakers may be asked to give evidence of people's entitlement to land based on ancestral interactions therewith.

When an *ibar-nain* is particularly competent, he can receive significant recognition. In some cases, there is a hierarchy among different ritual speakers, and some houses respect different kinds of *ibar-nain*. One speaker, said to be "sitting by the pole inside the house," deals with internal issues for example, while another talks "outside the house." Side-houses are subsumed into a larger house structure in such a way that during important rituals, when the speakers of the higher-ranking houses perform, the ritual speakers of the side-houses "sit at the back of the house."

The skills of ritual speakers are a subject of frequent discussion, and many adults draw a clear distinction between a competent ritual speaker who "knows" (*ni natada*) and one who "does not know" (*ni bi natada dar*).[9] Ritual speaking is often carried out under the influence of a considerable amount of alcohol, and there are many ritual speakers who say they cannot speak without drinking (however, there are also a few renowned speakers who boast about being able to speak without consuming

---

Anthropology 11 (1982): 287–313; and Lars Højer, "Absent Powers: Magic and Loss in Post-Socialist Mongolia," *Journal of the Royal Anthropological Institute* 15, no. 3 (2009): 575–91.

[8] The term *haha-nain* can be translated as "master of words," "owner of words," or "person of words." David Hicks describes ritual speakers as "lord(s) of the word"; see Hicks, *Tetum Ghosts and Kin*, 28.

[9] Compare with Traube, *Cosmology and Social Life*, 33–34.

alcohol). Ritual speeches are delivered in a monotonous tone at a high speed and involve raising the voice at the end of each sentence, placing extra stress upon the last words. These rapid bursts of speech are greeted by a loud, approving "eeehhh" sound from the audience, which tends to become louder and more enthusiastic as more palm wine is consumed. Nonetheless, while ritual speakers are performing their words, not everyone in attendance is necessarily paying attention. Members of the audience commonly have private conversations at the same time, while also generally socializing, smoking, drinking, or soothing crying children.

Encounter between two ritual speakers and some members of their house groups, Manehiak and Manekaoli (2007; author's photo)

One factor that determines whether a ritual speaker is rated highly relates to the speed of delivery. On several occasions, men from the audience pointed out to me that a certain ritual speaker "really knew [how to speak]" because he was speaking very rapidly. Hesitation is interpreted as a sign that the speaker is not especially skilled. Once, during a mortuary ceremony, the speaker of a side-house was told off publicly by the other men present because he was stuttering as well as speaking quietly and slowly. The style in which the speeches are performed seems to be as important as their content. Skillful and competent ritual speaking may elevate the authority and prestige of the speaker and his origin house.[10]

During a meeting that aimed to resolve a dispute about the land on which the government offices in Laclubar Town were built, ritual speakers from a variety of Laclubar *sucos* were invited to speak. Afterward, one of the participants told me that listening to the ritual speaker of the *suco* Batara had convinced him that the ritual speaker's ancestors had given the land to the Portuguese government, and that it

---

[10] James Fox argues that in some eastern Indonesian societies, such as those of Sumba, ritual speech performed appropriately elevates the speaker's status, whereas in others, such as those of Roti, ritual language ability does not change a person's social status (Fox, *To Speak in Pairs*, 14).

therefore did not belong to the *liurai* of Orlalan, who also claimed it. The ritual speaker from Batara had spoken so fluently and truthfully during this meeting that he had managed to change this listener's mind about the issue. The fact that the ancestors of Batara were said to have given the land to the Portuguese government meant that today it must belong to the independent East Timorese government and not to individuals or other origin houses trying to claim it. Narratives about the past that are recounted by "persons of words" are closely connected to the way in which claims to land ownership and to status are made.

In several types of ritual, two speakers from different origin houses speak in turn, usually while facing each other (see photo, opposite page). The speech itself is rhythmic and normally begins with expressions of mutual respect. Ritual speech involves both reference to a set format of phrases, which people can easily recognize, and the improvisation of phrases that respond to the requirements of a particular situation. The phrases uttered are characterized by a parallel structure that James Fox has called "speaking in pairs."[11] The following is an example of this sort of parallelism, taken from a mortuary ritual in Funar:

meta halik, buti halik [black banyan tree, white banyan tree][12]

Ritual speech in Funar and Laclubar has strong similarities with the ritual languages found in other areas of Timor and eastern Indonesia. Using a comparative model, Fox has defined some of the common features of ritual languages in Austronesian societies as "highly metaphoric in nature," having a "formal, formulaic, and parallelistic" structure.[13] Fox maintains that the dyadic structure of ritual speech "contributes to a dualistic perception of the world."[14] The symbolic dualism of ritual speech, he argues, reflects the dual classificatory systems of the political and ritual organization in the region.[15]

In the Idaté language, ritual speaking is called *sede* or *amula*. Although it is mainly performed in Idaté, it is often combined with Tetum, Portuguese, and Indonesian loan words, though these are rarely recognized by Idaté speakers as having a non-Idaté origin.[16] Despite the abundance of foreign loan words in ritual speech, such terms are considered local, since it is believed that they have been handed down directly from the ancestors. In various contexts in Southeast Asia (especially in eastern Indonesia and Timor), ritual speeches are represented as the unchanging "words of the ancestors,"[17] even though there is little agreement regarding the extent to which these words are affected by social change. In Funar,

---

[11] Fox, *To Speak in Pairs*, 1.

[12] The banyan tree (*hali* or *nunuk*) represents the origin houses, with the ancestors seen as the trunk of the tree and the descendants as the flowers/fruits or tip.

[13] Fox, *To Speak in Pairs*, 12.

[14] Ibid., 26.

[15] As identified, for example, by Franciscus A. E. van Wouden, *Types of Social Structure in Eastern Indonesia*, trans. Rodney Needham (The Hague: Martinus Nijhoff, 1968 [1935]), 165.

[16] There is one type of ritual speech (known as *malakar*) that people say is an entirely separate language. To my knowledge, there are only a few people in the Laclubar region who can speak it, although several people could quote one or two sentences.

[17] Fox, *To Speak in Pairs*; Joël C. Kuipers, *Power in Performance: The Creation of Textual Authority in Weyewa Ritual Speech* (Philadelphia: University of Pennsylvania Press, 1990).

people also maintain that ritual speech is connected to the ancestral realm, and—more significantly—that ritual speakers are vehicles through which the ancestors' words are expressed.

By denying that they are the authors of ritual speech and thereby disembedding words from their social context, Funar's "masters of the mouth" transfer authorship to the ancestors. Moreover, the subject matter of these highly formalized speeches does not always directly relate to the occasion for which they are performed. In his careful study of Weyewa ritual speech performances on Sumba, Joël Kuipers refers to this phenomenon as "entextualization," suggesting that, compared with other forms of speech, the "words of the ancestors" are marked by "growing levels of (apparent) detachment from their immediate pragmatic context."[18] In Funar/Laclubar, this kind of detachment of ritual speech from its immediate social context strengthens the ancestors' agency and authority. Kuipers notes a fundamental shift in the Weyewa language ideology, which has occurred alongside a transformation of the structure of authority and involves a weakening of the connection between ritual speech and the enactment of a fixed ancestral past.[19]

Webb Keane has further examined the moral and political dimensions of ritual speech in relation to its material dimension, thereby developing the concept of "semiotic ideology."[20] This term refers to the study of the functioning of signs—the ways in which words and things are coordinated—without assuming any particular relationship between subjects and objects.[21] This concept is exemplified through Keane's research in Sumba, where he distinguishes between the semiotic ideology of Sumbanese ritualists and Dutch Calvinists. The latter attempt to draw a clear line between humans and nonhumans and between the world of agency and that of natural determinism.[22] The former, just like residents in Funar, imbue objects with agency. Speech ("words") is only authoritative if transacted alongside specific material objects ("things").[23]

According to Keane, ritual speech performances are representational acts. Ritual speech, which is grounded in representation, is used alongside specific material practices to reproduce authority. For Sumbanese ancestral ritualists, *sacra* and words handed down by the ancestors index the absence of those whom these heirlooms make present. This is because however "present" the ancestors may be during rituals, they are not present in the same way as the living. Hence, everything hinges on replicating ancestral *forms*, such as speech, exchanges, and performances.[24] The presence of the ancestors thus remains a matter of ambiguity, and the efficacy of any performance is never assured, since ritual produces identities that are portrayed as already existing.

---

[18] Kuipers, *Power in Performance*, 4.

[19] Joël C. Kuipers, *Language, Identity and Marginality in Indonesia: The Changing Nature of Ritual Speech on the Island of Sumba* (Cambridge: Cambridge University Press, 1998), xii. Kuipers builds on the work by Judith Irvine who initially developed the notion of "language ideology" as connecting people's ideas about language to the maintenance of power relations and interests; see Judith Irvine, "Ideologies of Honorific Language," *Pragmatics* 2, no. 3 (1992): 252.

[20] Keane, *Christian Moderns*, 16–17.

[21] Ibid., 16.

[22] Ibid., 7.

[23] Keane, *Signs of Recognition*, 9.

[24] Ibid., 18–20.

Representational acts are inherently unstable. They are prone to certain vicissitudes, attributing agency to a realm beyond human intention. Ritual speech, which can structure authority, exemplifies the problem of agency and the ambiguity of authorship.[25] Drawing on Charles Peirce's theory of signs, Keane argues that signs of authority should not be recognized as symbols (which signify by virtue of social convention). They must seem natural to be effective, thus locating agency outside the individual. Ritual speech, for example, must index the presumed existence of links to the ancestors.[26] Scenes of encounter are exercises of power, but only because participants anticipate the possibility of failure and show how to overcome risk. They dramatize risk by constantly anticipating that something could go wrong and that this would bring misfortune.

The idea of knowledge here is characterized by a sense of vulnerability and is thus quite different to that found in Funar. As Keane puts it, the very image of ritual speech following a path laid down by the ancestors implies the possibility that knowledge may be lost and rituals may fail. Inadequate knowledge is a significant feature of ancestral ritual, such that the possibility of failure is implicit in the very structure of ritual in these contexts. This understanding of knowledge as vulnerable and fragile is also put forward in Traube's description of ancestral knowledge amongst Mambai: "Mambai sometimes voice a fear that this knowledge might someday be lost, buried beneath the dense, tangled branches of an increasingly rootless discourse."[27] While maintaining the notion of a cosmological wholeness embodied in ritual speech, Mambai assimilate historical influences such as Portuguese colonialism into their origin narratives.[28]

In Funar, too, ritual speech delegates authorship to the ancestral realm. "Trunk words" must be recognized as authentic ancestral words beyond human intention, so that a speech act is considered to be authoritative. However, in comparison to the case described by Keane and Traube, Funar residents expressed less concern about the perpetual danger of losing truthful words, although they were confronted by the very real possibility of such loss. Residents of the Laclubar subdistrict were preoccupied with the notion that ancestral words existed out of time, unaffected by past wars and conflicts. Simultaneously, they needed to assimilate new historical events into their accounts and needed others to recognize such "new" trunk words as authentic.

Unlike other regions of the world, where drastic historical and social upheavals have produced an acute awareness of a void or gap in local knowledge,[29] many of my research participants exhibited a certainty that they were the guardians of valuable words. Despite the tragic losses of life and the suppression of public gatherings during the Indonesian occupation, there was a sense that the "words of the ancestors" could never be lost. This was beautifully illustrated by a story told to me by Edu, a man from Funar, when I asked him whether the death of ritual speakers during the occupation meant a loss of cultural knowledge.

---

[25] Ibid., 24.

[26] Ibid., 133–34.

[27] Traube, *Cosmology and Social Life*, 32.

[28] Ibid., 7, 51.

[29] See, for example, Højer, "Absent Powers," 149, on post-socialist Mongolia.

In the past, there was a respected ritual speaker who "knew how to speak truthfully." He was from the ruling house (*liurai*) and was in unique possession of invaluable words concerning the history of his origin house and the origins of humanity. His son, however, was not interested in these "traditions" (*tradisaun*) and left Laclubar to join the Portuguese military. As part of the *segunda linha* (reserve troops), he was stationed in Oecussi (the small enclave situated in Indonesian West Timor). When the father became very ill, it was impossible for the son to visit him, as this was the time when the border area with Indonesia was becoming increasingly insecure and required a greater military presence. So the father died without having seen his son one last time.

You might think that the old man's words were lost forever because the son had had no interest in learning any lessons of history and culture from his father. After all, he had lived far away from his ancestral land for a long time. Just before the ritual speaker died, however, he chewed a betel nut, asking his wife to keep the betel rind safe until his son came back from the military. When the son did finally come back for his father's funeral, the mother asked him to chew on his dead father's betel nut. At first the son refused, saying, "Why should I chew this old betel nut?" But eventually he gave in because his mother insisted that they would not bury the old man until the son had chewed the betel. From the moment that the son put his father's old betel chew into his mouth, he suddenly "knew how to speak." He had never learned about the origins of his ancestors from his father because he had never listened to any of his father's words, but the words were passed on to him through the betel nut. Like his father, he became the region's most respected "master of words."

Edu told this story to illustrate that the words of the ancestors cannot be lost through war and death, and that they are not transmitted through learning.[30] Rather, words are transmitted as part of material objects, such as the betel nut that enabled the son to become a ritual speaker. Words exist outside the human body and are unaffected by historical events and ruptures.

Even though this point of view was widespread and was variously reiterated by a number of men I spoke to, some had different opinions on the matter. Aristides, for example, an important ritual speaker from Laclubar Town, told me that he was scared that the narratives he knew would be lost when he died. Because of this, he was writing them all down (in Tetum) in a small black book, which he wanted to preserve for his grandchildren. When I met him, he gave me this book without hesitation and encouraged me to take it to the capital city to photocopy. He said he was happy for me to share its content with "foreigners in other countries," but warned me not to show it to anyone in Laclubar. "Many people have stolen my words before," he explained, and for this reason he did not want others to get hold of the book.

I want to emphasize the coexistence of quite diverse assumptions about the role of speech within the same context. On the one hand, there is a suggestion that "words of the ancestors" cannot be lost through war and conflict. On the other hand, there is a fear that words can be stolen, which conflicts with the idea that they persist in an unchanging form through time. The conception of the fixity of "trunk

---

[30] Compare with Kuipers, *Language, Identity and Marginality in Indonesia*, 151.

knowledge" has been further accentuated by the experiences of loss during the Indonesian occupation and the suppression of customary practices. The inability to perform many rituals during the Indonesian occupation when public gatherings were prohibited may have further bolstered an essentialized understanding of knowledge. The repressive atmosphere during the occupation may have inadvertently fueled the need for representing words as indestructible; at the same time, this may have promoted conditions in which knowledge and the authority over it have come to be increasingly challenged and contested.

SPEAKING LIKE ONE PERSON

Speaking is gendered as a male activity, whereas silence is female. Immobility or "sitting" is likewise considered to be a female activity, and the person guarding the *lulik* house is described as a woman, even though this person is often a man. Ritual speakers are nearly always men; their role is an active one that is juxtaposed with the quiet immobility of women. This gendering of ritual offices or responsibilities is common in the region, throughout which there tends to be a ritual division between active male roles and inactive and silent female roles.[31] Silence and immobility do not necessarily connote inferiority, however, since these characteristics are associated with spiritual superiority in many Southeast Asian contexts.[32]

The symbolic dualism of the ritual organization and the paired oppositions of ritual speech have been conceptualized in terms of complementarity.[33] Errington argues that complementary oppositions are a common way of organizing difference in the "Exchange Archipelago" (which includes eastern Indonesia, Timor, and some areas of northern Sumatra), which is quite different from the nondichotomous constitution of gender in the "Centrist Archipelago."[34] Moreover, Errington identifies the notion of a unified and undifferentiated ancestral origin, which later becomes fractured, as a common theme in island Southeast Asia.[35] This fracturing can produce two types of difference: complementarity, which is instantiated through the

---

[31] Compare with: Errington, "Recasting Sex, Gender, and Power," 18; Andrew McWilliam, *Paths of Origin, Gates of Life: A Study of Place and Precedence in Southwest Timor* (Verhandelingen van het Koninklijk Instituut voor Taal-, Land- en Volkenkunde 202) (Leiden: Brill, 2002), 149; and Schulte Nordholt, *The Political System of the Atoni of Timor*, 186.

[32] See, for example, Signe Howell, "Many Contexts, Many Meanings? Gendered Values among the Northern Lio of Flores Indonesia," *Journal of the Royal Anthropological Institute* 2, no. 2 (1996): 263.

[33] A common notion in Southeast Asia, discussed in detail in: Errington, "Recasting Sex, Gender, and Power," 48; Fox, *Speaking in Pairs*, 26; and Joël C. Kuipers, "Talking About Troubles: Gender Differences in Weyewa Ritual Speech Use," in Atkinson and Errington, *Power and Difference*, 155. Another way of conceptualizing the symbolic constitution of difference in this region is "categorical asymmetry," which means that one element in a pair of opposites is considered to be superior (see Traube, *Cosmology and Social Life*, 4).

[34] The centrist archipelago includes the Malay Peninsula, Java, Kalimantan (Borneo), Sulawesi, Mindanao, the Visayas, Luzon, and other Philippine islands. See: Errington, "Recasting Sex, Gender, and Power," in Atkinson and Errington, *Power and Difference*, 39, 55; and Jane M. Atkinson, "How Gender Makes a Difference in Wana Society," in Atkinson and Errington, *Power and Difference*, 66.

[35] Errington, "Recasting Sex, Gender, and Power," in Atkinson and Errington, *Power and Difference*, 47.

difference between men and women, and hierarchy or seniority, which is exemplified by the difference between older and younger siblings.

In Laclubar/Funar, can we speak about the symbolic constitution of speech and movement as male, and of silence and immobility as female, in terms of complementarity? Recall the claim that ritual speech is the words of the ancestors. The ancestral realm, however, is associated with *lulik*, with the indigenous "inside" that is gendered female. Hence, the source/origin of speech (which is gendered male) is the realm of the ancestors (which is gendered female through its association with the indigenous inside). It seems, then, that at the source/origin there are no dichotomies, but that the ancestral realm instead encompasses, produces, and precedes male-gendered speech. The relationship is analogous to that between a trunk and its branches: it is nondifferentiated at its source, but then becomes differentiated.[36] The relationship between these two opposites is not simply one of complementarity, but one of encompassment and different levels: the oppositional entities are the encompassing whole (the trunk) and the encompassed part (the tip).[37]

On one occasion, I saw a woman publicly uttering ritual speech (or something that sounded like it). This was during the election campaign in Laclubar Town, when the presidential candidate José Ramos-Horta had come to visit. Ramos-Horta, who lived in the region for part of his childhood, received a formal welcome from a number of prominent ritual experts by means of short ritual speeches. A number of women dressed in woven sarongs then presented him with gifts made from plaited palm leaves (see photo, next page). Ramos-Horta was offered betel nut by the wife of one of the ritual speakers, and she also made a small speech inviting the prestigious guest to chew betel.

When I visited the woman and her husband later, they asserted that women can also be ritual speakers.[38] Yet other villagers, especially those from Funar, vehemently denied that women could ever be ritual speakers; instead they emphasized women's equally important role of "holding the betel basket" (*akahu dadebuk/mamar hatin*). This role, although it can include the utterance of some words of respect, is in no way the same as that of ritual speaking. Any woman can be allotted the ritual function of holding the betel basket, but women are usually chosen for this office if they "know how to receive people," that is, if they are hospitable and know how to look after guests. Offering betel nut to guests is a vital part of any ceremony, for it is a demonstration of hospitality.

---

[36] See Errington's discussion of the fusion of dichotomous elements in relation to ideas about a unified ancestral source in ibid., 51. Hoskins argues that, in Kodi, gender is united at the highest level (the level of deities) and dichotomized at the lower level of alliance and exchange; see Janet Hoskins, "Doubling Deities, Descent, and Personhood: An Exploration of Kodi Gender Categories," in Atkinson and Errington, *Power and Difference*, 205.

[37] A similar argument has been made by: Valerio Valeri, "Reciprocal Centres: the Siwa-Lima System in the Central Moluccas," in *The Attraction of Opposites: Thought and Society in a Dualistic Mode*, eds. David Maybury-Lewis and Uri Almagor (Ann Arbor: University of Michigan Press, 1989), 117–41; and Elizabeth Traube, "Obligations to the Source," in Maybury-Lewis and Almagor, *The Attraction of Opposites*, 325.

[38] Compare with Keane, who maintains that in Anakalang it is not forbidden for women to perform ritual speech, but it is seen as inappropriate (*Signs of Recognition*, 101). See also Kuipers on the way that men's speech among the Weyawa is directed toward the ancestors and women's speech toward a human audience ("Talking About Troubles," 156).

Welcoming the presidential candidate (2007; author's photo)

The gendering of immobility and silence as female does not imply an actual silence or exclusion of women from ceremonies. During one marriage negotiation that I witnessed late in 2006, both the wife of the ritual speaker from the woman's origin house and a number of elderly women constantly interrupted the speeches being delivered by two ritual speakers, demanding that the amount of the marriage payments (*helin*) should be raised. They shouted numbers into the crowd—for example, "*Eey, ruanulu* [twenty]"—while happily drinking palm liquor, laughing loudly in the middle of the speeches, complaining and gossiping, and smoking as many cigarettes as they could get their hands on, which they discreetly took from the woven palm basket provided by their hosts. It was generally older women who interrupted the proceedings with sarcastic remarks or brazen demands to raise the *helin*, while the young women tended to behave more diffidently. It is not clear whether women's interruptions have a real impact on the amount agreed upon by men. There is, nonetheless, a clear contrast between male and female behavior at such events. Male elders who were negotiating the *helin* were not allowed to name any numbers, as this would be impolite. They limited their discussion to passing grains of maize between one another without mentioning any actual numbers out loud.

Apart from the one example described, women are generally not considered "masters of the mouth." Nonetheless, women were central in mediating my relationships with the male "persons of words." Halfway through my stay, Maria, the woman I lived with, offered to organize a communal meeting with several of Funar's important ritual speakers as a way to aid my research. By that time, I had already spoken to a variety of different ritual speakers and was increasingly aware of the tensions among them. Maria stressed that to find the most truthful account, I would have to bring together all of the different ritual experts from Funar. By so doing, I would ensure that no one would be able to recount stories that were untrue. She wanted the experts to "speak like one person" (*koalia hanessan ema ida deit*, T.), which she thought they would be compelled to do if they spoke in each other's presence.

To welcome the guests, I bought some buffalo meat and asked my neighbor to help me to pick out some particularly beautiful betel nuts at the market. On the day of the meeting, my tape recorder was fully charged and spare batteries and paper had been set aside. I waited the whole day, but no one came. Some children were sent to find the men who had been invited, but they had little success. Several invitees simply did not come without ever giving any further explanation. Two men did provide an explanation a little later, however. Marco, for example, one of Funar's most prominent ritual speakers, came the following day and explained that he had been busy working in his field when the meeting was held. He sat down in our front room and recounted the origin narratives of his origin house, Bamatak, which I had already heard from other villagers (Chapter 1).

The ancestors of Bamatak, he said, came to Funar from Wehali, having traveled up the river on the back of a crocodile and later on the back of an eel. The narrative included a series of names for the places that the ancestors visited on their journey, as well as accounts of the potent objects that they brought with them and of how they came to lose a piece of land to the traditional rulers, the *liurai*. Marco ended the interview by telling me that there was much more to tell, but that he could not do so there and then.

A few days later, Manuela, the wife of Paulino, another renowned ritual speaker, came to our house to explain why her husband had not attended the meeting. She said that she felt too embarrassed to speak to me directly, so she communicated via one of the teenage girls who lived with me. Manuela said that her husband and the other ritual speaker, Marco, had some disagreements and that her husband had not wanted to provoke a fight. I learned that Paulino disagreed with Marco on several issues. First, he maintained that his ancestors had already established their presence in Funar before Marco's ancestors arrived, and, second, Paulino felt that Marco's claim that his ancestors arrived on the back of an eel was a fabrication designed to make them seem powerful, since eels are frequently considered to be *wer-nain* (water spirits) and therefore *lulik*. According to Paulino, Marco wanted to portray his origin house as "bigger" and more important than it really was. For both men, there was just one true account of the journeys and interactions of the ancestors, yet they failed to agree on what precisely this entailed. As a consequence, the only way the two men could avert a public altercation was to avoid speaking in front of one another.

There was another dimension to this dispute, however. Paulino's wife, Manuela, was also Marco's sister. Indeed, this may be a reason why she felt compelled to mediate between the two men. Since Paulino related to Marco as a wife-taker, he was obliged to treat him as his superior. As part of the *liurai*, however, Paulino was at the same time in a senior position to Marco. On a number of occasions when I met Marco, he was nonetheless adamant that the members of his house "do not have to listen to orders from the *liurai*," and thus he was not in a position of inferiority with regard to his brother-in-law. By contrast, members of Paulino's origin house often told me how Marco was trying to "become big"—that is, to assert a status that they felt he did not have, according to their own interpretation of the ancestral narratives.

The fact that Maria wanted to invite the ritual speakers to "speak like one person" in the first place indicates that she was aware of the disagreements between them. Unwilling to concede to her wishes, the ritual experts simply decided not to attend the meeting, or else to arrive at different times.[39] Ritual speech and ancestral narratives are generally considered to be opposed to the sphere of national or regional politics, which is negatively referred to as "just *politik*."[40] Nevertheless, ritual speakers seem to be deeply implicated in disagreements about the status of their house groups, and these disputes have a strong political dimension. Despite their refusal to speak in front of each other in this instance, there are certain occasions when ritual experts do need to converse at the same gathering, such as during the inauguration of an origin house—a situation that can lead to severe social tension.

Disagreements over the status of different houses did not only revolve around origin narratives. A member of Bamatak explicitly connected the origin narrative that recounts the contest between Bamatak's and Lawadu's ancestors to present-day events. With a sense of frustration, he told me that today the members of Lawadu think they are more important than they really are: "The truth is that they cannot order us about" (*Loloos, sira labele manda ami*, T.). Despite this, he said, people of Lawadu seemed to think they were better than members of Bamatak.

During the Indonesian occupation, a girl that belonged to Bamatak had gone to Dili to attend school. There, she was to live with two men from the ruling house Lawadu, who were also her mother's brothers.[41] When she moved in, however, one of the uncles told her, "You can live here, but you have to have a separate kitchen." This was clearly an insult—after all, they shared the same ancestors and her grandparents were the uncles' parents. The statement effectively meant that he had no desire to support the girl, and that she would not be able to do her schoolwork because she would have to prepare her own food. This led to a falling out between the girl's parents and the two *liurai* men, a conflict that continued for more than ten years and that gradually merged with other disputes. This incident was interpreted as a sign that the members of Bamatak did not receive the respect they deserved and that the *liurai* did not want them to become educated. Today, those family members have begun to reconcile, although this earlier issue of not supporting the niece has not been fully resolved.

Unlike ritual speech, narratives of ancestral origins are known and recounted by people who are not "masters of words." Moreover, claims to place, precedence, and status are usually made in private, and people are aware that others adhere to different versions of these accounts of the past. Conflicts in the present tend to be framed in relation to origin narratives. The conflict about the girl from Bamatak who moved to Dili, for example, was framed as a continuation of past conflicts between these two houses.

The tension between Bamatak and the ruling house was just one of a series of disagreements among ritual speakers that I noted. Throughout the course of my fieldwork, I was referred to several different "masters of words" to learn about "history and culture" (*istoria no kultura*). When I documented their stories, inconsistencies emerged in the various accounts, thereby challenging the hierarchical

---

[39] I suspect that another reason why some of the ritual speakers did not attend the meeting was that they were too shy to come to Maria's house, since Maria was also a member of the *liurai*. They were more forthcoming when, later in my fieldwork, I went directly to their houses. Another reason might be that they did not want to share their knowledge with an outsider, namely, me (although this was never expressed directly).

[40] Compare with Keane, *Signs of Recognition*, 2.

[41] The significance of the reversal of the direction of exchange implied by this example is further discussed in Chapter 5.

relations among the house groups that the accounts were supposed to explain. The inconsistencies may well have been a result of the competition among house groups. Whereas members of the *liurai* house asserted their superior status, members of other houses tended to emphasize their independence. I was not able to reconcile their various narratives or establish an overarching model that could accommodate all of the different accounts. Inconsistencies were apparent not only among accounts provided by different narrators, but also within accounts deriving from a single narrator. For example, in one of his accounts, the ritual speaker of the ruling house maintained that his ancestors had originally come from Wehali. Later, he claimed that they had emerged from the land in Funar and only went to Wehali to collect a potent spear. When I pointed this out, he said, "But Menina, we don't know whether this is really true or not—it is just a story we tell."[42] In spite of the insistence that these are words of the ancestors, he seemed to acknowledge the possibility that it was the people themselves who authored these narratives.

In the dispute between Marco and Paulino, the point of disagreement was a question of precedence concerning not just the ancestors' mode of travel, but also the sequence of their arrival. I knew of many other cases where narratives of ancestral journeys recounted by ritual specialists contradicted the claims of others. Another common source of dispute concerned the interpretation of origin narratives. Some ritual experts would use their accounts to stress that their ancestors were autochthonous, while others emphasized the potent objects that their ancestors owned, using this as evidence of their superiority. Land claims based on ancestral connections were also contested. During the construction of Manekaoli's named origin house, ritual experts from three different houses told me independently how the land on which it was being built belonged to their respective origin houses. Nonetheless, they worked together peacefully on the construction of the building. It seemed remarkable that these competing and contradictory claims could coexist without leading to more regular and overt conflict.[43]

Despite the emphasis in this region on the fixity of knowledge, there is actually a great deal of contestation. This is only tacitly acknowledged, as people from different houses tend to avoid recounting their narratives in front of each other. Nevertheless, they strive to maintain the notion of the disembodied permanence of ancestral words. One way of sustaining this is by persistently concealing the actual content of these words, revealing them only on certain occasions.

NARRATED JOURNEYS

Ritual speeches and origin narratives typically include the recounting of the place names connected with the founding ancestors of an origin house. When such journeys are described, the ritual speaker does not normally provide the context necessary to understand what the places stand for.

Earlier in this chapter, I mentioned the ritual speaker's wife who invited Ramos-Horta to chew betel nuts when he visited Laclubar for the election campaign. The day after this event, I asked her and her husband about the speeches they had given.

---

[42] I was usually addressed as "Menina," which is Portuguese for "Miss." This title was used both as a substitute for a proper name and as a term of endearment. When I introduced my host family to my boyfriend I became "Senhora Menina."

[43] Compare with Michael W. Scott, *The Severed Snake: Matrilineages, Making Place, and a Melanesian Christianity in Southeast Solomon Islands* (Durham: Carolina Academic Press, 2007), 72.

Her husband, Célio, decided at this point to tell me about the origins of his ancestors in Laclubar. He recounted the journey of two ancestors called Bita Loin and Leki Roma via a series of place names:

> Susuk Huhun, Himin Laun Ro Mi Malaek, Orlau Ha'hauk Tula, Larek Matan Suhu Roma, Ahauk Huun, Tarababa, Ai Mera Huu, Ahoti Huun, Turilalan, Bere Hunu Matan, Tuur Usi, Ai Leti Loo, Ai Leti Lidu, Ai Leti Hou Hada

These place names were uttered without any explanation and in a rapid and monotonous tone of voice. Each is associated with a story of what the ancestors did there, although this context was only explained to me when requested. Célio said that in Turlilalan the land had been so "hot" (*banas*) that his ancestors had not been able to have any children and that their hair had gone white, and because of these problems they had moved on. In Bere Hunu Matan, they had to cross a large river. In Ai Leti Hou Hada, the ancestors had parted: Leki Roma went elsewhere and founded his own origin house, while Bita Loin, Célio's ancestor, stayed and cut down three trees to build his origin house, which was called Ada Rota. Bita Loin had a spear and a sword, which he put inside the house, and a scepter (Célio used the Tetum term *rota*), which he passed on to the ancestors of the *liurai*. Several other ritual speakers in Laclubar Town told me in private that their ancestors had been the original owners of the scepter and were thus entitled to "rule" in Laclubar, or that their ancestors had passed it on to the current *liurai*. In Laclubar Town, too, power relations were contested, and people referred to origin narratives to make claims to status and political leadership. Whenever I carefully pointed out these inconsistencies, I was told that the others must be lying.

Because narratives of ancestral journeys are limited to certain place names, they can be recounted in front of other ritual experts without necessarily causing open disagreement. The context necessary to understand the ancestral journeys and their interpretation was usually revealed to me in private. Célio also emphasized that his story was not yet complete and that if I wanted to hear all of the words he had to recount, I would have to come back another day.

The recitation of place names reflecting ancestral journeys has been called "topogeny" by James Fox, who notes that this is a widespread practice among Austronesian populations.[44] Rather than being preoccupied by genealogies, he argues that Austronesians are concerned with ordering succession through place names; this holds true for Idaté speakers, too. Topogenies relate the entire history of a large group in a semantically condensed form, establishing "precedence in relation to a particular starting point—a point of origin."[45] Moreover, according to Fox, topogenies represent a "projected externalization of memories" and "a distinct means for the ordering and transmission of social knowledge."[46]

Through these topogenic accounts, house groups create attachments to specific places, anchoring themselves in a distinct territorial environment. I agree with Fox that topogenies represent an intricate part of the way personhood is constituted,

---

[44] Fox, "Place and Landscape in Comparative Austronesian Perspective," 8.

[45] James J. Fox, "Genealogy and Topogeny: Towards an Ethnography of Rotinese Ritual Place Names," in Fox, *Poetic Power of Place*, 91–102.

[46] Fox, "Place and Landscape in Comparative Austronesian Perspective," in Fox, *Poetic Power of Place*, 8.

since it is through the recitation of ancestral journeys that house groups constitute themselves as territorially rooted units.[47] Furthermore, through the topogenic recitation of place names, house groups position themselves in relation to other groups. Therefore, topogenies do not just reflect existing social relations, they are also involved in producing them. According to the semiotic ideology of people in Funar/Laclubar, speech, which represents the words of the ancestors, must be embedded within the material world, which includes specific places that the ancestors visited. It is through the potent combination of words and places that house groups constitute themselves vis-à-vis both others and the ancestral realm.

The recounting of ancestral journeys through the recitation of topogenies is a way of telling the history of a house group. This close connection between history and the landscape has been observed not only for Austronesian speakers, but also among other groups, such as the Apache. According to Basso, Apache history is constructed and refashioned through people's relationship with the landscape.[48] Place names, for example, can allude to historical events that illustrate someone's wrongful behavior, and thus add a "moral dimension" to the inhabited environment.[49] Certain places are both a source of historical knowledge and a source of morality, and as such have the ability to transform people's perceptions about the world and how to act within it. This moral dimension was also important in Funar/Laclubar and came to the forefront in historical accounts about Indonesia's occupation.

I collected a few historical narratives from people who were not "masters of words." When I interviewed Justino, a man from another *suco* of Laclubar who was active in the resistance movement against Indonesia, he structured the account of his resistance-related activities around certain places. He described a journey that he, his uncle, and his mother undertook when the Indonesians reached Laclubar Town in 1976:

Fatu Siduk, Muklaku, Buku, Natabora, Mota Diloot (Lacluta), Barique, Laclubar

When Justino told me this story, he simply said that he had to go into hiding and then told me the places he visited. I had to ask explicitly what happened in each place, since he did not offer the information. He told me that when they were at Buku (near Bora), the Indonesians commenced aerial bombing of the region and he saw many people killed. In Natabora, he witnessed people starving, including four of his siblings. The journey lasted for three years, and he and his family finally surrendered to the Indonesians in Laclubar in 1979. Justino was in his forties when I did my fieldwork, and so he must have been a child when he undertook this journey. It is therefore probable that he learned some of the details from the adults who accompanied him. When he became an adult himself, he decided to join the resistance against Indonesia and helped to set up a clandestine network in the Laclubar region. The account of his involvement in the resistance was also organized around place names. Here, I have summarized one particularly interesting section of his account, which took him several hours to narrate:

---

[47] Fox, "Genealogy and Topogeny," in Fox, *Poetic Power of Place*, 91.

[48] Keith H. Basso, *Wisdom Sits in Places: Landscape and Language among the Western Apache* (Albuquerque: University of New Mexico Press, 1996).

[49] Ibid., 124.

When the Indonesian military learned of Justino's connections with the armed resistance (FALINTIL), he could no longer sleep at home, so together with some friends he left to hide in the forest. They undertook a four-day journey, traveling first to Funar (Ruu Duan) and then to the river Dambua Loo before sleeping at Kai Tetik, where they cut down wood to build a shelter. They were hungry and had no provisions, so they roasted corn. They then continued to a field named Wer Meran, where they found some bananas to eat. Then they came to a river and the house of the catechist. They had no guns, only a *lulik* sword. At the house of the catechist, they boiled water with honey and bananas. They were very tired, but continued the journey anyway and reached Failacor, where they received peanuts and coffee. Failacor's inhabitants shared food because they realized that they were related to Justino, since his mother was from there (*ami ni uun enia*, "this is where our trunk/origin is"). Then the men traveled to Ai Kurus and Ai Mera, where they felt particularly hungry because they had no food. They proceeded to Metinaro and Hera, from where they could see the militias in the valley. They cut their hair so that they would not arouse too much suspicion and went into Dili. In Dili, they came across a man from Laclubar (Batara) who was a member of the pro-Indonesian militia and who would recognize them if he saw them. So, silently ("internally" — *iha laran* T.), they uttered words of ritual speech directed at their origin house and asked not to be seen.

They remained in hiding in Dili for some time, but when militia activities there intensified, Justino decided to return to Laclubar. However, during the journey someone recognized him and took him to the headquarters of the Mahadomi militia. It was ten o'clock in the morning, and they started punching and beating him. They hit his face, his legs, and his whole body and tied his legs and feet with cord. (At this point, Justino showed me his scars and the deformations on his legs.) They continued to beat him until three in the afternoon, at which point an Indonesian TNI (Tentara Nasional Indonesia, Indonesian National Armed Forces) commander arrived. He took the opportunity to interview Justino, after which the soldiers continued to torture him for three more days, leaving lasting scars all over his body.

The rest of the story is a detailed account of the torture and imprisonment that Justino received at the hands of the Indonesian military and the militias over several weeks. The account was structured around his movements between the prison cell and the place where he was questioned. He was eventually released from prison because his cousin, who was a commander in the Indonesian military, put in a good word for him, and also because of pressure from the Red Cross, which had visited the place where he was being held.

Although this story does not consist only of place names, it nonetheless shares many features with topogenic accounts of ancestral journeys. Justino and his companions carried a *lulik* sword during their travels, just as some ancestral accounts include a *lulik* sword. They chopped down trees to build a shelter. They uttered words of ritual speech for protection, just as two of Laclubar's ancestors had done when they were imprisoned by the rulers of the neighboring domain. It is easy to imagine how future generations might only remember the account via the names of the places Justino visited during this journey.

Justino's account was something of an exception, since those people in Funar/Laclubar who were not actively involved in the resistance rarely spoke so openly about the Indonesian occupation. When they did, however, many of them spoke about it as the time they had to "run away" (*alari*) from the Indonesian military in the late 1970s. Yet their accounts also tended to be structured around place names in a similar way to Justino's account. Many such accounts were simply lists of place names, and people were often not forthcoming with any further details, although when I asked specifically, there would usually be references to hunger, physical exhaustion, and the loss of children and siblings. Sites in the landscape thus provide the core around which narratives are structured—not only narratives about ancestral origins and journeys, but also those about the more recent past. Such sites are sources of power and pain; they inspire utopian as well as dystopian imaginaries.

SECRECY AND CONSPIRACY

On my first visit to Laclubar Town in 2005, I traveled with Valmir, a man in his early forties who was from Laclubar but lived in the capital city, Dili. Valmir, a member of the monarchist PPT party, was the son of a traditional ruler (*liurai*). In one of our first conversations, Valmir told me that he knew many secrets: "I know many secret words that other people would like to have … You do not need to speak to anyone else for your research. It is enough if you just speak to me." The conversation continued with Valmir making various insinuations about possessing authoritative knowledge of this region. The conspiratorial way in which he spoke indicated that these secret words were not just powerful, but also potentially dangerous. Nevertheless, throughout this first visit to Laclubar Town, Valmir never actually divulged the valued and potentially perilous words he claimed to possess, instead tempting me with little snippets of information that "no one else knew."

Initially, I thought that this way of alluding to secret and powerful knowledge without ever actually disclosing it was something unique to Valmir. However, I soon revised this assumption. In the months that followed, I had countless similar interactions with other relatively prominent residents of Funar and Laclubar. Secrecy was an important aspect of the way in which people disclosed or concealed words. It was common for a person, usually a man, to inform me that he (or someone he knew) was the owner of invaluable words that I needed to record, stressing that after hearing these words, I would not have to do any more research. People also had very specific ideas of what my research was about, or at least of what it *should* be about— namely, to uncover the nature of these truthful and powerful words. They emphasized that these words were secret (*segredu*) and that other people in the Laclubar subdistrict must not find out about them, even though, needless to say, everybody was keen to get hold of them.

One of the ways in which the desirability of the secret words could be increased was by revealing small pieces of information while keeping the core concealed. For example, one man, a member of Laclubar's police force, alluded to the possibility that the United States had a special interest in Timor-Leste due to the presence of oil in Pualaka (near Laclubar Town), though he refused to give further details.[50] Noting

---

[50] Given Australia's claims to Timor-Leste's oil resources in the Timor Sea, such fears are not entirely unfounded. However, at times such trepidation becomes entangled with unsubstantiated claims, such as the suspicion that foreigners want to steal "uranium" from Timor-Leste (located underground). See, for example, Kammen, "Fragments of Utopia," 406.

my skepticism, he proffered some more "evidence," confiding that the Peace Corps volunteers in Laclubar were actually CIA agents. Why else, he argued, would they own such big satellite phones?[51] He said he knew all about their plans, but could not tell me about them right there and then, indicating that his knowledge could have drastic consequences. Instead, he referred me to one of the ritual speakers, whom he thought might be able to shed some light on the issue.

The words of some ritual speakers were themselves considered to be potent. One teenage schoolboy suggested that when his father "pulls words," he could sit on the tip of a sword without being hurt. A local schoolteacher maintained that when his relative uttered ritual speech, his words could kill a buffalo without him touching it. Similarly, a number of narratives revolved around the protection that powerful words offered people during times of conflict, such as Justino's account discussed earlier. "Words" have the potential to unleash real and tangible effects on the world; they are "ritual technologies," to borrow a term from Albert Schrauwers, through which hidden potency can be tapped into or released.[52]

One of the reasons that several people in Funar gave for supporting the former East Timorese president Xavier do Amaral in the elections of 2007 was the suggestion that he held a secret key (*chave*, Pt.) to Timor-Leste's *kultura*. Some even made an explicit connection between the Portuguese term *chave* and his name, Xavier, or Avô Xavier. The people I spoke to were secretive about this key, but several villagers compared it to secret words that would enable Xavier do Amaral to release *lulik* from the land (*asai lulik*) and thus bring wealth and well-being to all once he was elected. Not everyone agreed that this key symbolized powerful words, but its exact nature was rarely discussed in any more detail. One man claimed that it stood for the fingers of one's hands needed for work in the fields, thus connecting the image of the key to the land.[53]

The idea that Xavier do Amaral possesses a powerful key is analogous to the suggestion, discussed in Chapter 1, that there is gold in Funar. Both are what Kammen calls "utopian visions," linking future prosperity with subterranean riches and *lulik*.[54] *Lulik* is a distinctively indigenous potency not only because of its connection with the landscape and the primordial ancestors, but also because the *lulik* house is referred to as the "Timorese house" (*ada timor*).

In 2006–07, it became quite common in Dili to frame internal political problems in terms of international political events. The 2006 conflict between easterners and westerners (described in the introduction), for example, was seen as akin to that between the US-led coalition forces and Iraq.

[51] Some also suggested that Peace Corps volunteers were land spirits, a belief that reflects the common representation of land spirits as foreigners (*malae*).

[52] Albert Schrauwers, "Through a Glass Darkly: Charity, Conspiracy, and Power in New Order Indonesia," in *Transparency and Conspiracy: Ethnographies of Suspicion in the New World Order*, eds. Harry G. West and Todd Sanders (Durham: Duke University Press, 2003), 127.

[53] Until his death just before the presidential elections in 2012, there was widespread support for Xavier do Amaral in Funar, especially among the autochthonous houses. The more educated *liurai* tended to support José Ramos-Horta because of his connection with outsiders. As one person put it, "Horta had traveled abroad and knew many countries." This reflects the distinction between the *liurai*, who valued connections with the foreigners, and the indigenous land-owners, who emphasized their autochthonous connections with the landscape.

[54] Kammen, "Fragments of Utopia," 405.

Showing support for "Avô Xavier" (2007; author's photo)

The diverse ways in which people in Funar/Laclubar speak about the potency of the landscape resonate with Meratus Dayak's ideas about the "Diamond Queen," who, according to Tsing, is a metaphor for everything local.[55] The Diamond Queen, a figure from a folk tale in South Kalimantan, is said to bring *adat* (custom) and well-being to local people, thereby leading to the restoration of an ancient kingdom. Just as the Diamond Queen is a metaphor for everything local, Xavier do Amaral's key is a metaphor for what is distinctively indigenous and connected to the land: *kultura* and *lulik*. Both metaphors are tied to visions of future wealth and well-being and incorporate certain millenarian elements. The source of the promised wealth is in both cases a local/indigenous one. Importantly, in Funar, this indigenous resource may be mobilized through cultural "words" (Xavier do Amaral's "key"). This could explain why people attributed the intention of stealing gold (a metonym for the *lulik*) to my endeavor of learning about "cultural words."

During my time in Timor-Leste, stories of possible wealth and prosperity coexisted with narratives about the prospects of mayhem and war. In 2007, for example, rumors were rife in Laclubar that members of FRETILIN were hiding sacks of rice in a secret deposit for distribution to their supporters. Several villagers claimed to have heard gunshots at night and alluded to the possibility of terrible and unspeakable things happening in the future. On a number of occasions while discussing the political situation in Dili, members of the house where I lived told each other to be quiet in case neighbors were listening in on them. The suspicion and

---

[55] Anna Lowenhaupt Tsing, *In the Realm of the Diamond Queen: Marginality in an Out-of-the-Way Place* (Princeton: Princeton University Press, 1993), 278.

mistrust directed toward others is doubtless connected to their experiences of the Indonesian occupation, when there was a constant and very real danger of people being accused of supporting the resistance (and shots were, indeed, fired at night).

Rumors and suspicions thus contained both a realistic and a "dystopian" element. During the 2006 crisis, for example, there were rumors in Funar and Laclubar that in Dili a pig had given birth to an elephant. This, people said, was a sign (*signal*) that much worse was to come. In the same vein, a number of villagers claimed that the "Three Lakes" (*Tasi Tolu*) near Dili had all turned blood red in color. This was also taken as a sign of impending war. Some said that terrible massacres had already occurred, which was why the lakes were filled with blood. Others maintained that the red lakes were signs of much worse to come, and that war and unthinkable mayhem would once again ravage Timor-Leste.[56]

What these utopian and dystopian visions have in common is the idea that behind the visible world there is an invisible realm full of deeper truths and richer possibilities—a realm that can also be a source of danger and disaster. This sphere is frequently (but not always) connected to the landscape and to the ancestors or other spiritual beings. In exploring the idea of the landscape as a cultural process, Hirsch contends that the distinction between its foreground and background is a cross-cultural phenomenon that separates the visible everyday reality (the foreground) from the invisible potential of social existence (the background).[57] In Funar, this would correspond to a separation between the everyday world of the living (the foreground) and the spiritual realm of the ancestors, *lulik* potency, and other beings associated with the landscape (the background). The "words" of ritual speakers are a way of mediating between the foreground and the background and thus of realizing the hidden potential associated with the latter. Because of the possibilities and dangers that are contained in this process, however, there is need for a degree of secrecy.

These narrative traditions illustrate that local ideologies about language, speech, and knowledge are part of a general sense that beyond the visible world there is an invisible realm that affects the way events unfold. The conception of the unseen ancestral "trunk" is part of a cosmology of the occult and the unseen, in which certain aspects of the world's workings remain hidden. As West and Sanders have noted, in social and political contexts where occult cosmologies remain strong, critiques of power can come to resemble the more familiar conspiracy theories of Euro-American modernity.[58]

Dystopian fears tend to increase in times of conflict, such as in 2006, and—as in other nearby conflict zones—rumors clearly have the potential to amplify existing tensions. Nils Bubandt has documented millenarian narratives that circulated in Maluku in 1999 predicting a battle the following year between Christians and Muslims that would lead to a radical transformation of the world.[59] Similarly, in the

---

[56] At the time, similar rumors were circulating in Dili that there was a massacre at Tasi Tolu and over sixty people had been killed and secretly buried.

[57] Eric Hirsch, "Landscape: Between Place and Space," introducion to *The Anthropology of Landscape: Perspectives on Place and Space*, ed. Eric Hirsch and Michael O'Hanlon (Oxford: Clarendon Press, 1995), 3, 22.

[58] Harry G. West and Todd Sanders, "Introduction: Power Revealed and Concealed in the New World Order," in West and Sanders, *Transparency and Conspiracy*, 6.

[59] Nils Bubandt, "Violence and Millenarian Modernity in Eastern Indonesia," in *Cargo, Cult and Culture Critique*, ed. Holger Jebens (Honolulu: University of Hawai'i Press, 2004), 92–116.

2006 conflict in Timor-Leste, rumors that unknown forces were instigating violence often created extreme anxiety. Even today, emotionally and politically charged rumors about invisible sources of power and potency continue to circulate within the country. In this sense, the practices of concealing and revealing knowledge, which may have been intensified by past experiences of persecution, have the potential to exacerbate existing fears and suspicions of both one another and outsiders.

A WAY OF BEING IN HISTORY

In an attempt to compare perceptions of "being in history" across cultures, Maurice Bloch describes two models representing either end of a spectrum.[60] The first model is exemplified by the Sadah of northern Yemen, who represent what Bloch calls the "Platonic" model. The Sadah regard themselves as privileged vessels of divine and legal knowledge. Despite the external pressures of historical change, the Sadah, as descendants of the Prophet Mohammed, see themselves as unchanging continuations of the past and, therefore, as the chosen vessels of God. Bloch contrasts this perception with the self-representation of the Bicolanos of the central Philippines, which corresponds more closely to what Bloch calls the "Aristotelian" view, according to which persons are shaped by outside influences. The Bicolanos, who define themselves as "those who have nothing," see their culture as an amalgamation of foreign influences and their personhood as modified by history and transformed by the influence of outsiders.[61] According to Bloch, the Vezo (and the Merina) of Madagascar represent an intermediate case, since their identity is thought to be fluid and malleable during life but becomes fixed at death.

Applying this model to Funar, we find a way of being in history that is largely Platonic: ritual speakers are the vehicles for ancestral words that are transmitted to them independent of historical events. People downplay the role of recent historical events in shaping their lives and their management of cultural words. However, this notion of the unchanging nature of words can give rise to a number of dilemmas and tensions.

In a place where people agree that their past can be told through truthful words that have been handed down from the ancestors, it is not surprising that there are some disagreements about the narratives' content. In Funar and Laclubar, there is evident competition among ritual experts, and altercations were often avoided by not revealing "words" publicly. Ritual speakers would frequently meet with me in private and would tell me not to pass on what I had been told. Withholding important words, then, was not just a way of presenting oneself as a powerful speaker, but also a means of avoiding conflict.

Initially, I conscientiously sought those to whom I had been advised to speak, and who were considered especially knowledgeable "owners of words." Yet I soon realized that the secrets people alluded to were rarely revealed, and that many potential interlocutors made great efforts to find reasons to postpone our meetings. I therefore stopped actively pursuing people, since I did not want to oblige anyone to talk to me against their wishes. I was also careful not to give the impression that I was there to take something valuable away from the people of this region.

---

[60] Bloch, *How We Think They Think*, 70.

[61] Fenella Cannell, *Power and Intimacy in the Christian Philippines* (Cambridge: Cambridge University Press, 1999), 248.

The idea that knowledge exists in an external realm independent of human authorship and intention stands in marked contrast to the anthropological emphasis on embodied, contextual, or relational knowledge, mirroring Bloch's distinction between Platonic and Aristotelian perspectives. In arguing that residents of Funar have an ideal conception of disembodied Platonic knowledge, I am not suggesting that there is no such thing as nonverbal, embodied, or relational knowledge, but rather that both kinds of knowledge can coexist within the same context. It is important to avoid the temptation to juxtapose disembodied Western epistemological ideologies with the supposed fluid, embodied, relational, or contextual epistemologies of non-Western societies. My case material has shown how specific historical conditions (in this case, violence, dislocation, and the suppression of customary knowledge) can accentuate particular aspects of people's ideological frames. It may well be that the suppressive conditions of the Indonesian occupation transplanted it to the unchanging realm of the ancestors. It also illustrates how the conception of disembodied knowledge is difficult to uphold, especially in situations where the political and social relations deduced from ancestral narratives are strongly contested.

Despite the assertion that knowledge has not been affected by the Indonesian occupation, some of the assumptions underlying people's epistemological practices have nevertheless been shaped by past conflicts and dislocation. Most notably, two key aspects of people's language ideology have been accentuated. First, the suppression of ritual practices and the death of eminent ritual speakers has reinforced an essentialized, disembodied understanding of knowledge as unchanging ancestral "words" that cannot be lost. Second, even though the comparative literature suggests that secrecy was already part of knowledge practices in the region before the Indonesian occupation, the repressive atmosphere during the occupation may have augmented the need for secrecy and hence drawn increased attention to the occult aspects of people's knowledge practices. In a self-perpetuating cycle, these developments in turn further intensify conflicts over who has the authority to speak and who is the rightful representative of *kultura*. If there is only one set of truthful words, clearly, there must be contestation over who their rightful guardian should be.

Prominent members of the community seek to stress their own status vis-à-vis others' by making claims to secret words and withholding knowledge, the existence of which is repeatedly invoked. This has the effect of creating a large number of competing claims about the possession of ancestral words and the legitimacy of those who claim to know them. Because these claims are made in private, the people who make them are rarely challenged. While many profess to possess words about the past, the claims to status that are made on the basis of these accounts remain fragile and contested, since there are always numerous competitors making similarly structured but categorically different claims.

For Keane, the representational vicissitudes inherent in ritual speech bring out an apparent paradox: supposedly permanent ancestral identities need to be constantly sustained and worked upon, since "self-assertion ... puts dependence on others."[62] Having to be acknowledged by others as competent and knowledgeable speakers puts the burden of dependence on "masters of words" when they perform

---

[62] Keane, *Signs of Recognition*, 27.

speech. This is especially true on occasions when the accounts of ritual speakers have to be publicly recognized. One of the most significant of these public occasions is the inauguration of origin houses, which I turn to in the next chapter, to explore the tension between autonomy and dependence.

CHAPTER THREE

THE HAZARDS OF HOUSE RECONSTRUCTION

When I returned to Funar in 2010 for a short visit, the impossible had happened. A man who came from an origin house deemed as having autochthonous origins as "people of the land" had been elected village chief (*chefe de suco*). During the 2007 national elections, several of my acquaintances had been adamant that only members of *liurai* houses, identified with foreign power, could hold political office. By contrast, members of houses of autochthonous origin had specific ritual responsibilities that were seen as diametrically opposed to the political tasks of "foreign" houses. Despite this, in 2009 a member of an origin house triumphed over his *liurai* opponent.

Origin houses combine the notion of ancestry and place, a common combination in Southeast Asia.[1] In Funar, these houses, which are said to have been founded by a number of ancestral brothers in the distant past, are referred to as "customary houses" (*ada lisan*), "head houses" (*ada ulun*), and "potent/sacred houses" (*ada lulin*).[2] An origin house brings the physical building together with human house-members who comprise both the ancestors and the living. Origin houses present a collective mode of being and identification that is a fundamental aspect of human existence in this part of the world. Yet, as residents returned to Funar, there was competition and contestation amongst house groups regarding the social status of their houses, and a transformation of the ways in which origin houses were perceived. This transformation established the conditions through which foreign and autochthonous origin houses—previously seen as distinct categories—came to be viewed as no longer mutually exclusive or incompatible.

During the civil war in 1975 and the Indonesian invasion that followed, the settlements belonging to Funar were destroyed and burned, and their inhabitants went to hide in the forest—some for months, others for years.[3] In addition to the residential structures that were razed, in 1975 all origin houses were destroyed as a result of the conflicts between political parties, and could not be rebuilt during the Indonesian occupation. When people returned to their ancestral land after nearly two decades of forced resettlement, there was a widespread preoccupation with reconstructing these houses.[4] During the course of my initial period of fieldwork (2005–07), most house groups in Funar were in the process of reconstructing their

---

[1] On the notions of origin, see Fox, Introduction, in *Origins, Ancestry, and Alliance*, 4–5.

[2] As discussed in Chapter 1.

[3] The conflict between FRETILIN (Frente Revolucionária de Timor-Leste Independente, Revolutionary Front for an Independent East Timor) and UDT (União Democrática Timorense, Timorese Democratic Union) and the Indonesian invasion are often collapsed into a single event.

[4] Compare with McWilliam, "Houses of Resistance in East Timor."

origin houses. Individuals involved in organizing the reconstructions repeatedly pointed out to me that this was a significant, as well as somewhat dangerous, affair.

What actually constitutes an origin house and the extent to which origin houses are autonomous or dependent on each other was profoundly contested. Houses can split and new houses can be founded. Sometimes, smaller houses are integrated into more powerful ones. Yet these splits and mergers are de-emphasized, because one of the most significant aspects of origin houses is precisely the notion that they have existed in their current form since the time of the ancestors.

The reconstruction and inauguration of origin houses involved not only the physical reconstruction of buildings, but also a reconstitution of assumptions concerning the nature (and number) of these houses. By the same token, people's collective modes of identification were transformed and reconstituted. The main issue in this reconstitution was the question of whether origin houses could contain within themselves both foreign and indigenous elements, or whether these two categories should continue to be segregated into distinct physical buildings.

After independence, houses that already had a diarchic structure (with Timorese/ritual and foreign/political elements) saw a further bifurcation into the same oppositional categories by producing foreign and indigenous houses out of one of the two terms, as I illustrate throughout this chapter. This tendency toward further splitting one element of a complementary opposition seemed to be motivated by a desire to establish autonomy from other houses and to undermine the hierarchies that dependency on others implies. In building and rebuilding the origin houses, house groups were creating self-sufficient entities that contained diarchic structures and their corresponding analogous oppositions. Exploring how these matters played out around the house reconstructions reveals how it became possible for a member of an autochthonous house (a "person of the land") to become village chief (occupying the role of the outsider). In other words, it brings to light the *reconstitutive* process that took place during the reconstruction period.

This issue of how post-conflict reconstruction of origin houses involved the transformation of existing social and political relations relates to broader concerns about the way collective modes of being and identification are affected by experiences of displacement and conflict. Anthropological accounts of the subjective experience of violence commonly portray conflict as destabilizing collective identities.[5] Violence is thought to shatter and destroy subjectivity, which subsequently needs to be "remade."[6] Often it is presumed that such "remaking" is a process of recreating what previously existed. The rebuilding of origin houses in Funar at first seems to confirm the interpretation that post-conflict recovery involves the reconstruction and renewal of previous forms of sociality and collective identification. Yet during the house reconstructions it emerged that, in specific historical circumstances, the assumptions underpinning these forms of collective identification can actively be transfigured.

BINARY IDEOLOGIES

The centrality of origin houses in the social organization of different East Timorese groups has been described by a number of anthropologists who carried out

---

[5] Kleinman et al., *Social Suffering*, x.

[6] Das et al., *Remaking a World*.

fieldwork before the Indonesian occupation.[7] In these studies, emphasis is put on the role of houses in defining social groups as well as in marriage exchange. Houses have been interpreted as repositories of cultural and symbolic meaning and as spatial structures that reflect and reproduce both social and cosmological relations.[8] Named houses as social groups are portrayed as a source of stability and cohesion.

By contrast, in Funar, the rebuilding and inauguration of origin houses was accompanied by a challenge to existing hierarchical relations, leading to the transformation of these relations. There were both open and covert conflicts about the nature of origin houses and the relationships between them. At the heart of the transformative process lay the reconceptualization of the relationships between foreign and indigenous categories. It seems that during the reconstruction, people tried to reinvent their houses in new ways—making it possible for a man from an autochthonous house to take on the role of village chief, which is usually associated with the domain of foreign houses. The reconstructions that I witnessed in 2005–07 laid the groundwork for the transformation and reinvention of binary ideologies, the consequences of which could be seen in the 2009 elections in which a person who was not a member of a *liurai* house became village chief.

Binary ideologies in island Southeast Asia are part of a widespread pattern of diarchic social organization. These diarchies emerge from a dualistic conception of foreign and indigenous sources of power, a complementary opposition that is common in eastern Indonesia and Timor-Leste.[9] As well as indigenous-foreign, diarchic oppositions are associated with a range of corresponding analogous oppositions such as inside-outside, female-male, immobility-mobility, and silence-speech. One element of the opposites is usually considered superior (here, the female over the male element and the indigenous over the foreign), giving rise to what has been called "categorical asymmetry."[10] Janet Hoskins, who examined the tension between indigenous and foreign authority on the island of Sumba, has emphasized that this "diarchic balance" is constantly shifting, contested, and reworked to accommodate the import of foreign models and objects of rule.[11] She maintains that

[7] See, for example, Brigitte Clamagirand, "The Social Organization of the Ema of Timor," in Fox, *The Flow of Life,* 134–51; Shepard Forman, "Descent, Alliance and Exchange Ideology among the Makassae of East Timor,"in Fox, *The Flow of Life,* 152–77; Hicks, *Tetum Ghosts and Kin*; and Traube, *Cosmology and Social Life.* For an overview, see McWilliam, "Houses of Resistance in East Timor," 29–34.

[8] For an overview of the anthropological literature on houses beyond Timor-Leste, see: James J. Fox, "Comparative Perspectives on Austronesian Houses: An Introductory Essay," in *Inside Austronesian Houses: Perspectives on Domestic Designs for Living,* ed. James J. Fox (Canberra: Australian National University, 1993), 1–28; Janet Carsten and Stephen Hugh-Jones, *About the House: Lévi-Strauss and Beyond* (Cambridge: Cambridge University Press, 1995); Signe Howell and Stephen Sparkes, *The House in Southeast Asia: A Changing Social, Economic and Political Domain* (London: Routledge, 2013); and Claude Lévi-Strauss, *The Way of the Masks,* trans. Sylvia Modelski (Seattle: University of Washington Press, 1982).

[9] See: Errington, "Recasting Sex, Gender, and Power," 47; Friedberg, "Boiled Woman and Broiled Man," 287; Hoskins, *The Play of Time,* 53; Schulte Nordholt, *The Political System of the Atoni of Timor,* 187; and Traube, *Cosmology and Social Life,* 102.

[10] James J. Fox, "Category and Complement: Binary Ideologies and the Organization of Dualism in Eastern Indonesia," in *The Attraction of Opposites,* 47; and Traube, *Cosmology and Social Life,* 4.

[11] Hoskins, *The Play of Time,* 118, 138.

the "pervasive duality of power in Eastern Indonesia is always and intrinsically contestable, unstable, and politically constructed."[12]

Similarly, James Fox highlights the complicated historical processes in which dualistic categories are implicated as social configurations form and transform throughout history. Dyadic structures are prevalent across eastern Indonesia and Timor-Leste, but there is such a large variety that we cannot reduce these dyadic forms to a single model of dual organization, as van Wouden and others have attempted.[13] Dyadic structures proliferate not just across the region, but also within a single context, where different dyads are invoked to suit a particular purpose. It is for that reason, Fox argues, that there is a need to study not "the products of classification, but [...] the *processes* of classification."[14] Post-independence Funar lends itself particularly well to the study of the process of dyadic classification that shaped the ways in which groups came into being, since the village found itself in a situation where new diarchies were being recreated, quite literally, in the form of newly constructed origin houses.

In some contexts, diarchic organization is related to another common theme: the outsiders who are "installed inside."[15] This theme features in a variety of origin narratives about outsiders becoming king, while the indigenous population maintains ritual responsibilities. Sometimes the outsider is a complete stranger; in other variants, as mentioned in Chapter 1, he is a returning younger brother.[16] According to Fox, "the installation of the outsider inside [...] effects a reordering of precedence whereby an outsider comes to represent the inside."[17] However, when a member of one of the autochthonous houses in Funar was elected village chief in 2009, it was not a foreigner who was integrated into indigenous arrangements; rather, an "insider" was installed in an office associated with the political power of the "outside."

The paradigm of the stranger-king, with its set of analogous oppositions, is a familiar one. The situation in Funar is interesting in that, through reconstructing origin houses, it appears that some people were attempting to reconstruct versions of this paradigm almost from square one. They were trying to rebuild social configurations characterized by a dual formulation, according to which everything is simultaneously one kind of thing *and* one of two kinds of things.

The desire to create self-sufficient houses corresponds to the generally competitive atmosphere in the period after independence. The local rulers (*liurai*) in the region were not as influential as they were once said to have been, especially during the time prior to the Indonesian occupation, when members of *liurai* houses loyal to the colonial administration managed to consolidate their power base. During the Indonesian occupation, many *liurai* moved to the capital city for education or work (and some continue to live there today), which meant that fewer members of *liurai* houses moved back to the ancestral land. In the 1970s, the majority of Funar's *liurai* had been in support of the pro-Portuguese Timorese Democratic Union party

---

[12] Ibid., 39.

[13] As argued in Fox, "Category and Complement," 35.

[14] Ibid., 39, my emphasis.

[15] Fox, "Installing the 'Outsider' Inside."

[16] Traube, *Cosmology and Social Life*, 53. See also: Sahlins, "The Stranger-King;" Caldwell and Henley, "Stranger Kings in Indonesia and Beyond"; and Scott, "Proto-People and Precedence."

[17] Fox, "Installing the 'Outsider' Inside," 202.

(União Democrática Timorense, UDT), whereas the *liurai* of Manelima (a *suco* near Laclubar Town) were notable supporters of the pro-Indonesian APODETI (Associacão Popular Democratica Timorense, Timorese Popular Democratic Association, East Timor), including the last governor of Indonesian-occupied Timor, Abílio Osório Soares.[18] After independence, supporters of the anti-Indonesian resistance were more likely to gain positions of political influence, which further weakened the position of the *liurai* in Laclubar. The relative weakness of *liurai* locally created a power vacuum that allowed other houses to make claims to influence—even though the members of the "foreign" *liurai* did attempt to assert their status. Yet the fragility of their position may have enabled autochthonous houses to make significant claims to political power, even leading to a member of these houses getting elected to the office of village chief.

The period immediately after the restoration of independence was a time of transition, during which different political actors sought recognition from the newly independent government and other national and international political actors. However, in contrast to other areas, which saw a noticeable influx of development agencies and national and international development projects, the Laclubar subdistrict received comparatively little support from government and aid agencies in the years immediately after independence. While most of Timor-Leste was subject to an influx of foreign aid and investment, Funar remained relatively cut off from these financial flows. In other regions of Timor-Leste, especially the capital city Dili, the Laclubar subdistrict is commonly identified as having taken a pro-Indonesian position, and this could be one of the reasons why during my fieldwork the region was relatively isolated and disconnected, with little attention paid to it by government officials and aid agencies alike.

Despite the lack of significant financial support, the reconstruction of origin houses was nevertheless a major preoccupation for all of the different house groups in Funar. Those involved in organizing these reconstructions repeatedly pointed out to me that this was an extremely important and delicate affair. Immense personal and financial efforts were invested in the house reconstructions, which culminated in elaborate inauguration ceremonies called "watering the house" (*ada wer*). As I discussed in the introduction, this phenomenon was not limited to Funar. Since the end of the Indonesian occupation in 1999, there has been an upsurge in origin house reconstructions across the country, reflecting a more general revitalization and revaluation of ancestral custom (*lisan*) akin to the renewed significance of *adat* in Indonesia and *kastom* in Melanesia.

In Funar, the rebuilding took place in such a tense atmosphere that one could almost say there was a race to reconstruct origin houses. At the crux of the disputes among origin houses was the question of whether houses identified as foreign (*malae*)—and hence associated with political power (*ukun*)—could at the same time be autochthonous "owners/people of the land" (*larek-nain*), and thereby associated with *lulik* and the ancestors. These root assumptions about the nature of origin houses were crucial because they were connected to the way houses related to each other: either as interdependent groups within a broader unity and hierarchy, or, by contrast, as autonomous, self-sufficient units that could each contain within

---

[18] See: Bovensiepen, "Entanglements of Power, Kinship, and Time in Laclubar"; and Bovensiepen, "Diferentes Perspectivas Sobre o Passado."

themselves these disparate elements of political and ancestral power (and associated oppositions).

HOUSE INAUGURATIONS

Depending on how they are classified, there are five or six main origin houses in Funar. As in other house-based societies,[19] Funar's origin houses are both physical buildings and units of social organization and identification. Each may contain within it several "side-houses" (*ada soran*), which are further subdivided into households or "hearths" (*wai-matan*). Origin houses and their side-houses have a distinct ritual and political role and are hierarchically ranked.

Every origin house in Funar is associated with a specific narrative account that describes the founding of the house, presented in terms of the need to store *lulik* objects that the founding ancestors had obtained. One (or more) of the male members of an origin house is considered to be a "master of words" (*haha-nain*) who has the task of speaking on behalf of the house on ritual occasions and acts as "keeper" of the accounts of the house's origin. These origin narratives are frequently kept confidential, and members of other houses often do not know the details of the origin narratives of houses to which they do not belong. Women tend to leave their origin house when they marry (because one cannot marry a person from the same house). The core of an origin house therefore consists of its male members, who are considered to be brothers. The sense of relatedness extends from the ancestors to the successors such that different generations are part of the same community.

Origin houses in Funar are assemblages of various human and nonhuman elements. Houses are usually associated with particular sites in the landscape that are significant in the ancestral origin narratives, and they sometimes carry the name of such a site. They contain valuable objects, such as plates, baskets, spears, and scepters, that have been handed down from the ancestors. Many of these objects, like the houses in which they are stored and the sites associated with ancestral settlements, are considered to be highly potent.

There are marked differences among origin houses both in terms of the socioeconomic status of their members and the position these houses are considered to have in relation to others. The low-ranking side-houses of an origin house are commonly described as the "children" (*anan*) of the highest-ranking "parent" (*ina-ama*) house. The house Manekaoli, for example, encompasses several low-ranking houses within it, which are described as its children. Similarly, relations between houses were frequently likened to those among older and younger siblings. For example, Manekaoli was said to be the older brother/older sister (*bou/kaan*) of the house Manehiak, and Manehiak was therefore the younger sibling (*walin*).[20]

Houses are not just ranked by using kinship terms or by describing them as being foreign or indigenous, but also according to a more straightforward hierarchical classification into rulers (*liurai*), nobles (*dato*), and commoners (*povu*, "the people"). Sometimes a fourth category is used, slaves (*atan*). The different modes of ranking houses are often employed simultaneously, depending on the context and

[19] See: Carsten and Hugh-Jones, *About the House*; and Lévi-Strauss, *The Way of the Masks*, 184.

[20] For explanations of how the language of kinship is used to subvert and naturalize rank differences in house-based societies, see: Carsten and Hugh-Jones, *About the House*, 10; and Lévi-Strauss, *The Way of the Mask*.

on what is being stressed. If hierarchy is de-emphasized, the language of kinship tends to be used. For more straightforward vertical differentiation, the rulers–nobles–commoners model is evoked. As will be seen in the next chapter, these different categorizations are further complicated by the relations of inferiority and superiority created through gift exchanges between houses, where wife-takers are inferior to wife-givers.

During the course of my fieldwork, all house groups in Funar were engaged in rebuilding their origin houses. Some had already completed and inaugurated their houses when I arrived; some did so during the period of my stay, and others completed the reconstructions after I left. These reconstructions were usually protracted affairs, taking place over several months if not years. House members are expected to contribute resources, money, and labor, the lack of which was the reason why some of the reconstructions took so long. Once a house was rebuilt, its members had to "ask for permission" (*lu'i licensa*) from the ancestors to inaugurate it. In addition to ancestral blessing, permission and recognition also had to be granted by other house groups in a public ceremony. For several days, elaborate feasts would be held, which included dancing and drumming outside the rebuilt origin house.

House inaugurations ("watering the house") were occasions when ritual speakers recounted the origin narrative of that house, while members from other house groups, sometimes hearing this narrative for the first time, publicly acknowledged the existence and status of the house. As will become clear, these quests for recognition were not always successful. Another aspect of the festive activities was the installation of potent ancestral objects inside the house. Some of these objects were said to have been given to the ancestors by *lulik* land when the house first came into being, while others were said to have been obtained from outsiders and then passed on from generation to generation. Objects that had been lost or stolen during the Indonesian occupation were replaced and re-inspirited (a process called *aluli*); in some cases, however, their physical absence intensified outsiders' suspicions about whether house groups truly possessed the objects and status that they claimed.

The following discussion of the reconstruction of three origin houses rebuilt during my initial fieldwork teases out the disparate assumptions that came to the surface on these occasions.

LAWADU: THE RULING HOUSE

Lawadu is the name of a mountain near the center of Funar, where the ancestors of the origin house Lawadu used to live. Members of this house maintain that they became the rulers (*liurai*) of Funar after their ancestors won a contest with another house (see Chapter 1). At the beginning of my fieldwork, I was told that Lawadu had a foreign origin, its founding ancestors having originally come from Wehali.[21] But later in my stay, this narrative was qualified. One man told me that Lawadu's ancestors were part of the autochthonous population of Funar, but that they had gone to Wehali to get a spear (or, in some versions, a sword). In addition to having a number of side-houses, Lawadu is split into the house of the "younger brother,"

---

[21] Wehali is a ritual center located on the border between West Timor and Timor-Leste; see Chapter 1, this volume; Therik, *Wehali: The Female Land*; and Friedberg, "Boiled Woman and Broiled Man," 287.

called Manehiak, and the house of the "older brother," called Manekaoli. Manehiak, the house of the foreigner (*ada malae*), is gendered male and is said to possess a scepter (*ua*) associated with Portuguese colonial rule. Manekaoli, gendered female, is the "indigenous" Timorese house (*ada timor*), embodying *lulik*.

During my fieldwork, a variety of male elders from Funar told me that their house possessed an object called *ua*. Because they described this as a long rod with a golden handle (or made entirely of gold) that was made "to rule" (*ukun*), I refer to it as a scepter. Alternative labels include cane, staff, rattan stick, or, in Portuguese, *bastão*. It may also have some resemblance to the Indonesian *tongkat*. In some accounts, other objects (such as metal plates) that signify political power are also referred to as *ua*.

When I first arrived in Funar, Manehiak had already constructed a "scepter house" (*ada ua*) and Manekaoli a "*lulik* house" (*ada lelo*).[22] I was never allowed into Manekaoli's *lulik* house because it was considered too potent for foreigners to enter (this would endanger both my life and the lives of the house members, I was told). In the course of my fieldwork, an interesting development took place. In addition to having a scepter house, the members of Manehiak started to build a *lulik* house; conversely, the members of Manekaoli started to build a scepter house to complement their *lulik* house. In this way, both houses—Manekaoli (Lawadu's indigenous house) and Manehiak (Lawadu's foreign house)—would each have foreign/political and indigenous/ritual elements. These endeavors gave rise to covert allegations and expressions of doubt as various people, both from Lawadu itself and from other origin houses in Funar, questioned whether this bifurcation of an already existing split was legitimate, and whether such branching was in accordance with ancestral wishes.

Manehiak, initially conceived of as Lawadu's foreign scepter house, was the first to (re)build a *lulik* house. Manehiak's ritual speaker maintained that this house needed to be built because Manehiak owned *lulik* objects that were stored inside the scepter house and these objects "did not want to be so close to the scepter" (associated with the political sphere). The assumption implicit in this claim is that *lulik* and *ua* (i.e., the *lulik* associated with the ancestors and political power embodied in the scepter) are two separate elements that cannot be contained together in the same building. Some maintained that Manehiak had always had both *lulik* and *ua* houses and that they were simply rebuilding what had been destroyed. Those who questioned the construction of the *lulik* house maintained that Manehiak was the foreign house of Lawadu and did not actually have a *lulik* house, thus, Manehiak's members were simply inventing it. The drowning of a young woman belonging to Manehiak in December 2006 cast new doubts on the legitimacy of the *ada lelo* house-building project, as some interpreted this as a sign of ancestral discontent.

Nevertheless, the house building was eventually completed and Manehiak's *ada lelo* was inaugurated in August 2007. In line with convention, Manehiak's members invited the people from Funar's other origin houses to witness the house inauguration. The first part of the ceremony took place in the house of the guardian

---

[22] The term *ada lelo* (literally, "house of the sun") is sometimes used interchangeably with *ada lulin* (*lulik* house). Whereas *ada lelo* refers specifically to a *lulik* house (opposed to the category of *ada ua*, scepter house), *ada lulin* is also used as a generic term for origin or customary house, including both *ada lelo* and *ada ua*. This kind of classification, whereby one component of a complementary pair (usually the superior category) stands for the whole, is a common aspect of categorical asymmetry; see Fox, "Category and Complement," 47.

of the *ada ua* of Manehiak. Before the *lulik* objects could be brought into the newly built *lulik* house, it was required that the members of the other origin houses come and visit in separate processions to acknowledge the inauguration. The members of the different houses arrived separately, led by their senior male members. When they approached the house of Manehiak, wearing woven cloth shawls around their shoulders, they walked carefully with reserved and humble body postures, keeping their heads low and stopping at a distance to ask for permission to approach the house. They were then welcomed by the male elders of Manehiak, who received them with equally humble postures. (See the first photo in Chapter 2, which was taken when the members of Manekaoli were received by the brothers of Manehiak in front of the house by means of an exchange of ritual speeches.)

The members of Manehiak did not mind me entering their house, so this was one of the rare occasions on which I was permitted to enter a house containing *lulik* objects. It was built on stilts, with a thatched roof and a single room. From the inside and the outside, the house looked like any other house on stilts—inside there were woven mats covering the bamboo floor and a small hearth in the middle of one of the sides of the room. The only difference was that on the right-hand side of the room (as viewed from the doorway) there was a hanging *lulik* basket. People did not point out any particular symbolic significance of the layout, as has been described in some of the comparative regional literature.[23] What mattered to members of Manehiak was that everything was built according to the customs of the ancestors. The buildings, the ancestral objects, and the words of ritual experts had to be recognized as true forms of ancestral authority. I was reminded that no "modern" objects could be brought inside, including shoes, cameras, recording equipment, and even cigarettes (although loose tobacco was allowed). One of the main risks during the inauguration of the origin house was offending the ancestors—for instance, by introducing objects into their realm that had not existed during ancestral times.

When the male members of the other houses had entered, betel nuts were chewed and small speeches exchanged. These mainly involved mutual expressions of respect and an acknowledgement of the authority of the house. The ritual speaker of Bamatak, for example, addressed Manehiak as "the owner of the drum, the owner of the flag, the owner of the scepter, the owner of the hat" (*bapa ni nain, bandeira ni nain, ua ni nain, xapeu ni nain*). When I asked whether the *lulik* house of Manehiak actually contained drums and flags, I was told that it did not and that that these expressions were forms of respect used for addressing a person of authority. The authority of Manehiak was thus publicly confirmed by the visitors from the other houses. Another ritual expert from Bamatak gave a speech, saying, "You are firstborn (*kaolik*), we are last (*hiak*). We listen to your orders." Again, this was interesting because several members of Bamatak had insisted on other occasions that their house was separate and that they therefore did not need to listen to the orders of the *liurai*. References to the ancestors of both houses were made, and the members of Manehiak were addressed by using the Portuguese military title *coronel*. The

---

[23] See: Clamagirand, "The Social Organization of the Ema of Timor"; Clark E. Cunningham, "Order in the Atoni House," *Bijdragen tot de Taal-, Land- en Volkenkunde* 120 (1964): 34–68; Forman, "Descent, Alliance and Exchange Ideology"; and McWilliam, *Paths of Origin, Gates of Life*. By contrast, the ritual speaker of an origin house called Ada Major, in Laclubar Town, told me about the symbolic significance of the layout of his *lulik* house, including a male and a female entrance.

surrounding men from Manehiak and Bamatak nodded enthusiastically at the speeches and became increasingly drunk, to the annoyance of some of the hosts.

Afterward, when members of Bamatak had left, the members of Manekaoli entered the house. Being the "older sibling," they were less deferential and the speeches they made consisted mainly of references to the common ancestors of Manehiak and Manekaoli (such as Romanraek and Romanmauk, Naikoli and Nainahak). Some of the women present also managed to squeeze into the house and crouched down in the rear next to me. One of them whispered into my ear, "The brothers of Manekaoli should have been invited into the house *first,* before Bamatak arrived." This meant that the high-ranking house (Manekaoli) should have been treated more respectfully by being the first to participate in the ritual.

In the previous chapter, I discussed Keane's argument regarding the representational vicissitudes of speech acts. In Sumbanese "scenes of encounter," risk is dramatized: there is always the looming possibility that things may not go to plan. The woman who pointed out the mistake in the order of guests who were welcomed was evidently aware of the possibility of the ritual's failure, similar to Keane's argument in the case of Anakalangese scenes of encounter. However, it seems that she not only anticipated ritual failure, but appeared to *expect* it. The expectation that things will go wrong goes beyond what Keane identifies as the hazards to which interaction is prone, as the following account of a *lulik* possession illustrates.

The stream of visitors was interrupted in order to hold a consultation with *lulik*—the spiritual potency associated with the ancestors. For this, members of the different houses all swarmed into the house. Many of the women who had been busy cooking until then and who had therefore remained in the kitchen also flocked indoors, bringing palm wine and *lulik* meat from the pig that had been slaughtered. The children were then sent out of the house—not because they were not allowed there, I was told, but because they would start crying upon feeling that "there are people [in the house] (*nain laa*)." Because of the fearful and respectful way in which this was said, I interpreted it to mean that this referred to people who could not be seen—presumably the ancestors. Just before climbing up the stairs, a member of Manehiak whispered into my ear, "There is gold [inside the house] (*osa meran laa*)." I did not say anything, and I did not see any gold—but again, he might have been referring to the strength of the potency of this house.

José, the newly appointed "guardian" of Manehiak's *ada lelo*, was sitting opposite the door, beside the ritual speaker (Paulino) and Basílio, the "ladder to the sun" (*lelo odan*), who was the spirit medium. All of them were wearing red headscarves and necklaces, thus "following the ancestors," the person beside me explained. Basílio was supposed to communicate with the *lulik* and with the ancestors. However, since he had only recently been chosen as the "ladder to the sun," potential problems were anticipated. In the past, the possession ceremony had not been successful, so the people sitting around me were nervous, stating that they hoped he would succeed this time.

This kind of "possession" by *lulik* is similar to the possession of people by the ancestors (an event called *ribola*), and people often talked about these two events in the same way. Still, when I asked specifically about this, I was told that possession by a person who has just died and possession by *lulik* are different matters. In this case, it was the *lulik* that was expected to "descend" (*teuk*) into Basílio's body, thus allowing the members of Manehiak to communicate with it. Full of expectation, everyone gathered around Basílio, a young and timid man in his early twenties who looked increasingly uncomfortable and scared as time went by. The participants, especially the men, were by now fairly drunk, and more and more people came pushing into the house to watch the *lulik* "descend." The men sitting at the front tried to create some order, but everyone kept on arguing and shouting above one another. All the people inside the house continued to stare fixedly at Basílio, who was expected to start shaking. But he did not move.

Felismina, who was huddled beside me, explained that the *lulik* needed to "descend" at exactly eight o'clock. *Exactly*, she emphasized, otherwise it wouldn't work. When I asked what was happening, she said, "The *dato* [here, guardian of the *lulik* house] and the mountain are descending (*dato nora hoho rateuk*)." Maria explained that Felismina was talking about the person who had guarded the *lulik* in the past and that "the mountain" referred to Mount Lawadu. In her statement, the ancestor thus merged with the place where the ancestors had lived. Felismina sat beside me with a knowing grin on her face, telling me that she knew how this worked since her father had once guarded this *lulik* house.

Paulino, Manehiak's "master of words," made three short speeches—as he was supposed to, I was told—but still nothing happened. Basílio did not move an inch. People started to get restless and agitated, with everyone in disarray and occasionally jumping up. Some people started to cheer and shout, while others laughed or giggled. Felismina stayed calm and kept on shaking her head. "They still haven't descended" (*bi rateuk hei*), she repeated. "They have already made a mistake (*sala ona*)." She told me once again that she knew from her parents how this was supposed to be done and that they weren't doing it right—above all, Basílio's body posture was poor and the timing was wrong. Some men jumped up and started heckling him, while others warned them to be quiet. With so much pressure on him, Basílio looked withdrawn and miserable. The risk of failure—the possibility that the house members would not be able to receive the *lulik* effectively—was particularly strong in this scenario, indicating that people not only anticipated the possibility of failure, but perhaps had even expected it.

Felismina was whispering nonstop to herself while admonishing others for interrupting the procedure. Gradually people started leaving the house in disappointment. Felismina told me that her father had had white hair and that the *lulik* of Manehiak was very "heavy" (*rihun*) and needed white hair to be received, but Basílio was still young.[24] Disappointed that Basílio had not become possessed, other ritual speakers decided to try their luck and started making ritual speeches, a departure from the protocol that seemed to annoy some of those present. We waited and waited, but nothing happened—Basílio just sat in the corner with his arms crossed, letting his head hang down and the red cloth fall over his face. People around me were whispering, "It is not descending." Some of the members of Bamatak, who only a few hours earlier had submissively (and ceremoniously)

---

[24] "Heaviness" is frequently associated with *lulik*. In Laclubar, I was told a narrative about two brothers. One brother in this narrative was too heavy to be picked up, so he became the guardian of the *lulik*. (Here the close association between *lulik* and the land is expressed succinctly.) The other brother was so light that he could be lifted above the ground and became the guardian of the *ada ua*, the *liurai*, which literally means "beyond/above/traverse the land" (*liu rai*). Regarding the association between *liurai* and mobility, see, for example: Janet Gunter, "Kabita-Kaburai, De Cada Dia: Indigenous Hierarchies and the Portuguese in Timor," in "Parts of Asia," ed. Christiana Bastos, special issue, *Portuguese Literacy & Cultural Studies* 17/18 (2010): 281–301; and Traube, *Cosmology and Social Life*, 259.

recognized the members of Manehiak as their superiors, were now laughing and cheering with a combination of disdain and hostile amusement. Tonho, one of the members of Bamatak, kept shouting loudly, "Descend! Descend!" (*Teuk! Teuk!*) He was clearly drunk and was told off by the women nearby; nevertheless, he could not be held back. This state of affairs continued for some time and people began to discuss why the possession had not worked. They argued that the *lulik* was just "too heavy" for Basílio, who had "only just been born."

All of a sudden, after many of the participants had already left, Basílio started to twitch and tremble. He fell into a corner of the room while shaking violently, his head moving up and down and his chest pushing forcefully against his head. Everyone fell silent and moved closer, filled with curiosity. Basílio started to calm down and gave his hand to José, the new guardian of the *ada lelo*. Then he gave his hand to all the other male elders sitting nearby. Interestingly, he did this in the way that is commonly done in Indonesia/Java, putting his hand on his chest after touching the hand of the other person.[25] There was a lot of tension in the room at this point and one of the women beside me was close to tears. Suddenly, Tonho, from Bamatak, blurted out, "Come on, speak! We can't hear you!" before being told off again by the others. Manehiak's ritual speaker started to give a small speech, but then Basílio began to twitch and shake again, his body convulsing as if he were going to be sick. A man beside me from Bamatak said (cynically, it seemed to me) that Basílio wasn't shaking properly and that his movements needed to be small, not large like they currently were.

Basílio started to make elaborate shaking movements and stamped on the ground. Felismina shook her head, though: "Aie, [he is] young, young (*aie, mori mori*)." Older men made smaller movements, she contended. José, the guardian sitting beside Basílio, began to laugh. Anxiously, he tried to hold himself together since everyone was looking at him, but he could not stop laughing. Basílio then started talking, but his red headscarf was in his face; he was only whispering, so I could not hear anything. People kept on yelling and interrupting while others told them off.

Basílio did not speak for a long time. After an extended pause, he gulped down three glasses of water, took off his *tais* (woven cloth) and his scarf, and seemed to be done. Maria, beside me, announced contentedly, "The *lulik* has descended (*lulik teuk*)." I asked several men nearby what had been said, but they did not know. People started to leave the house; the possession was over.

In the evening, Maria summarized what the *lulik* had communicated through Basílio. According to her, it had been communicated that the members of the Bamatak hamlet (which includes people from both Manehiak and Bamatak origin houses), especially the hamlet chief (David), should speak carefully and truthfully. David should be careful not to speak randomly (*arabiru*); otherwise, the people (*povu*) would revolt against him. Moreover, the members of Manekaoli should build their scepter house quickly. The message delivered through the possession seemed to reflect the tense and competitive atmosphere that surrounded the event. What had started out as an expression of mutual respect rapidly deteriorated into a drunken scene containing both overtones of disobedience and a tinge of mockery.

---

[25] This is a rare way of greeting people in this region, but no one around me seemed to find it odd that the *lulik* from the ancestral past would greet people Indonesian-style.

A fight did, indeed, break out later on in the evening of the first inauguration day, graphically illustrating the existing tensions. The reasons for this fight are complex and will be discussed in more detail in the next chapter. Through the inauguration of Manehiak's *lulik* house, however, it had become clear why the construction of origin houses is a risky affair: the members of the other houses have to acknowledge and agree with the inauguration, thus confirming the status position of the house group within the social hierarchy. There are many things that can go wrong: not following the ancestors can lead to misfortune, illness, physical fights, and even death. Moreover, the person receiving the ancestors might be too young or inexperienced for the role he has been assigned. And vitally, as we have seen, other observers can decide to obstruct the inauguration ceremony, implicitly challenging the public recognition of the origin house in the wider social arena.

The reconstruction of Manekaoli's scepter house was not completed before I left. Later, I learned from an acquaintance that when the house was finally inaugurated, the ritual speaker had not spoken truthfully about the history of the house and had become ill as a result. Members of the other houses were angry with him, his wife had bad dreams, and tensions in Funar intensified. As an acquaintance of mine commented, "Only the *liurai* and the *dato* [nobility] are allowed to sit on a chair, but nowadays everyone tries to grab power. They do not recognize each other's position any more. They just want to overthrow and destroy each other."

At issue in the rebuilding of Lawadu's houses were not only the relationship between foreign and autochthonous elements, but also their political and ontological status. Was Lawadu one house with different branches (foreign and autochthonous) that encompassed and ruled over all the other houses in Funar? Or, on the contrary, were Manehiak and Manekaoli themselves separate autonomous house groups that contained within themselves both foreign and autochthonous elements? During Manehiak's inauguration, both positions were advocated by those attending the ceremony, contributing to a general atmosphere of uncertainty and risk. There was the danger of offending the ancestors by not following their ways, as well as the possibility of not being recognized by the others as a legitimate, ontologically discrete house group.

On one level, the situation in Funar is akin to Hoskins's description of the urn and the staff in Kodi (West Sumba). Just as Manehiak's *lulik* and *ua* had to be separated out, some Kodinese attempted to separate the *staff* (associated with foreign power) from the urn, which was guarded by the "Sea Worm priest" and signified the indigenous/ritual sphere.[26] In the same way that scepters in Funar are associated with the political power of outsiders (especially the Portuguese), the staff in West Sumba was introduced by the Dutch, who sought to displace the value of the "founding objects" and thereby weaken the political position of local rulers (*ratu*).[27]

The division between indigenous and foreign spheres in both Funar and Kodi is undoubtedly contested and subject to historical transformation.[28] The current conflicts over origin houses in Funar were exacerbated by the interventions of the Portuguese and Indonesian governments, whose political interference benefited some house groups at the expense of others and thereby fueled suspicion and contestations among them. When houses were reconstructed, their very existence as

---

[26] Hoskins, *The Play of Time*, 128.

[27] Ibid., 56.

[28] Ibid., 118.

distinct entities was at stake. To quote my acquaintance again: "They do not recognize each other's position any more. They just want to overthrow and destroy each other."

BAMATAK: THE NOBLES

The ancestors of the origin house Bamatak, a name that means "green settlement," are said to have come from outside of Funar. I was told that this house originally contained within itself foreign/political and indigenous/*lulik* elements that were identified with a younger and an older brother, respectively. In ancestral times, the younger brother, Avô Na'i Leikau-Malikau, looked after the scepter house (*ada ua*), which contained a drum and a flag, while the older brother, Avô Na'i Lahuibere-Hahinaleu, was the guardian of the ritual sphere. When the founding ancestors of this house arrived in Funar from Wehali, the younger brother is said to have gone back to Wehali to fetch a golden plate they had forgotten. The older then tricked his younger brother by blocking the way back to Funar (a cavity in the ground) with a stone. That is the reason why the house group Bamatak today only has a *lulik* house: the younger brother was prevented from returning to Funar. Because of their prestigious origins in Wehali, however, Bamatak's members maintain that they are nobles (*dato*) or *aristocracia*, who elect the *liurai*. While the members of Bamatak are considered to have a foreign origin, they do not have a foreign house, only a *lulik* house, called *Ada Lulin*.

Again, I found that the initial account provided to me of Bamatak's origins was modified by subsequent further information in the middle of my fieldwork, when the guardian of Bamatak's *lulik* house mentioned that he was guarding both *ua* (scepter) and *lulik* in this house. He said that the *ua* was a golden plate that the ancestors had brought with them to Funar. The plate fulfilled the same function as a scepter, indicating that the house group that owned it was entitled to political rule. This is why the ritual speaker of Bamatak later initiated the construction of a scepter house that would form the counterpart to the *lulik* house. This caused disagreements within Bamatak and also provoked criticism from members of other house groups. Some argued that Bamatak already had a separate scepter house; others maintained that this was not a "true" house, since its guardian was looking after a metal rod (*besi*) used for plowing fields.

In the middle of the reconstruction of Bamatak's scepter house, a dramatic incident occurred. Bamatak's ritual speaker fell ill at his field hut and died within three days. This shocked the members of Bamatak and other house groups in Funar, and many saw his death as a sign (*signal*) of the ancestors' discontent. Some suggested this discontent stemmed from the fact that the ritual speaker had made claims to a house that did not exist, trying to increase Bamatak's influence and status within Funar. Following weeks of negotiations among house members, it was decided that the project of building the scepter house would be abandoned, even though the main structure of the house had already been erected. Unlike the case of Manehiak and Manekaoli, where *ua* and *lulik* were successfully separated, Bamatak's attempt to build a separate scepter house failed. Bamatak, a house with a foreign origin, therefore only maintained its indigenous *lulik* element, since it was unable to establish its claim to foreign political power in a distinct building.

In a way, this case presents the inverse of Hoskins's argument about the tension inherent in the Kodinese diarchy resulting from the fact that objects, like the urn, associated with the indigenous sphere were obtained from the outside (in the Kodinese case, China). In Bamatak's case, a house group with foreign origins came to be associated exclusively with the ritual *lulik* sphere, but was not able to externalize its foreign/political element. Even though in both cases there is a tension between the notion of local origins and foreign authority,[29] Bamatak's case cannot be explained in terms of "contestation" or "competition" alone: the confrontation over Bamatak's scepter house challenged its very right to exist. The continuity and integrity of house groups in Funar were connected to the endurance of objects and origin houses. Yet where Bamatak failed to successfully establish autonomy by externalizing its diarchic elements in two separate houses, other house groups succeeded.

BERLIBU: PEOPLE OF THE LAND

The origin house Berlibu is one of several houses in Funar that claim to have autochthonous origins; its members say that they are "owners/people of the land." Compared with the *liurai* house Lawadu, those villagers belonging to Berlibu (and other autochthonous houses) were relatively poor in monetary terms, as they had little access to education and employment and were not well connected to networks in the capital city, Dili. From my general observations, it can be said that *liurai* were relatively wealthy: they lived in larger, better-equipped residential houses than did members of Berlibu, and some lived in stone houses in Laclubar Town. Several members of *liurai* houses were educated through the university level, enabling them to work in Dili and remit money to their relatives in Funar. In contrast, members of the autochthonous houses, also known as *povu* ("commoners" or "people"), had access to vast stretches of fertile land and, in this way, were able to provide the resources needed for house reconstruction and inauguration. People of the land were much more numerous, so there was a large base of voters for a person of the land wanting to stand for village chief. Those belonging to the "nobles" (*dato*) were in an ambiguous category, since they were aspiring to high status but had not managed to achieve the socioeconomic influence of the *liurai*.

Early in my fieldwork, Berlibu's ritual speaker, Elísio, initiated the "watering" of Berlibu's scepter house (*ada wer*). In front of the house, a large marquee had been erected using wooden posts and a sizable plastic cover. On the large grass-covered field in front of the house, the members of Berlibu were dancing. The women were dressed in woven cloth (*tais*) and shiny bright shirts. They formed a line and, like the hand of a clock, walked in tight circles so that the women near the line's outside end had to step farther and faster than those on the inside, at the center of the circles. While walking rhythmically to the beat, they banged on drums (*bapa*); one of them played the gong (*dadii*). Their body movements were reserved and minimal. By contrast, the men danced freely around them, making expansive gestures, waving swords (*laha'a*) in the air, and pounding their feet on the ground. The type of movement performed by the women is called *dahur*, while that of the men is called *lore*. These styles of dance would seem to reflect the gendering of immobility as female and mobility as male.

I attended the watering ceremony with a group of people from Manehiak and Manekaoli. They waited politely at the entrance of the tent, displaying the characteristic modesty and unassuming body posture that is commonly adopted

---

[29] Ibid., 29.

when approaching another house group during ceremonial occasions. The members of Berlibu who were inside invited us to enter. When we were seated, betel nuts and cigarettes were provided, followed by coffee, biscuits, fried bananas, and peanuts. The men with whom I had arrived were then asked to join the men of Berlibu at the back of the house. When I asked whether I could join them, one of my companions indicated that I should not go. Weeks later, however, Elísio told me off for not having joined them, telling me that it was on this occasion that he had recounted the origin narrative of his house and that he would not be able to tell those narratives again on just any other occasion. From the tent, I could see the men inside sitting on braided palm mats in a circle. Several wore red headbands. Elísio was uttering words of ritual speech, leading the other men to respond with a loud, approving "eeeeh."

Meanwhile, the women and some of the other men were sitting under the canopy in front of the house, drinking, smoking, and chatting. After about two hours, just before food was served, I joined the women in the kitchen. Elísio's wife pointed to the dishes they were preparing for the men: boiled rice in the form of a large round block, surrounded by meat. She said that the other guests were allowed to eat other kinds of food, but that the male elders had to eat as the ancestors did. The same types of explanation were given with regard to the actual "scepter house," where no "modern" objects were allowed inside, which meant no shoes, no tobacco, and no cameras. This house could only be built from types of material that had existed in the time of the ancestors, because otherwise the ancestors would be offended. Throughout the celebrations, this was the single most important explanation given for why people carried out the procedures in the way they did. People said that they were "following the ancestors" (*tuir avô sira*, T.).[30]

One of the aspects that made Berlibu's reconstruction such a precarious undertaking was the fact that not everyone in Funar agreed with the assertion that Berlibu's scepter house had ever actually existed. This becomes clear when we consider how the evening of the house inauguration proceeded. After we finished eating, the male elders inside the house joined the others in the tent in front of the house to socialize, drink, and chat. Edu, one of the men I had arrived with, came from inside the house and sat beside me. He told me that he was surprised by what he heard in the back of the house. He had always thought that Berlibu was just a side-house of the *liurai*, but the elders of Berlibu revealed that day that they, in fact, had a separate origin.

While we were talking, Elísio, who appeared quite drunk by then, started walking up and down the tent, shouting loudly, "We are people of the land; we emerged from the land!" He went on to say that members of Berlibu had given land to the *liurai*, but they were the true people/owners of the land. According to him, his ancestor Bere Mesak had received a scepter from the *malae* (foreigners) together with José do Espirito Santo (a former *liurai* of Funar from Manekaoli). Elísio continued walking up and down, repeating his words and nearly tripping over people because he was so drunk. The surrounding guests laughed with a slight sense of embarrassment, but generally did not pay him much attention.

Later, as we walked home following the dim glow of my flashlight, Edu tried to make sense of the narratives he had heard during the inauguration, attempting to

---

[30] On this occasion, they used the Tetum expression *tuir avô sira* ("to follow the ancestors"). On other occasions, they used the Idaté expression *lahelo avô sira* or *lahelo avô sira lalainak* ("to follow the ancestral ways").

reconcile them with the origin narrative of his own house. Edu started with the fact that his own ancestor, José do Espírito Santo, had received a scepter from the Portuguese, which entitled members of Lawadu/Manekaoli "to rule" (*ukun*). So how could Berlibu also claim to have a scepter? He reasoned that Elísio's ancestor, Bere Mesak, must have accompanied José. So the scepter would have come from foreigners, he continued, but this then conflicted with Elísio's claim that his house group represented "the people of the land." Elísio maintained that his scepter was *lulik*. Edu took the stance that these categories were opposed and mutually incompatible. Commenting on the diverse views about this issue, Edu came to the following conclusion:

> These days the elders are confusing things. The people of the land do not have political power, and now they are claiming to have a scepter. Then they say the scepter is *lulik*. In truth, scepters are not *lulik*; they are signs of rule. The elders today just confuse *lulik* and *ua*.

In this statement and in the earlier discussion of house inaugurations, we find two disparate positions. According to the first, *lulik* and *ua* are two separate and mutually exclusive categories that, defined by their origin (foreign or autochthonous), are connected to two distinct types of power: political rule (*ukun*) and ancestral potency or ritual powers (*lulik*). The second position holds that the category *lulik* is, indeed, associated with autochthony, but precedes and encompasses *ua* (associated with foreign political rule) as an element of itself. The latter view entails the possibility that scepters can be *lulik*. It is important to note that we cannot attribute these two positions to specific house groups. Some members of the same house held both positions, while sometimes the same person adopted different views in different contexts.

In the days after Berlibu's inauguration, other villagers commented somewhat sarcastically on Elísio's claim that his ancestor had received a scepter, saying that this ancestor was just the *ajudante* (helper) to the *liurai* and that his scepter was not actually for political rule. The doubts about Berlibu's authenticity were typical of the tense and suspicious atmosphere in which house reconstructions took place. Even though members of other Funar house groups attended the ceremony, they showed a degree of disdain and disbelief toward Berlibu's claim to have a scepter house because one simply could not have an autochthonous *and* a foreign origin at the same time.

THE RECONSTITUTION OF DIARCHIES

The expectation that origin narratives be publicly recounted during house inaugurations brings the tensions, uncertainties, and disagreements about the nature and number of origin houses in Funar to the surface. While it is likely that such contestations were present in the past, it seems that the interventions of the Portuguese colonial government, which distributed "scepters" to select rulers, further exacerbated existing tensions. The long absence from the ancestral land during the Indonesian occupation made it impossible for the villagers to rebuild their houses. Any existing tensions or disagreements seem to have been largely repressed during that time, emerging with new virulence when Timor-Leste gained independence. Reviving ancestral customs in Funar thus entails vulnerability, risk, and the danger of offending the ancestors or other house groups. The sense of risk here is not limited to what is arguably an inherent part of all ritual interaction,[31] but rather reflects wider historical, political, and economic tensions in the region. Underlying disagreements about status turned into open disagreements (as in the case of Manehiak's inauguration) and led to private expressions of disbelief (as in the case of Berlibu) or even to the termination of the construction process (as in the case of Bamatak).

The main locus of uncertainty and disagreement is the relationship between foreign and indigenous sources of authority, embodied in the scepter and *lulik* houses and associated with corresponding binaries (the younger and the older brother, political rule and *lulik*, male and female, etc.). This chapter began by questioning how it could be possible for a member of an autochthonous house to become village chief, a political office previously associated with the "outside." Here, I offer an answer: the view that allows for the combination of foreign and indigenous elements in one house—that allows houses to be both autochthonous and foreign—was gaining currency in 2007 and had become more widely accepted two years later.

The contrasting premises about the nature of origin houses that emerged during reconstruction may be posed in both political and ontological terms. Underlying the accounts of origins in Funar are two disparate assumptions: one takes dualism as its starting point, while the other is essentially monist. First, there is the idea that there exists a fundamental division between two different categories, namely, foreign houses and autochthonous houses.

The ancestors of the autochthonous groups emerged from the landscape, whereas the ancestors of the foreign houses came from "outside." This idea of two essentially different house categories was in effect the perspective put forward by Edu when he said that elders in Funar were confusing *lulik* and *ua*. Interestingly, those who endorsed this position, which was based on an original distinction between foreign and autochthonous houses as categories of being, tended to do so to emphasize the current *unity* of all origin houses in Funar, achieved through their being subsequently encompassed within a greater hierarchy. The political consequence of this dualistic root assumption is an emphasis on hierarchy and unity rather than differentiation. In the case of Funar, the unity is not based on an essential similarity/identity. On the contrary, unity is *achieved* out of an initial differentiation.[32]

A second set of presuppositions also emerged during the house inaugurations, one that was more concerned with autochthony and ancestral origins. In describing the ancestral house brothers as having emerged from different sites in the landscape, the narrators of these accounts assumed and emphasized a primordial unity between people and place. This was most apparent in the origin account of Berlibu, but was also evident in that of Lawadu. The emphasis on autochthony, which at first sight seems to be a typical case of precedence, is actually invoked to present Funar's house groups as autonomous units with separate origins. At the same time, however, this emphasis is deployed to represent the split between *ua* and *lulik* houses as resulting from an *internal* division within the autochthonous house category. Therefore, houses can be *both* autochthonous *and* foreign; scepters can also be *lulik*. The indigenous category (being autochthonous/people of the land/guarding *lulik*) *precedes* the foreign (*ua/ukun*) element *and* encompasses it. This can be seen, for example, in

[31] Keane, *Signs of Recognition*, 9.
[32] Compare with Scott, *The Severed Snake*, 23.

Elísio's emphasis on Berlibu's ancestors having "grown" from the land while at the same time guarding a scepter. This set of presumptions was also associated with the perceived electability of a member of the autochthonous house to a political office.

When mobilizing notions of autochthony, the underlying assumption is an original state of consubstantial unity between people and place, followed by subsequent differentiation when house groups emerged from distinct sites in the landscape. On this premise, distinction emerges out of an original state of unity where land and people are of the same kind. This was implicit when people emphasized the autonomy of house groups vis-à-vis each other. By contrast, when taking differentiation (foreign versus autochthonous houses) as the starting point, the unity and interconnection of Funar's house groups today was underlined.[33]

This tension between monism and dualism is the focus of Gregory Schrempp's study of Maori cosmogonic myths, the variants of which, he claims, may be interpreted as supporting both monistic and dualistic ontologies.[34] According to Schrempp, different theories of ancestry and identity may coexist in the same concrete social unit despite their dissonance. He argues that what seem to be disjunctive and incompatible logics are, in fact, variants of a common schema, "the one and the two." This schema is rooted in a "primordial paradox": "is the first 'thing' really one or two?" This ensures the "possibility of a dualism behind every seeming monistic formulation and vice versa."[35] Schrempp introduces the term "dual formulation" to refer to "the coexistence of two different conceptions of the essential character and identity of a given concrete social unit."[36] This makes possible what he calls an "optative system," in which Maori, who are always simultaneously people of the land and people of the sea, can choose which side of their being to instantiate in specific social or ritual contexts.[37]

In light of Schrempp's analysis of the coexistence of dualist and monist conceptions that can be variously instantiated in a given social unit, the seemingly disparate assumptions that came to the fore during origin house reconstructions could be seen as a comparable dual formulation: house groups are simultaneously foreigners and people of the land, instantiating in a given moment either the one or the two. Interpreting the movement between unitary and binary forms in Funar from this perspective, it is possible to see how origin houses can be either exclusively autochthonous or autochthonous and foreign at the same time. However, in contrast to Schrempp's claim that monistic and dualistic root assumptions are not logically incompatible, it seems that, for some people in Funar, these two disparate ways of conceptualizing houses did pose a problem—as became clear during the multiple tensions and conflicts that surrounded the reconstruction process.

Discussing processes of dyadic classification, James Fox notes the occurrence of what he calls "recursive complementarity," a concept he develops via Forth's study

---

[33] Ibid., 18.

[34] Gregory A. Schrempp, *Magical Arrows: the Maori, the Greeks, and the Folklore of the Universe* (Madison: University of Wisconsin Press, 1992).

[35] Ibid.; quoted material from 63, 60, and 62, respectively.

[36] Ibid., 68.

[37] Ibid., 65.

of Rindi exchange goods in eastern Sumba.[38] Here we find a situation where a category that is gendered in one way (e.g., bride-wealth objects, which are classified as masculine and opposed to feminine dowry goods) contains an internal split into differentially gendered goods (e.g., bride-wealth objects include male-gendered horses and female-gendered metal valuables). Fox argues that "by this principle of recursive complementarity, nothing is exclusively of one category; anything that is categorised according to one component of a complementary pair can *potentially* contain elements of its complement."[39] That means one category always potentially contains its opposite (e.g., inside contains outside and vice versa). Similarly, origin houses in Funar always potentially contained their opposite: foreign houses contained both foreign and indigenous elements, and indigenous houses also contained both foreign and indigenous elements (and their analogous oppositions). However, this dual formulation based on the logic of recursive complementarity was contested in Funar, since not everyone agreed that a house could be *lulik* and *ua* at the same time.

During the inauguration and rebuilding of origin houses after independence, it was possible to observe the very process and production of dyadic classifications. Several origin houses in Funar sought to realize one possibility inherent in the logic of their binary ideology by claiming for themselves the condition of being self-sufficient wholes. Yet in what circumstances is each side of the dual formulation instantiated? Faced with a local power vacuum and with the necessity of re-emplacing themselves in the land, as well as the new possibilities that this entailed, a main concern in Funar appears to be the establishment of permanence and autonomy from one another in an attempt to escape the hierarchies that dependence on others imposes. The logic of recursive complementarity, according to which every one element contains the potential of the two, lends itself particularly well to such endeavors.

Yet inherent in this productive process was a tension, namely, the need to discount the fact that what Funar residents were doing by materializing houses based on the logic of recursive complementarity departed in any way from previous social configurations. This meant that historical changes, including mass conversion to Catholicism and interventions by the Portuguese colonial government and the Indonesian state, had to be negated to make an effective claim to authenticity and originality. Houses were said to have been built exactly as they had existed during ancestral times. Yet connections with the outside could never be fully negated. The recursive internal dualism of indigenous and foreign houses allowed house groups to implicitly acknowledge their connection with outsiders through the foreign element.

Unlike Schrempp, my emphasis is not on the ontological tensions and possibilities inherent in existing cosmologies, but on the material and historical conditions that have shaped such identification. As they found themselves relatively excluded from nation-building processes that could have tied them to another center on the "outside," the inhabitants of Funar expressed their mode of being as house groups in terms of an infinitely replicating "relation-of-two." This was not just a

---

[38] See: Fox, "Category and Complement," 45–47; and Gregory L. Forth, *Rindi: An Ethnographic Study of a Traditional Domain in East Sumba* (Verhandelingen van het Koninklijk Instituut voor Taal-, Land- en Volkenkunde 93) (The Hague: Martinus Nijhoff, 1981).

[39] Fox, "Category and Complement," 46.

particular historical instantiation of a self-reproducing schema. Instead, it emerged at a specific historical moment at which houses strove toward autonomy and self-sufficiency. Several months after Berlibu's controversial inauguration of its scepter house, Elísio told me that he, too, was planning to build a *lulik* house. In an effort to establish Berlibu as independent from the *liurai*, Berlibu's members sought recognition as an autonomous and dual-sex whole that contained within itself autochthonous and foreign elements and was therefore self-sufficient. Lawadu's split into Manehiak and Manekaoli, each of which contained a scepter and a *lulik* house, can be interpreted as a similar move toward self-sufficiency. And I would not be surprised if Bamatak, too, has by now been able to (re-)build a scepter house. Despite the existence of a model of unity among the fraternally related origin houses, the reterritorialization of Funar involved the creation of small-scale sites of *coincidentia oppositorum*—the reunion of all of their analogous oppositions—that allowed them both to claim self-sufficiency and maintain a diarchic element.

It seems no coincidence that the move toward establishing autonomous units that combine within themselves analogous oppositions took place at the moment when Timor-Leste as a nation regained independence. Several members of autochthonous house groups in Funar drew on the nationalist slogan of "self-determination" (*ukun rasik aan*, T.) to express their wish to be independent from one another. Out of the experience of forced dislocation, war, and independence, alternative forms of conceptualizing their collective mode of being emerged.

Nationalist discourse since independence draws a distinction between those who supported the Indonesian occupation ("opportunists") and those who opposed it (the "oppressed"), but are united in their suffering and opposition to colonial powers.[40] While this rhetorical dichotomy could hardly be expected to correspond to complex political realities—particularly in the Laclubar subdistrict, where political affiliation varied widely—it nevertheless influences perceptions. The move toward the creation of self-sufficient autonomous house groups reflects the comparative geographic and economic isolation of the Laclubar region as a whole. In the post-independence period, the inhabitants of this region cannot be categorized as either opportunists or oppressed, containing instead both elements within. Similarly, during the conflicts that broke out in Timor-Leste in 2006, which exacerbated divisions between people from the eastern districts (*lorosa'e*) and the western districts (*loromonu*), the inhabitants of the Laclubar subdistrict emphasized that this distinction did not apply to them, since, as they belonged to the "middle land" (*rai klaran*), they contained elements from both sides. This drive toward replicating relations of two therefore seems to be not only historically contingent, but also reflected at different levels of identification.

REBUILDING THE PAST

Since at least the 1980s, anthropologists have recognized that cultural and ideological frames are not simply reproduced in an unchanging way through different historical periods, but are constantly being made and remade. It is possible that the binary ideologies underlying people's understanding of origin houses have been subject to transformation before, yet little comparative ethnographic or historical material is available to verify this. The process of reconstructing origin

---

[40] Kammen, "Master-Slave, Traitor-Nationalist, Opportunist-Oppressed."

houses involved both the negation of such changes and a search for the means to accommodate them. Thus, the process of reconstruction made visible the intense efforts that go into the reproduction of specific ideological frames and the challenges that are involved in such attempts.

In his study of magic in post-socialist Mongolia, Lars Højer describes the creative aspects of absent knowledge.[41] Unlike Funar villagers who maintained that, despite the physical destruction of origin houses, the houses never ceased to exist, Mongolians were filled with a certainty that, post-socialism, something had changed and had been lost. In spite of this, as Højer describes, the absence of knowledge can be procreative, since absence is a precondition for the efficacy of certain religious images and practices. In Funar, absence—the absence of physical buildings—can also be creative, engendering new possibilities of collective identification, including the possibility of transforming status relations.

This relates directly to Webb Keane's examination of how the authority of ritual is grounded in representation. The presence of ancestors in ritual performances is a matter of ambiguity as ancestral words and things make the ancestors present by indexing their absence. To do so, words and things have to be transacted and coordinated in tandem. In Funar, however, there was a double absence, as people were not just confronted with the ambiguity of the ancestral presence, but also by the absence of the "things" (ancestral objects and buildings) that made them present.

Keane describes how Sumbanese ancestral ritualists both instigate and seek to overcome the risk inherent in action. The destruction of the material forms that index ancestral authority has made it especially hard for Funar villagers to control or overcome the risks to which representational acts are prone. It may even be that the destruction of ancestral origin houses and objects has intensified the way that the hazards of ritual action are experienced. Because the material signs that make ancestors present had to be remade from scratch, the ancestors' presence in ritual performance was a matter of increased ambiguity.

The predicament that people in Funar faced as they moved back to their ancestral land was related to the fact that they were rebuilding houses that were considered to have existed since the time of the ancestors, yet not everyone could agree about the nature and number of these ancestral houses. The reconstruction of origin houses was conceptualized as the materialization of houses that had existed in an unchanging form since the time of the ancestors. This gave rise to a tense atmosphere in which people challenged and criticized each other's attempts to rebuild certain houses, expressing uncertainty about the way houses were supposed to relate to one another and accusing each other of inventing houses that did not exist in the past.

The reconstruction of houses involved the materialization of a version of the "stranger king" paradigm, characterized by a dual formulation according to which houses were simultaneously one kind of thing (autochthonous) and one of two kinds of thing (either autochthonous or foreign, female or male, *lulik* or *ua*). According to the recursive logic that characterized this dual formulation, every claim to be one kind contained the possibility of a further split into two, so that one is always potentially two. The impulse behind this splitting seems rooted in attempts to escape an overarching hierarchy or to lodge claims of independence from the *liurai*, foreign powers, an older brother, or superior other. Since claims to authority could be made

---

[41] Højer, "Absent Powers."

on the basis of having a foreign origin, as well as on the basis of being autochthonous, the best strategy was to be always potentially both. Houses were able to reinvent themselves precisely because the chaos and dislocation of the Indonesian occupation had left the previous configurations fragmented and nebulous.

However, there was a problem. Claims by origin houses to be both foreign *and* autochthonous were hindered, or even undermined, by the need to host other house groups at inaugural ceremonies and to be recognized and legitimatized by them. There is a deep irony here: an origin house's quest for independence is dependent on recognition from others. The very attempt to lodge autonomous self-sufficient units depends upon the principles of relationality and dependence that origin houses are seeking to escape. This idea is nicely expressed in Keane's suggestion that self-assertion requires dependence on others, emphasizing the mutual dependence that eliciting recognition generates and the effort that goes into producing signs of authority.[42]

The social and political implications of these disparate claims are most apparent in the shift in power relations that took place in Funar following house reconstructions. The successful reproduction of autonomous houses that combine within themselves analogous oppositions echoes the transformation that led to the possibility of electing a "person of the land" to the outsider's office of village chief. Ultimately at stake during the house reconstruction were political independence and influence, based on a presumed ontological autonomy that could subsume autochthonous and foreign elements within itself.

"Unstable places" undergoing dramatic political change are thought to be particularly suitable sites for the study of the fragmentation and fluctuation of identities.[43] As is apparent in the examples discussed in this chapter, however, experiences of violence do not just destabilize existing identities; they can lead to the formation of different modes of identification. The case I describe shows how the reconstruction process in response to the destruction of the origin houses was used to create new possibilities of identification, which were actualized during house inaugurations. In this sense, conflict and displacement not only destroy people's modes of being, they also contribute to their transfiguration. However, the tension and anxiety surrounding house reconstructions illustrate that this constitutive process was itself hazardous, conducted in an atmosphere of uncertainty, disagreement, and conflict. Thus, identity formation is not only engendered by conflict, but can also provoke novel forms of antagonism.

The Indonesian occupation involved not only large-scale displacements, but also mass conversion to Catholicism. Interestingly, there was hardly any reference made to the Catholic Church during the reconstruction of origin houses, as Funar villagers sought to discard the idea that recent historical events had a significant impact on the nature of ancestral houses. There is a potential tension between the claim to permanence and the transient experience of division and destruction—a tension that emerged in the reconstruction process when houses needed to be physically rebuilt. I once asked an acquaintance of mine in Funar what happened during the Indonesian occupation when the origin houses no longer existed. At first he was confused by my

---

[42] Keane, *Signs of Recognition*, 16.

[43] Carol J. Greenhouse, Elizabeth Mertz, and Kay B. Warren, eds., *Ethnography in Unstable Places: Everyday Lives in Contexts of Dramatic Political Change* (Durham: Duke University Press, 2002).

question. Then he told me that the houses never stopped being there; the houses were there, but one could not see them. Thus, houses do not cease to exist when the edifice is destroyed. I was told that, as long as members of a house are still alive, the house exists. An origin house only becomes "extinct" when all its (male) members have died.

The reconstruction of origin houses essentially involved mediating the tension between, on the one hand, the radical historical transformations that took place in the country over the previous centuries, and, on the other, the need to maintain the view that these houses endure in an unchanging way throughout time. The friction between the ideal of the houses' permanence and the experience of their transience, between the claim to continuity and the need to continuously reconstruct and repair houses, may be an inherent aspect of material culture in this region.[44] Yet this tension was particularly pronounced in Funar, given the total destruction of buildings. When Funar's inhabitants moved back to their ancestral land, they were confronted with a kind of *tabula rasa*. The buildings that embodied the house groups had to be rebuilt from scratch, while the notion that they had never actually disappeared had to be maintained. House reconstruction in Funar was viewed as a means to make origin houses once again visible and tangible. The problem was that not everyone agreed on the precise nature of that which was invisible. This led to doubts and suspicions about the invention of houses, which came to the surface during the planning of origin house reconstruction and inauguration. The conflicts that emerged during the inaugurations, however, did not only concern the number and nature of houses; other kind of problems and disagreements also surfaced during these events, as will be explored in the next chapter.

---

[44] See, for example, Roy Ellen, *Nuaulu Ritual Practices: The Frequency and Reproduction of Rituals in a Moluccan Society* (Leiden: KITLV Press, 2012), 196.

CHAPTER FOUR

ON THE PAIN OF SEPARATION

The inauguration of Manehiak's *lulik* house, described in Chapter 3, lasted several days. After the members of the other origin houses had come to pay their respects, the next stage of the inauguration was initiated, which involved carrying the *lulik* objects to the new house. During this procedure, the women of Manehiak lined up proudly in front of the newly built house, drumming and dancing, all of them beautifully dressed in sarongs, woven shawls, and their most precious blouses (see photo, below).

Waiting in front of the rebuilt *lulik* house (2007; author's photo)

The men of Manehiak, with woven cloth wrapped around their shoulders, formed a group and started transporting the *lulik* objects, which included swords, spears, metal plates, and a basket, to the new house (see photo on next page). Among those leading the procession were Basílio, the "ladder to the sun" (*lelo odan*); and José, the guardian of the *ada lelo*. José had originally belonged to a different origin house, one called Ada Soran, a side-house of Bamatak. The origin house Bamatak encompasses a number of side-houses (its "children"), including Ada Soran, which was described as its "firstborn son." The evening before the inauguration, however, José was appointed guardian of Manehiak's *lulik* house, and his participation was thus an essential part of the ceremony.

The men were slowly approaching the *ada lelo* when an unexpected incident occurred. As the procession moved toward the house, large teardrops began to roll down José's cheeks. His crying grew louder and louder. Before long, his mother, sisters, and aunts, who were standing nearby, joined in, weeping in a truly heart-rending manner. At the moment when José was about to enter the newly built *lulik* house, his older brother, Rafael, overcome by tears, suddenly burst from the group and embraced José in an attempt to pull him back. While holding his brother and weeping, Rafael cried out, "My younger brother, my younger brother. Now the two of us are separated! Ayeeeh, my younger brother!" (*U walik, u walik. Ita nain-rua tahahe roo. Ayeeeeh, u walik!*)

Carrying *lulik* objects to the house (2007; author's photo)

To me, this emotional outburst did not appear to be part of the inauguration ceremony, since none of Manehiak's members were crying. Indeed, the brothers of Manehiak did not tolerate Rafael's behavior for long, quickly dragging him away to enable the inauguration to continue. As the ceremony proceeded, the loud sobbing of José's relatives gave way to more subdued crying. Meanwhile, José's father and paternal uncle danced frantically in front of the *ada lelo*.

This incident caused considerable upset in Funar, and it soon became clear that two things had been occurring simultaneously: the inauguration ceremony of Manehiak's *lulik* house and the culmination of an exchange that had taken place between Manehiak and Ada Soran. The night before the inauguration, a small ritual had been carried out at the cemetery to determine who should become the guardian of the newly built *ada lelo*. During this consultation, the ancestors announced that José, a member of the origin house Ada Soran, should be given to the origin house Manehiak and become the guardian of its *ada lelo*.

José's mother, Felismina, was originally from Manehiak and had married a man from Ada Soran. In Funar, children ideally are integrated into the father's origin house, provided that the correct marriage payments are made. In this case, however, no marriage payments had been made to compensate for the loss of José's mother, which is why the members of Manehiak were within their rights to ask for a descendant from Ada Soran to make up for this. Due to this outstanding debt, Ada Soran's members were obliged to "give" José to Manehiak. The emotional outburst of José's relatives during the ceremony was in response to this exchange, their tears expressing their pain at the loss of one of their members.

Why did the incident involving the change of José's house membership represent such a dramatic event for the members of his origin house? By examining the background to this event, I will explore that question and also explain how an origin house's membership is decided and defined. Origin houses are organic entities whose members are considered to share the same body. When members change house affiliations, they become disconnected from that organic unity. How do people deal with this separation, how are they compensated for the loss of a house member, and what is the historical context within which these emotional responses must be understood?

The most common reason for changing house affiliation is marriage. Marriage, exchange, and alliance—classic subjects of anthropological enquiry—were the focus of much of the early ethnographic work on eastern Indonesia and Timor, most notably Franciscus van Wouden's *Types of Social Structure in Eastern Indonesia*. In this book, van Wouden argues that the alliances created through cross-cousin marriage provide the key for understanding the organization of cosmos and society in the region. This interest in comparative work was later taken up by contributors to the volume *The Flow of Life*, edited by James Fox, which is concerned with the examination of kinship and classification in Eastern Indonesia and Timor. The flow of life, they argue, is maintained through alliances and exchanges between groups.

This approach has been criticized by Catherine Allerton, who suggests that its proponents were overly concerned with the rules governing social action and with demonstrating links between cosmological beliefs, ritual activities, and structural order. She contends, therefore, that these ethnographers paid insufficient attention to people's personal experiences.[1] In her analysis of "marriage paths" among the Manggarai of Flores, Allerton proposes an examination of marriage exchange as place-based practical action rather than a practice that follows certain rules and regulations. My investigation combines both approaches by showing the importance of marriage exchange for the social and hierarchical relations between house groups, while also examining the way in which these exchanges are experienced by those involved.

CHANGING HOUSE MEMBERSHIP

Descendants

At first it was hard for me to understand the grief displayed by José's paternal relatives at the inauguration of Manehiak, since he was going to remain in the village and would continue to live only a few meters from his parents' house. The only difference was that he would no longer be part of their origin house. To comprehend

---

[1] Allerton, "The Path of Marriage," 339–40.

their sadness, it is necessary to examine why the loss of a person from one's origin house is considered to be so painful.

Avó Bea, who lived with us for some time, told me again and again how proud she was to have over thirty grandchildren. The Idaté term for grandchild (*buu*) refers to both the grandchild and the grandparent and is therefore descriptive of their relationship.[2] Avó Ludovina also had a large number of grandchildren. When she died, the mortuary celebrations were particularly elaborate and a large number of buffalo were killed in her honor. Members of other origin houses were impressed by the grand ceremony, saying how lucky the old lady was to have so many children and grandchildren. Similar comments were made during the celebrations held to mark the end of the mourning period (*kore metan*) for Avó Bertha, a woman who had died in Laclubar. Again, people fondly noted her impressive number of progeny, which meant the celebration was particularly elaborate. In all cases, having many grandchildren was considered to be an admirable achievement and was interpreted as a sign of the strength and wealth of the origin house in general. Members of origin houses with fewer members occasionally commented, somewhat enviously, that those houses were "rich" and had a lot of influence in the region.

In contrast, members of small origin houses, such as Bubai, were widely pitied. Bubai had few living members and very few men, which was considered to be an unfortunate situation that made them "poor." Another house in Funar, Ada Malae, was said to have died out entirely, since only one male member and his daughter remained. Both male and female grandchildren were valued, and I never noticed any special preference for sons over daughters. Nevertheless, a house with no male descendants was considered to be extinct, suggesting the paramount importance of male descendants for the continued existence of the house group. This is because sons usually remain in their origin house, while daughters tend to leave when they marry.

Descendants are thought to be connected with the ancestors in rather concrete ways. Let me illustrate this by means of a short vignette. During the rainy season, there were times when it would rain for days and weeks without interruption. People had little to do during the day, so the women would keep themselves busy braiding mats while the men would gamble by playing cards. The people I lived with would spend quite a lot of time at home, either sleeping or just lying in bed listening to the rain drum on the tin roof. One day, between the endless showers, a small sliver of sunlight slipped through the clouds and everyone eagerly came out of their houses. My neighbor Dilma greeted me with disheveled hair and a disgruntled expression. Wrapped up tightly in her faded sarong, she said, "I could not sleep at all, because the ancestor was crying," pointing to her three-year-old son, Oscar.

By means of this statement and gesture, Dilma's son was directly identified with his dead ancestor. This type of conflation occurred on a number of occasions. When a child cried, it was common for parents to say that the ancestor was crying. Descendants are supposed to carry the names of their ancestors. Nowadays, since many people are actually given "Christian names" (*naran serani*), parents often add an ancestor's non-Christian "heathen name" (*naran jentiu*) after it. If children do not carry an ancestral name, the ancestors might cry through their descendant. This happened in the case of Oscar, according to his mother. When the ancestor cried, his

---

[2] Compare with Forth, *Beneath the Volcano*, 243.

descendant cried. Thus, there seems to be a physical connection between ancestors and descendants, similar to that between a tree trunk and the tip of its branches.

In many situations, male descendants would be spoken about as if they *were* the ancestors. When men spoke of their fathers or grandfathers, they made no distinction between themselves and members of their male origin line. Similarly, a woman whose husband used to guard an origin house in Orlalan spoke about her son and his male ancestor (Bita Loin) as though they were the same person. When I wanted to find out about her origin house, she said I would have to ask Bita Loin when her son, Tilo, came back. Through Tilo, she indicated, I would be able to communicate with Bita Loin. There is no strict linguistic separation between fathers, sons, and grandsons, and these people are frequently spoken of as the same person.

Although men tend to be permanent members of their origin houses while women are more likely to leave following marriage, the latter are considered to remain physically connected to their brothers' origin houses. This became clear to me when I witnessed the resolution of a conflict between a wife and her husband from the hamlet of Lawadu. During an argument, the husband had beaten his wife and pushed her down the ladder leading up to their house, which was raised on stilts. As a result, the woman suffered extensive bruising and cuts to her head. The conflict was resolved through a meeting involving the hamlet chief and a police officer from Laclubar Town, during which statements were taken from both parties. The hamlet chief demanded that the man give an animal to his wife. A point of contention was whether the man should also be obliged to give an animal to his wife's origin house (his wife-givers). The police officer argued that this was not necessary. The wife's brothers, however, who were also present at the meeting, insisted that, because the wound had involved lacerations that had caused the woman's blood to be spilled, their origin house also deserved an animal since it was their blood, too. In this case, the woman remained physically connected to her natal origin house, allowing her brothers to demand payment when her blood had been spilled.

"Our Daughters and Our Mothers' Trunk"

Members of the same origin house are considered to be siblings, which is why they cannot intermarry. Since one cannot marry and have children with a sibling, one has to find a marriage partner from a different origin house. Origin houses (or their side-houses) are thus the transacting units of exchange during marriage.[3] In Funar, matrilateral cross-cousin marriage (i.e., a man who marries his mother's brother's daughter, a person referred to as *tuananga*) used to be the preferred type of marriage.[4] As Elizabeth Traube has shown in the case of the Mambai, the house is an "alliance group" that plays a pivotal role in marriage and exchange.[5] Today, however, matrilateral cross-cousin marriage is less common in Funar, since the Catholic Church has redefined cross-cousin marriage as incest (at least, this was the reason people gave me for its decline).

---

[3] Compare with Signe Howell, "The Lio House: Building, Category, Idea, Value," in Carsten and Hugh-Jones, *About the House: Lévi-Strauss and Beyond*, 152; and Traube, *Cosmology and Social Life*, 82.

[4] See Fox, *The Flow of Life*; Traube, *Cosmology and Social Life*, 81–97; and Franciscus A. E. van Wouden, *Types of Social Structure in Eastern Indonesia*, trans. Rodney Needham (The Hague: Martinus Nijhoff, 1968).

[5] Traube, *Cosmology and Social Life*, 81.

In most marriages, the woman leaves her origin house to join that of her husband. In Idaté, the members of the giving origin house are called *naiuun*, which may be translated as "my mother's trunk/origin" (*u inaik uun*). The members of the origin house that receives a member are called *anamahinak*, which means "female children" (*anan mahinak*, i.e., "daughters"). As with the relationship between ancestors and descendants, the terms for exchanging groups indicate a sense of growth and diversification, as the mother's trunk/origin produces and encompasses its female descendants. I translate these as wife-givers and wife-takers, even though I am aware that these terms are problematic and do not entirely capture the way the Idaté terms are employed.[6] As the donating party, the wife-givers (*naiuun*) are considered to be socially superior to the wife-takers (*anamahinak*). This is a nontransitive relationship, meaning that the wife-givers of the wife-givers do not represent the highest-ranking group. The superiority of the wife-givers is produced and expressed in the relationship between two origin houses: the donors and the recipients.

For a woman to become a permanent part of her husband's origin house, the husband and his relatives need to compensate the members of her origin house for their loss. This compensation is called *helin* (or *folin* in Tetum). In Funar, the *helin* given by the receiving house to the giving house consists of items that are gendered male (such as money, buffalo, horses, goats, and palm liquor). The quantity is determined through negotiations between the ritual speakers of the houses involved and can range from one to one hundred. The giving house reciprocates with presents that are gendered female, such as pigs, woven cloth, and rice.

Helin or *folin* can be literally translated as "price," yet, despite the frequent translation as "brideprice," this translation does not adequately capture the way people use this term because "price" seems to indicate that women are exchanged as commodities. In Funar, the wife-givers emphasize that they are not "selling" women.[7] Rather, the *helin* is seen to be compensation for the loss of a person from the house.[8] When I asked villagers why a *helin* had to be given upon marriage, I was told that it was necessary to compensate the parents for their hard work and the resulting "tiredness" (*kole*), as well as to compensate the house as a whole for the loss of a member. I was reminded, moreover, that this was not a one-way payment, since the wife-givers also had to give gifts. Valerio Valeri has analyzed Huaulu marriage in Seram, eastern Indonesia, in terms of a dialectical relationship between commodity and gift exchange.[9] After having received the marriage payment, the commodity transaction is negated when the wife-givers reciprocate with gifts. Huaulu alliance,

---

[6] The terms "wife-givers" and "wife-takers" seem to privilege the perspective of men who exchange women amongst themselves—a notion not implied by the Idaté terms. Moreover, Fox has criticized the terms "wife-givers" and "wife-takers" for failing to capture the dynamic and fluid nature of these groups, proposing "progenitor" and "progeny" as alternatives. See Fox, "The Transformation of Progenitor Lines of Origin," 132. My preferred solution would be to use the Idaté terms, but this would make it hard for English speakers to follow the argument and comprehend the way in which people are transferred from one origin house to another.

[7] Compare with Valerio Valeri, "Buying Women but Not Selling Them: Gift and Commodity Exchange in Huaulu Alliance," *Man* 29, no. 1 (1994): 1.

[8] Compare with da Silva, "Negotiating Tradition and Nation," 460.

[9] Valeri, "Buying Women but Not Selling Them."

just like marriage in Funar, involves a commodity transaction (a "price"), but also entails the denial of this commodification through subsequent gift exchange.

It was rare for an origin house to be able to pay the *helin* in one go, as it usually takes time to amass the necessary resources. In many cases, it actually took several years to complete payment. A woman can only truly "enter" (*tama*) her husband's origin house once the *helin* is complete, a process called *arisa*. Completion also means that the children of the couple will become part of the man's origin house. The final payments are made when the woman dies; it is at this point that she becomes a permanent part of her husband's house, since she is buried on the same plot of land as the other members of this group (see Chapter 5). The process is therefore gradual, and it remains flexible which house the woman and her children are affiliated with until the *helin* is fully honored. However, even when the *helin* is paid in full and a woman thereby enters her husband's house, this process can still be reversed when there is a conflict, which can involve the repayment of the *helin* and the return of the woman to her brothers' house.

During my fieldwork, I witnessed only one case of formalized marriage exchange. This involved my neighbor's daughter, who went to marry a man from Fatumekerek, a village that is several hours' walk from Funar. In this case, part of the *helin* was handed over immediately. For as long as it had not been paid in full, the woman continued to live with her parents, while her husband came to visit her occasionally. Over the course of the following months, the members of the husband's origin house continued to bring parts of the *helin*, so the wife started to move back and forth between her parents' house and that of her husband. When she was ready to take up temporary residence in her husband's house, the wife-takers (i.e., members of her husband's origin house) came to collect her. They approached the house of the wife-givers with caution, giving verbal assurances of their humility and respect at every stage of the encounter between the two house groups.[10]

House groups are indebted to the origin houses of the women married to their male members, which is why it is regarded as essential to be respectful toward the wife-giving house groups, approaching them with deference. Encounters between wife-givers and wife-takers are often strained and thus necessitate certain etiquette to avoid conflict. On such occasions the wife-givers always receive the privilege of drinking, eating, and chewing betel nut first. People are worried about offending their wife-givers, since this could affect them negatively (for instance, by reducing the fertility of the women who came from that house).[11] They said it was vital to show respect toward one's wife-givers, since problems and conflicts with them were thought to lead to infertility and infant mortality.

This point cannot be overemphasized, since there are countless cases I know of where personal problems such as infertility or premature death were attributed to an offense that was committed toward the wife-givers. On one occasion, for example, a woman's brother (and hence wife-giver) was made directly responsible for her childlessness. I also know about a case where a woman blamed her brother for the

---

[10] Upon the departure of the daughter, the members of the wife-giving house were inconsolable even though they knew that she would continue to return to the house for the whole of the following year and when she had her first child, since the *helin* had not yet been paid in its entirety. There was a clear parallel here with the way members of José's paternal origin house mourned his loss during the inauguration of the *lulik* house. The loss of a member, whether a man or a woman, is expressed as a painful event.

[11] Compare with McWilliam, "Exchange and Resilience in Timor-Leste," 746.

death of her child. The two of them had had an argument, and, when subsequently she lost her baby during childbirth, she maintained that his "hot mouth" was the cause, as her brother had "spoken" to his *lulik* house. I was told again and again how crucial it is to fear and respect one's wife-givers.

"Going Back and Forth"

The relationship between wife-givers and wife-takers has, of course, been a key topic in the anthropological literature on Southeast Asia, with particular attention being paid to the structural asymmetry that is created through matrilateral cross-cousin marriage as well as the political relations and alliances that this asymmetry is thought to produce.[12] According to van Wouden, *connubium* (marriage exchange) is asymmetric "if affinal relationships are unilateral: in this case, a descent group gives women to another but cannot receive women from the same group."[13] Several residents of Funar told me that "following the truth" (*tuir loloos*), the men from an origin house should never marry women from an origin house whose members had married their mothers, grandmothers, or sisters. In other words, the direction of exchange should be maintained and never reversed. Several female elders told me that through their marriages they had "followed their female ancestor/grandmother" (*lahelo avô mahinak; tuir avô feto*, T.), thus replicating exchange relations that existed in the past.

Today, however, marriages take place in both directions. The ritual speaker of the *liurai* house, Paulino, who was married to his *tuananga*, commented on this with both amusement and embarrassment: "It goes back and forth [*ba mai*, T.]. We give them buffalo and we get them back again ... Then we give them buffalo and later we get them back again." Nowadays, he said, people in Funar take wives from and give wives to the same origin house.[14]

Reversals of the direction of exchange were fairly common in Funar in recent years, but they did not characterize every exchange relation. Some origin houses maintained a single direction over several generations (e.g., Berlibu and Bubai). It was not possible to generalize regarding the kinds of houses that allowed the reversal of the direction to take place. Changes in the direction of exchange occurred between two *liurai* houses (i.e., Manekaoli and Manehiak), for example, but also between *liurai* and lower-status house groups (e.g., Bubai and Manehiak, Ada Soran and Manehiak). This reversal meant that during death rituals, when exchanges between wife-givers and wife-takers are completed (see Chapter 5), the exchanging house groups were sometimes simultaneously wife-givers and wife-takers. The

---

[12] See, for example: Fox, *The Flow of Life*; van Wouden, *Types of Social Structure in Eastern Indonesia*; and Susan McKinnon, *From a Shattered Sun: Hierarchy, Gender, and Alliance in the Tanimbar Islands* (Madison: University of Wisconsin Press, 1991).

[13] Van Wouden, *Types of Social Structure in Eastern Indonesia*, 7.

[14] In *Origins, Ancestry and Alliance*, James Fox compares systems of marriage exchange across the region, revealing how there are some cases where the unidirectionality of exchange is maintained (e.g., among the Mambai and the Ema of Central Timor-Leste). For the Rotinese, however, although the directionality of exchange is maintained for two generations, it may be changed thereafter. Among the Atoni Meto of West Timor, a two-way directionality of marriage is also common, meaning that "lines of precedence" are constantly shifting. See Fox, "The Transformation of Progenitor Lines of Origin," 149.

participants would tend to laugh about this fact albeit somewhat coyly, as it meant they would take both male and female presents to the mortuary ceremony.

According to Traube, the potential reversal of the direction of exchange is given by Mambai as a reason for why *patrilateral* cross-cousin marriage is prohibited.[15] Similarly, Andrew McWilliam argues that among Fataluku, exchange only ever takes place in one direction (matrilaterally), which makes marriage unions "profoundly asymmetric."[16] This is relevant because we can see in Funar that, in the cases where the direction of exchange has been reversed, the alliances between these groups are less permanent and hence less asymmetric. Janet Hoskins makes a similar observation in Kodi, where the direction of marriage is not fixed and alliances are contested, unstable, and shifting. There seems to be a correlation between the ability to reverse the direction of exchange and competitive social and political organization.[17] Hoskins also holds that maintaining the direction of exchange is a strategy of the wealthy.[18] Changing the direction of exchange in Funar may be a way of dealing with the inability to pay *helin*.

This is in line with my general observations in Funar, where political and status relations between house groups are generally contested. The possibility of reversing exchange relations seems to be one further aspect of the overall competition and contestation between house groups.

LIVING TOGETHER

Relations between wife-giving and wife-taking house groups in Funar not only fluctuate at a structural level, but are also contested with regards to practical concerns. The union between two people is usually described as "living together" (*mori amutuk*) or "residing together" (*diuk amutuk*). However, the question of where a couple will live—and hence where their children will live and possibly what origin house they will belong to—is contentious.

In Funar and Laclubar Town, children do not necessarily grow up living in the house of their birth parents, as many move frequently among households or spend months or years living with other relatives. The reasons for this are varied: sometimes children are sent to live in a place that is closer to their school, and sometimes they go to live with a childless couple to help them with domestic and agricultural work. What is most common, however, is for children to live for some time with their father's brother, who is also considered to be their father (either their "big father," if the father's brother is older; or their "little father," if he is younger). There are also cases of children living with unrelated adults. The couple I lived with, for example, had taken in a number of children whose parents lived far from the center of Funar so that the children could attend school. I also knew of cases where children had gone to live with their mother's relatives, the wife-givers.

Living temporarily or permanently with adults who are not from their origin house does not mean that these children's origin house affiliations change, as happened in the case of José. However, when children continue to live with their wife-givers because no *helin* has been given by the child's father or his relatives, their

---

[15] Traube, *Cosmology and Social Life*, 82.

[16] McWilliam, "Exchange and Resilience in Timor-Leste," 750.

[17] Hoskins, *The Play of Time*, 18, 24.

[18] Ibid., 20, 25.

origin house membership is somewhat ambiguous. Usually, the mother's relatives with whom the child lived would contend that the child belonged to them because of the father's family's failure to pay a *helin*. The father's relatives, meanwhile, would stress that this was a temporary arrangement. During a child's lifetime, his or her affiliation to an origin house may not be entirely solidified, since it has the potential to be changed in certain circumstances.

The fluidity of kinship affiliation is a phenomenon that has been observed in numerous Southeast Asian contexts[19] and has led to the general suggestion that social identity in Austronesian societies is fluid.[20] Maurice Bloch takes up this suggestion about the fluidity of social identity in Southeast Asia and relates it to perceptions of "being in history."[21] In Chapter 2, I discussed Bloch's contrast between "Aristotelian" and "Platonic" models of knowledge and history, which he relates to the equivalent perceptions of identity and kinship. The Bicolanos of the Philippines, with their "Aristotelian" view of history, also have a fluid concept of identity, since they regard themselves as molded by outside influences. This stands in contrast to the "Platonic" view of history of the Sadah, whose kinship system is a "descent type"[22] and whose identity is considered to be made up of certain essential immutable qualities that are imparted to people at birth and connect people through time.

According to Bloch, the "intermediary" model is that of the Vezo in Madagascar, studied by Rita Astuti.[23] In analyzing different forms of identity among the Vezo, Astuti argues that, during life, Vezo kinship is cognatic and identity is fluid, as it is shaped by what people do.[24] Upon death, however, a person becomes part of a unilineal descent group and identity is fixed. In Funar, house membership becomes fixed upon death, that is, when a person is buried at the site where other members of the same house are buried. During a person's lifetime, membership of an origin house may be altered depending on the kinds of exchanges that are carried out between origin houses. Whereas for the Vezo, not being part of a descent group during life is structurally possible and even desirable, for the adults of Funar the fluidity of house membership is largely a result of their inability to pay the *helin*. In Funar, people strive to solidify their house membership during their lifetime, but they frequently fail to do so when they cannot raise the resources for the *helin*. If these villagers' lived reality resembles that of the Vezo (i.e., house membership is fluid in life and fixed upon death), their ideals differ, since in Funar people would prefer to resolve house membership during life by raising a *helin*. This is especially true for men and wife-takers.

---

[19] See, for example, Janet Carsten, "The Substance of Kinship and the Heat of the Hearth: Feeding, Personhood, and Relatedness among Malays in Pulau Langkawi," *American Ethnologist* 22, no. 2 (1995): 224.

[20] James J. Fox, "The House as a Type of Social Organisation on the Island of Roti," in *De la Hutte au Palais: Société "A Maison" en Asie du Sud-est Insulaire*, ed. Charles Macdonald and members of the ECASE (Paris: Edition du CNRS, 1987), 174.

[21] Bloch, *How We Think They Think*, 77.

[22] Ibid., 76.

[23] See: Ibid., 78; and Rita Astuti, *People of the Sea: Identity and Descent among the Vezo of Madagascar* (Cambridge: Cambridge University Press, 1995).

[24] Astuti, *People of the Sea*, 7.

Moreover, during a person's lifetime, the fixity of affiliation varies, since as a woman gets older she tends to become a more permanent member of her husband's origin house and may even become its guardian. The house membership of children is more fluid than that of their elders; with age, house affiliation becomes more permanent.

"My Younger Brother, the Two of Us Are Being Separated"

If house membership is fluid in early life, how do we explain why the incident concerning José, with which this chapter began, was so problematic? Why was the loss of José such a painful moment for his fellow house members? In the 1980s, José's father, who was a member of Ada Soran, married Felismina from Manehiak, whose parents used to be the guardians of Manehiak's *lulik* house. José's father told me that, during their time living in Laclubar Town, they lost all of their livestock and wealth due to resettlement and the Indonesian invasion, and that was why he had been unable to raise the *helin*. These tragic circumstances did not lead to a reevaluation of the *helin*, and, in 2007, José was "given back" to Manehiak as the guardian of their *ada lelo* to compensate for the loss of his mother from Manehiak. These exchange relations were embedded within the wider social hierarchy, since the socially superior wife-givers had the power to demand a child from the wife-takers.

Many of Manehiak's young members lived in Laclubar Town or Dili where they went to school or worked, and this could be the reason why Manehiak had to ask for a member from a different origin house to become the guardian of the *lulik* house. Before José assumed this role, his little brother, Teus, had already been living with his wife-givers from Manehiak, and it was he who was supposed to have become the guardian. However, Teus was too naughty (*nakar*) and was returned to his parents. The ancestors were consulted in order to choose a new guardian, which resulted in José's appointment.

José's relatives perceived the obligation to give away a son as a final and painful separation, as if a part of their body had been lost. "José is no longer part of us," his father's unmarried sister had exclaimed while crying in front of the *ada lelo*. José's brother Rafael was also overcome by the pain of separation when he tried to hold José back, crying loudly, "My younger brother, the two of us are being separated." Some hours after this incident, following the consumption of a substantial amount of palm liquor, a fight broke out between José's paternal relatives and several young men from Manehiak. Members of Ada Soran were upset that there had been no ritual at their origin house in order to ask permission for José to become a member of Manehiak. José's sister commented bitterly, "Oh, those people from Manehiak are so stupid [*beik*]. They think they are clever because they went to school and all that. But this time they were really stupid, because they did not ask our *lulik* for permission."

Some members of Manehiak denied the accusations, stating adamantly that the dead ancestors had made the decision that José should be given to Manehiak, and thus tried to absolve themselves of blame for the dispute. Some also denied that José had been given to Manehiak because of the failure to raise the *helin*, while others simply chose to mock José's brother for his dramatic interference by imitating his crying. After all, they said, members of Ada Soran had taken part in the ritual at the cemetery where the decision was made. There, José's dead maternal grandfather, who had been the guardian of the *lulik* house in the past, had told them to give José to Manehiak. They saw no reason for José's relatives to be upset.

Arguments between members of the two origin houses continued until late in the evening, and throughout the night one could hear crying that closely resembled the sobbing heard at funerals. The fight between Manehiak and Ada Soran illustrates how tense the relationship between wife-givers and wife-takers can be. José's younger, unmarried sister told me that now that her brother was part of Manehiak, he was her *naiuun* (wife-giver) and she had to respect and fear him because of this. The morning before the conflict, José's older brother, Rafael, had met with the brothers of Manehiak. During this encounter, he had publicly recognized José's incorporation into Manehiak by kneeling in front of José and stating, in a respectful and submissive manner, "You are now my *naiuun* (wife-giver)," assuring his younger brother that he would accord him with the appropriate respect. José's social position vis-à-vis his paternal relatives changed markedly as a result of this exchange. He went from being a submissive younger brother to a wife-giver deserving of his (older) brother's respect.

José's case was not unique; there were a number of other children who lived with their wife-givers. In many cases, however, the children's affiliation remained ambiguous during their lifetime. I knew of one man, for example, who had to give his daughter to the wife-givers because he was unable to pay the *helin*, but when his wife died, he simply demanded his daughter back, much to the dismay and consternation of the wife-givers. In Funar, the house membership of children whose fathers had not paid a *helin* often remains unknown, just as on Roti the integration of progeny into the maternal line is actively obscured.[25] Both on Roti and in Funar, the integration of offspring into the maternal house is only fully acknowledged when mortuary payments are made, a topic that will be discussed further in Chapter 5. José's case was unusual because his incorporation into the wife-giving house was rendered permanent during his lifetime, following his appointment as guardian of Manehiak's *ada lelo*.

In contrast to common portrayals of patrilineality, the entitlement of the wife-giver in Funar to ask for a child as compensation for the loss of a woman points to the primacy of the relation through the mother. Even though a married woman and her children are ideally integrated into the husband's origin house, if a *helin* cannot be paid, a child may need to be given "back" to the maternal relatives. Funar is not an exception in this respect. Traube describes, for example, how a Mambai man who gets married may live with his wife's parents. He does not have to give a bridewealth, but has to carry out low status duties for his wife's kin. The husband's children, Traube notes, will be affiliated with the wife's kin as well.[26] During a 2015 visit to Suai, on the south coast of Timor-Leste, I was told by a Kemak man that they also "return" a child to the wife-givers if a bridewealth cannot be paid. This, he stressed, would never happen amongst matrilineal Bunaq, where men enter into the woman's house. Similarly, Forth notes that among the Nage and Keo of Flores, children may be incorporated into the wife-giving house if appropriate marriage and death payments are not made.[27] According to Forth, this demonstrates the connection that children retain to their mother's group, which "continues to

---

[25] Fox, "The Transformation of Progenitor Lines of Origin," 138–39.

[26] Traube, *Cosmology and Social Life*, 88.

[27] Gregory Forth, "Separating the Dead: The Ritual Transformation of Affinal Exchange in Central Flores," *Journal of the Royal Anthropological Institute* 15 (2009): 560–63.

encompass them."[28] Forth's conception of affiliation as encompassment may also be employed to understand the way in which the relationship between wife-givers and wife-takers in Funar is described: the wife-givers are the trunk that encompasses the children/daughters. Despite the separation that occurs through marriage, descendants retain a primary relationship with their trunk. This notion of encompassment seems to capture the logic of actually occurring house membership much more adequately than do notions of patrilineality or matrilineality, which are commonly used to classify East Timorese language groups.

In Funar, the preferred marriage is one whereby women are integrated into the husband's group—what one may call patrilineal or patrifileal descent. Yet matrilineal principles are implicit, since, when the *helin* is not paid, the default house membership of a child is in the mother's origin house.[29] The coexistence of seemingly opposed principles, such as patrilineality and matrilineality, is supposedly a defining feature of "house-based societies," a concept first proposed by Lévi-Strauss and further developed in the volume edited by Carsten and Hugh-Jones.[30] The house as a social group is thought to unite opposing principles, such as those of patrilineality and matrilineality, filiation and residence, hypergamy and hypogamy, and close marriage and distant marriage: "[T]he house is therefore an institutional creation that permits compounding forces which, everywhere else, seem only destined to mutual exclusion of their contradictory bends."[31] While rejecting the evolutionist aspect of Lévi-Strauss's approach, which presents house-societies as a transitional stage between elementary and complex kinship structures, Carsten and Hugh-Jones emphasize the continued relevance of the suggestion that the house brings together antagonistic principles.[32]

There are clearly both matrilineal and patrilineal principles at work in Funar. Ideally, children are integrated into the paternal origin houses, but, despite this preference, the connection to the maternal origin house remains primary. For Funar's residents, patrilineality and matrilineality are not antagonistic principles, but form part of the same process: every person's origin is in the mother's origin house ("the mother's trunk"). By giving a *helin*, house affiliation can be changed so that a person can become part of a different house ("our daughters").

Living with the Wife-givers

Giving children "back" to the wife-giving house is one way of dealing with the inability to raise a *helin*; another way is to give oneself. In some of the other *suco* of Laclubar, people practice *abani* (*habani*, T.), whereby the man moves in with the woman's relatives and the children are divided between the origin houses of their parents. No *helin* is given in these cases; just "one or two" gifts are given "out of

[28] Ibid., 563.

[29] For a more detailed discussion of this argument, see Judith Bovensiepen, "Ich gebe dir mein Kind: Verwandtschaftsbeziehungen und Pflegschaften in Osttimor," in *Verwandtschaft Heute*, ed. Erdmute Alber, Bettina, Julia Pauli, and Michael Schnegg (Berlin: Reimer, 2010), 73–92.

[30] See: Lévi-Strauss, *The Way of the Masks*; and Carsten and Hugh-Jones, *About the House: Lévi-Strauss and Beyond*.

[31] Lévi-Strauss, *The Way of the Masks*, 184.

[32] Carsten and Hugh-Jones, *About the House: Lévi-Strauss and Beyond*, 9.

respect."[33] Such an arrangement is equally a possibility for Mambai men, as mentioned before, but also for Tetun of Wehali, in southwest Timor, and the Ata Tana'Ai of Flores. In these cases men can take up residence in the woman's house, in compensation for which a child is returned to the man's relatives.[34]

Most villagers I spoke to maintained that there was no *abani* in Funar because the men "do not want to leave." The reason given by several men as to why they did not marry women from the neighboring region of Lacló was that they did not want to move there, but the people of Lacló would not let their daughters move to Funar. According to the ideal marriage arrangement, men are immobile (i.e., the ones who stay) and women are mobile.[35] This is antithetical to the gendered division of ritual speech and dance, since silence and immobility are gendered as female and speaking and movement as male. Even though men emphasized that they preferred to pay *helin* to avoid living on someone else's land, they complained bitterly about the difficulties involved in raising the requisite money and livestock.

Despite the assertion that people in Funar did not practice *abani*, I knew of several village men who lived with their wives' parents because they were unable to pay the *helin*. Even though some of these men were already quite old, they all insisted that theirs was a temporary impasse resulting from a momentary lack of money and livestock for the *helin*. When I asked one man from the hamlet of Bamatak which house his children belonged to, he told me that they formed part of his origin house. When I later spoke to his wife's parents, however, they said that the children were part of *their* origin house, demonstrating yet again that a child's house membership is not always fixed and may vary depending on the context.

The inability to pay a *helin* did not automatically lead to uxorilocal residency or the obligation to give a child. I also knew of other cases in which no *helin* was paid, but the couple built their own house on the land of the husband's origin house. In other cases, however, this practice would lead to conflict between wife-givers and wife-takers. In January 2007, there was a severe rice shortage in Timor-Leste and elsewhere in Southeast Asia. The price of rice in the Laclubar subdistrict doubled, then tripled, and eventually the supply dried up completely. This period coincided with a particularly difficult "hungry season" (*moat*), which was intensified by the fact that the rains had come late and rats had destroyed many villagers' corn harvests. This dire situation led to a food shortage.

This food shortage brought existing conflicts further to the surface, including tensions between wife-givers and wife-takers. Jorge and Eva, a couple I know, could usually easily afford to buy rice, yet, due to the rice shortage, they had problems securing food for their household. This led to severe tensions with Eva's brother, who lived in the neighboring house next to the couple. Jorge complained bitterly that Eva's brother, along with his wife and children, were depending on him to feed them and decided that Eva's brother and his children should from now on have a separate kitchen—as until then the two households were sharing the same kitchen.

This conflict had more complex roots, however. Jorge is not from Funar, but from a different *suco*. During the dispute, he mentioned that he wanted to take his

---

[33] *Abani* is also used as a verb and is contrasted with *aheli*, which means "to give a *helin*." See also Hicks, *Tetum Ghosts and Kin*, 72, 95, for *habani* amongst Tetum of Vikeke.

[34] See: Fox, "The Transformation of Progenitor Lines of Origin," 143; and Traube, *Cosmology and Social Life*, 88.

[35] Compare with McKinnon, *From a Shattered Sun*, 107.

wife, Eva, with him to his natal *suco*, where he had more land and would not have to feed his wife's brother's children. Eva's brother, however, maintained that Jorge had not given the appropriate *helin* for Eva, and thus could not take her away. Jorge complained endlessly about sharing the kitchen with his wife's brother, saying that he had been supporting his wife's brother's family for so long that he no longer owed a *helin*. According to Eva's brother, these previous provisions were in no way sufficient, since Jorge was obliged to give him appropriate compensation in the form of a buffalo if he wanted to take Eva away.

Eva positioned herself somewhere between the two men, trying to play down the conflict as much as possible. In the end, Eva and Jorge went to stay at a relatives' house elsewhere in the sub-district for considerable time until the rice shortage was over. The food shortage thus proved to be the trigger for the escalation of preexisting conflicts about Eva's rightful origin house. Several people commented that Jorge had been foolish to move so close physically to his wife-givers in the first place, since this degree of proximity would inevitably lead to quarrels. I observed that the residency of couples and their children was a continuous source of disputes, some of which had deep political and historical roots.

GIVING CHILDREN TO THE *LIURAI*

Children living with people who were not part of their own origin house were at times referred to as *anan kiak*, "poor children" (or *oan hakiak* in Tetum, best translated as "foster children," since *hakiak* means "to raise"). Some of those to whom these terms were applied had lost their parents during the war, but in other cases the birth parents were still alive. One person referred to as *anan kiak* was a grown man named Alexandre, who became an orphan during the Indonesian occupation. His daughter told me her father's story over coffee.

Alexandre was originally from Maubisse, the area around Mount Ramelau, to the west of Funar. During the Indonesian invasion and the civil war that preceded it, people withdrew to the mountains to hide or join the resistance. It was during this chaotic time that Alexandre lost his parents. A man from Funar who had joined the resistance eventually found Alexandre, who was only a child at the time. This man tried to sell Alexandre as a war captive. However, the village chief of Funar intervened and took the boy in himself as a *oan hakiak*. Later, Alexandre married the village chief's sister and went to live on his land, becoming part of his origin house. Alexandre feels "lucky," his daughter said, and also indebted to the village chief. I was told that during local conflicts it was common to take captives, who ended up working as slaves for the families of the victors. Alexandre barely escaped such a fate.

Another interesting case is that of Nicolau, whose story was told to me by his grandchildren, since he is no longer alive. In the past, the Portuguese imprisoned Funar's *liurai*, who was called Dom João da Cruz.[36] He had sired no children prior to his arrest, so the other members of his origin house, Manehiak, asked the Dom's sister for her child, named Nicolau. Thus Nicolau, who was originally part of Ada Lulin (the high-ranking *lulik* house in Bamatak), was given to Manehiak (the *liurai*).

---

[36] Belo notes that in 1905 the *liurai* of Funar was a man called Dom João da Cruz. See Carlos Filipe Ximenes Belo, *Os Antigos Reinos de Timor-Leste (Reys de Lorosay e Reys de Lorothoba, Coronéis e Datos)* (Baucau: Tipografia Diocesana Baucau, 2011), 187.

There are several different versions of this story. Some argue that a *helin* was given for Nicolau.[37] Others held that Nicolau was given without compensation, but was instead given for his mother in return. When Nicolau was given to Manehiak, two unrelated children, Carlos and Domingas,[38] from low-ranking side-houses, were also given along with Nicolau in order that they would "carry water and cook" for him.

When Carlos died during my fieldwork, he was buried as a member of the origin house Manehiak. At his funeral ceremony, people went to great lengths to obscure the fact that he had been given to Manehiak together with Nicolau. Indeed, this was only made explicit when mortuary exchanges were made between Manehiak and Ada Lulin. Eventually, a member of Ada Lulin told me in private that Carlos and Domingas had been given to Manehiak as slaves (*atan*) to serve Nicolau. Most members of Manehiak, however, referred to Carlos as their "brother," even though it was clear that he and his family were considerably poorer and less educated than the other brothers of Manehiak.

There is ambiguity to the term *oan hakiak*, since some children potentially moved into the category of slave or domestic worker. Others, as in the case of Alexandre, who became part of the village chief's origin house, enjoyed relative prosperity and well-being. That Carlos and Alexandre were both referred to as "poor children" (*anan kiak*) or "foster children" (*oan hakiak*) attests to the close connection between being a war orphan, a foster child, and a slave or domestic worker. Slavery was an extremely sensitive topic in Funar, as it is in Timor-Leste as a whole.[39] Whereas many inhabitants of Funar categorically rejected the term "slave" (*atan*), in private, several individuals did use the term, especially when talking about foster children. The connection between slavery and fostering was made explicit by a young man who told me that "there are two types of foster children [*oan hakiak*]: real foster children and slaves. But no one talks about this anymore. Nowadays we just call them all *walin* [younger siblings]."

This ambiguity is not unique to Funar. In analyzing ideas about slavery on Sumba, Hoskins differentiates among three different types of slaves—namely, war captives, those who have inherited their status, and those who have recently been purchased.[40] On Sumba, as in Funar, former slaves are frequently represented as "poor relatives" or as those "without family." According to Hoskins, fostering, slavery, and marriage exchange are connected, since each establishes debt and obligation. Marriage is a form of debt, as men who are unable to raise the marriage payments may temporarily become bond slaves of the bride's father in a way not unlike uxorilocal residence in Funar.[41] In this sense, women have a "price" and may be "costly," although their status as a commodity is negated, as noted earlier, through the mutual giving of gifts during marriage exchange.[42] This offers an

---

[37] The inadequacy of the translation of *helin* as "brideprice" becomes clear here, since a *helin* can also be paid for men.

[38] Carlos and Domingas are pseudonyms, as they were still living in Funar when I started my fieldwork.

[39] See Kammen, "Master-Slave, Traitor-Nationalist, Opportunist-Oppressed."

[40] Janet Hoskins, "Slaves, Brides, and Other 'Gifts': Resistance, Marriage, and Rank in Eastern Indonesia," *Slavery and Abolition* 25, no. 2 (2004): 96.

[41] Hoskins, "Slaves, Brides and Other 'Gifts,'" 97.

[42] See: Ibid., 98; McWilliam, "Exchange and Resilience," 751; and Valeri, "Buying Women but Not Selling Them."

important insight for understanding the exchanges between origin houses in Funar, since they also involve debts between houses that at times are reimbursed through the transfer of a person.

The examples from Sumba provide another insight, this one concerned with the connection between slavery and hierarchy. Similar to the term *atan* used to refer to slaves in Funar, *ata* means "slave" in the more stratified domains of East Sumba and Kodi. In ten other languages of West Sumba, where a more flexible competitive social organization is the norm, *ata* means "human being."[43] There, the transfer of gifts during marriage and mortuary ceremonies is closely connected to rank and prestige, as exemplified by Hoskins's discussion of the gift of a slave girl during a royal funeral in East Sumba.[44] Giving a slave girl at the funeral was considered to be a continuation of transfers that included brides in the context of marriage negotiations.[45]

When I spoke to some villagers in Funar about *atan*, one man from the autochthonous house Bubai told me that when members of *liurai* intermarried during colonial times, it was common for the wife-givers to give one or two children from the *povu* (the "people") to work for the *liurai* along with the woven cloth and pigs that they were required to give together with their daughters. According to this information, in Funar, too, giving slaves was part of the marriage exchange between high-ranking houses. In addition, several villagers confided that they themselves (or their parents) had been given as children to the *liurai* because their parents had not been able to pay the taxes that the local rulers had collected for the Portuguese colonial government.[46] These children, called *ornassa*, carried out housework in the *liurai* houses. When I spoke to members of the *liurai* about this, they said that they took the children in so as to send them to school. It seems that the *liurai*, whose position was strengthened under the Portuguese system of indirect rule, and who were charged with the task of collecting taxes, were able to create relationships of debt that allowed them to command domestic labor. Today, the *liurai*'s elevated social position may partly be due to the economic advantages they have managed to accumulate (such as ownership of buffalo, education, and employment in NGOs in the capital).

When children change origin house affiliation today, these past experiences still resonate. At the beginning of this chapter, I mentioned the pain of José's relatives when their son was given to the wife-givers. After the inauguration of the *lulik* house, José's father told me, "I have to give my son to my *naiuun*." Then he added, "I have to give my son to the *liurai*." The pain and resignation of José's relatives when he was given to Manehiak was thus not only an expression of frustration about the nature of their obligation toward their wife-givers, it was also an expression of frustration directed at Manehiak in its capacity as the ruling house. In the past, when taxes could not be paid, children from origin houses that were ranked low in the

---

[43] Hoskins, "Slaves, Brides and Other 'Gifts,'" 95.

[44] Ibid., 93.

[45] Ibid., 99.

[46] There were also a number of people who told me that they had had to sell their buffalo to the *liurai* so that they could pay their taxes. Interestingly, there is historical evidence that suggests that the Portuguese invaded Funar at the beginning of the twentieth century precisely because they were interested in the buffalo herds that Funar's residents had managed to raise. See Zola, *Quatorze Annos de Timor*, 27–28.

social hierarchy had to be given to *liurai* families whose origin houses were ranked highest.

Members of Manehiak were not only the wife-givers of Ada Soran; they were also *liurai*, who in the past could ask for children to work for them when the tax payments they collected for the Portuguese were in default. Today, these same people can ask for a child when the *helin* cannot be paid. When José was given to the *liurai*, his father's origin house lost a male descendant. Descendants, as I argued earlier, not only ensure the continuation of a house group, but also make up the strength and wealth of an origin house. This could help to explain the unusually wild and uncontrollable dancing of José's father in front of the *lulik* house during the inauguration. Once the inauguration had finished, members of Manehiak made contemptuous comments about the overly emotional reaction of José's relatives, insisting that the ancestors had made the decision that José should guard the *lulik* house of Manehiak. The crying of José's kin might have been a socially expected reaction, given his change of affiliation, and/or a sincere expression of personal grief. However, despite the insistence of Manehiak's members that they were simply following the wishes of the ancestors, the tensions and historical inequalities among the different house groups seem to have affected the way this separation was perceived by members of José's paternal house group.

Cases such as José's, in which wife-takers remain indebted to the wife-givers, and repayment involves the "gift" of a child, were not the exception. I know of several instances where children were given "back" to the wife-givers. The wife-takers in these instances were always from low-ranking houses, and those requesting children were members of the *liurai*. When *liurai* intermarried without paying *helin*, no demands of children were made. In one example, a man from the *liurai* house Manekaoli married a woman from the *liurai* house Manehiak. The husband was a teacher in Funar's primary school and thus had a decent income. His wife-givers (the same house-group that had requested the transfer of José from Ada Soran) did not insist on receiving a *helin* or a child as compensation, instead suggesting that the couple use their money to send their children to high school.

As noted above, during the later part of the Portuguese colonial period, the *liurai* were able to command labor from low-ranking houses to work in their fields and carry out domestic work. While this is no longer practiced, there is nevertheless an element of continuity (or at least structural similarity) with past practices. Today, *liurai* houses that receive children as compensation for unpaid *helin* may use these children to perform a considerable amount of domestic labor. Alternatively, as in the case of José, they may assume certain ritual responsibilities that the children of *liurai* houses are unable to take on due to their educational commitments.

When the transfers of children to *liurai* houses are represented as part of marriage exchanges, these transfers represent the assertion of political and economic status through the idiom of kinship. According to Carsten and Hugh-Jones, following Lévi-Strauss, the "subversion" of the language of kinship to naturalize rank differences and the competition over wealth and power is a defining feature of house-based societies.[47] In these societies, houses are thought to act as vehicles for the naturalization of rank, although they may also play a vital role in the social

---

[47] See: Carsten and Hugh-Jones, *About the House: Lévi-Strauss and Beyond*, 10; and Lévi-Strauss, *The Way of the Masks*. See also Chapter 3, this volume.

organization of more egalitarian societies.[48] In Funar, when *liurai* houses ask for children from the wife-takers, these transfers are represented through the idiom of kinship, but they are also expressions of status inequalities that have deep historical roots.

Sometimes, after an interview or a social visit, people from poor households would bid me farewell by saying "Menina, I [will] give you my child … I don't have anything else to give to you." At times, people even picked out one of their children and said, "Here, have this one!" Even though this may have been a figure of speech—a way of emphasizing their own poverty—poor villagers did often end up sending their children to wealthier residents, hoping this may improve the children's life chances.

ON THE PAIN OF SEPARATION

Anita was a woman in her late twenties whose husband was from Funar. She belonged to an origin house in Sananain that had long-standing marriage exchanges with her husband's origin house. Due to the fact that Anita's husband, Abel, had found work in Laclubar Town, the couple did not return to the ancestral land after independence, even though Anita's parents and brothers had all returned to Fatumakerek (about an eight hours' walk from where she lived). One day, while I was in Funar, news reached us that Anita had fallen ill with malaria. This was quite unusual, since Laclubar Town and Funar are situated in the highlands where malaria is rare, and Anita had not traveled to Dili, where one is more likely to contract the illness. Along with some of the teenage girls from my household, I walked to Laclubar Town, first stopping at the house of Anita's husband's mother. On this visit, Anita's mother-in-law told us that Anita had become "mad" (*bulak*), that her words made no sense, and that there was not much hope for her.

When we reached Anita, she was lying in bed under a mosquito net, holding a large plastic bag full of pills that she had received from the health post. She looked tearful, but in contrast to her mother-in-law's account of her state of mind, she seemed lucid and her words were clear and easy to follow. She told me that she was very tired because she had no one to help her in the house. Her three children were all very young, under the age of six, and were therefore unable to help her with cooking and cleaning. She complained that her husband spent his salary on alcohol and that when he came home he beat her. She did not know how to feed the children and often had to subsist on food that her parents sent her from their own fields.

Anita mentioned that at the beginning she had not really wanted to marry Abel, but that he had been very insistent. To ask for her hand in marriage, Abel had gone to speak to members of her origin house, telling them, "There is a sweet flower in your house that I like." Since there were past marriage ties between his origin house and Anita's, Anita's parents swiftly agreed to the marriage. Abel told me on another occasion that he had had to promise his father just before he died that he would marry a woman from Anita's house; it was for this reason that he had gone to Sananain to ask if there were any suitable marriageable women. Anita stressed that living far away from her parents and the fields made it particularly hard for her to bring up her children, since this meant that there was no one there to support her.

---

[48] Roxana Waterson, "Houses and Hierarchies in Island Southeast Asia," in Carsten and Hugh-Jones, *About the House: Lévi-Strauss and Beyond*, 51.

From her own account, there was some ambiguity as to whether she was truly ill with malaria, just exhausted, or perhaps both. It seemed to me that her illness was a way of protesting against her difficult situation. She recovered within a matter of days.

Anita's account was unusual because most women did not openly complain about their marriages, even though they frequently told stories about other women's experiences of domestic violence and separation. This does not mean, of course, that all women experienced domestic violence. If they did, though, living far away from their relatives meant that they received very little support. As illustrated by the earlier example of the man pushing his wife down a ladder, a woman's brothers may well complain about domestic violence and make claims for compensation. This would suggest that for women, virilocal residence is not actually valued in the same way that it is valued by men because it can involve moving far away from natal kin. Children who went to live with their maternal relatives (that is, with their fathers' wife-givers) recounted similar stories. They found themselves in an inferior position, since wife-givers are considered to be socially superior to wife-takers. Despite this supposed status inequality, the children themselves would usually emphasize their equality vis-à-vis their new siblings. Nonetheless, it seemed to me that, in reality, they often took on more of the housework than the other children in the same household.

Rosa, for example, was a teenage girl who lived with members of her father's wife-givers, who were *liurai*. Her birth father, who was noticeably poor, had not been able to pay the *helin* for his wife. In the company of strangers, Rosa was shy and would nervously serve tea or coffee to guests when required to do so, but when no strangers were around, she was very talkative and engaging. When I asked her why she did not live with her birth parents, she explained that Tina, the woman with whom she now lived, loved (*adomi*) her so much. Rosa said that Tina had specifically asked to raise her; Tina had felt lonely, not having many children herself. Nonetheless, I noticed that Tina's birth children completed their schooling while Rosa stayed home to help Tina with housework. Rosa said that she did not do very well at school, because she missed (*anoin*) Tina so much when she was there. Missing Tina badly, Rosa would run away from school in Laclubar Town to go home to Funar, a two-hour walk. It was apparently for this reason that she never finished school.

Rosa explained that, as a young child, she was very naughty and cried all the time. According to her, her (birth) parents fought because they were so tired from her constant crying. It was therefore her fault, she maintained, that her father would frequently beat her mother. When she first moved to live with Tina, she continued, she was very unhappy, cried frequently, and did not want to eat; and her new siblings beat her. Later, Rosa said, she learned how to help out around the house. Her siblings laughed at her because she was so nervous when serving food that her hands shook, but they also looked after her. Rosa said that she did not know whether she belonged to Tina's origin house or to that of her birth parents, but she wanted to be part of Tina's. Nonetheless, her birth parents often called on her to help during the harvest or to cook at ritual occasions, and at these times she worked as part of her birth father's origin house.

The director of the secondary school in Laclubar Town told me that many of her pupils complained about the amount of household work they had to do, which was one of the reasons they gave for quitting school early. She maintained that children who lived with their maternal relatives (i.e., the wife-givers) were required to do more work than did the other children of these households, even though, of course, all children (especially girls) had to do some work at home. Birth parents often lived far away, to be near their fields, so many children did not have parental support.

In these interactions, however, not all children were passive. A young boy, about nine years old, was sent to live with the wife-givers (who were *liurai*). There, he had to fetch water in the morning for a family of ten while the other children were still asleep. In tears, he eventually told his new mother that he would no longer live with her since his (birth) mother needed him at home. Later, however, the other children in the household told me that he had grown tired of carrying the water by himself and thus renegotiated his situation to some extent. José's little brother, who was initially given to Manehiak, had to return to Ada Soran because he was "too naughty" and didn't do what he was told. It seems that children develop strategies to exert influence on the situations they live in—for example, by avoiding work, being "naughty," or delegating chores to other siblings.

Adults' ill treatment of children is a recurring theme in harvesting songs. During the corn harvest, people sleep in field huts that can be several hours' walk from the center of Funar. These dwellings are built on stilts to prevent rats from stealing the harvest. During the night, everyone who takes part in the harvest huddles together by the fire, binding corn into bundles for storage above the hearth. In order to stay awake and keep the work going, people tell stories, which are interspersed with verses sung by the whole group. In one of these stories, the children are mistreated by a woman who is not their "own mother" (*inan rasik* T.). As a result, they die and turn into birds. In the accompanying verses, the children complain about the lack of food. On one occasion, when I participated in the harvest, these verses caused some of the old women present to cry. They explained that they could not listen to these songs without crying, because the songs made them feel so sorry for the children who missed their own mothers so much. They explained that these verses provided encouragement to work carefully when harvesting corn. If one forgets to pick the small corncobs, the "corn-children," they cry for their "mothers," the big corncobs. At night the souls (*sumanar*) of these child corncobs will come to haunt you, looking for their mothers who were picked and taken to the house.

Parents' worries about being separated from their children were intensified during times of political conflict due to limited communication and transportation options. One day, a female neighbor came to see me in a state of anxiety and distress. Her daughter had accompanied her son to Dili because he was ill and had been taken to the hospital by ambulance from Laclubar Town. This mother was extremely anxious, both because her daughter had never been to Dili before and did not know her way around, and because the security situation there was tense. She asked to use my phone so that she could call relatives in Dili to tell them to look for her daughter and grandchild at the hospital. This incident made me aware of the distance—both geographical and emotional—between Funar and the capital city, which was heightened by the fact that no telecommunication services were available, and people who could not afford transport had to walk for several days to get there.[49]

---

[49] When I visited Funar in 2012, many villagers had mobile phones, and some people could get an internet connection through a memory stick. When I first arrived in the Laclubar sub-district in 2005, I seemed to be the only one with a mobile phone (see the epilogue).

More serious instances of separation took place in 1999. Several women recounted how their families were separated during the chaos of the post-referendum violence, and many mentioned that at some point they thought that their children, who had remained elsewhere, were dead. This loss of contact occurred when, for example, villagers were transported to West Timor in large trucks as the Indonesian military tried to move people across the border. It took many people weeks (and sometimes even months) to find out who was alive and where they were. The same happened during the conflict in 2006, when people were separated from their loved ones who were working in Dili, and were unable to find out whether they were safe. During the 2006 *krise* the public transport system had broken down and there was no way of making contact with anyone living far away. Several women from Funar told me that during that time they worried their children living in Dili might be dead.

Separation was an important preoccupation for many of the inhabitants of Funar. During the first year of my fieldwork, villagers never stopped commenting on the fact that I had come to Timor-Leste by myself. Older women, especially, would tell me that they could not understand why I would leave my family behind to live in a faraway country by myself. Whenever I passed through the village, the women would exclaim, somewhat dramatically, "Ayeeee! Menina is so young, only just born and now so far away from home." Others said to me, "When I see Menina, I have to cry and worry. Menina's mother must be crying every day and worrying. Ayeeeh, Menina!" These remarks about my "pitiable situation," which were expressed with a monotonous regularity for several months at the beginning of my stay, seemed to point to a more general preoccupation with the separation of parents from children and to worries about loved ones who were far away.

The combination of limited economic resources and the lack of transportation, information, and communication facilities (telephone and radio), combined with high infant mortality and episodic violent political conflict, may have made people feel particularly vulnerable and exposed to the constant threat of loss and separation. Voluntary separation from close kin is something that is hard to comprehend for people who, during wartime, were forced to go for weeks or months without any news from their children, siblings, or parents. Even though there is a clear difference between losing someone through marriage/exchange and losing someone through war, it seemed to me that "worrying/thinking" and "crying" about lost (and potentially lost) ones was a persistent preoccupation in Funar.[50]

GIVING AND TAKING: SEPARATION AND INEQUALITY

Losing a member of one's origin house is always a painful experience, since—as I have argued—the dead and the living members of an origin house are thought to be directly connected to one another. This resonates with Carsten and Hugh-Jones' suggestion that the house is itself "an extension of the person."[51] These authors maintain not only that self and social organization are projected onto the house, but also that the house and the bodies of its members are intricately linked. In Funar, house members are perceived to have an organic unity, as they are linked by virtue

[50] Compare with Sakti, "'Thinking Too Much.'"

[51] Carsten and Hugh-Jones, *About the House: Lévi-Strauss and Beyond*, 2.

of a common trunk. It was this close connection between house members that made José's separation especially painful.

José's case also illustrates the tense relationship between wife-givers and wife-takers. A major source of conflict is the problem of coming up with the *helin*, which is aggravated by the poverty and loss of livestock that many experienced during past conflicts and the concomitant dislocation. One way of dealing with the inability to raise a *helin* is to "give oneself"—that is, to live with one's wife-givers (which resembles *abani* practices in bordering regions, but is rarely recognized as such in Funar). An alternative is to give a child "back" to the wife-giving house, a practice that is common when wife-givers are *liurai* and wife-takers are of lower standing. Differences in status affect the bargaining position of exchanging groups, so that when the wife-givers are *liurai*, they are better placed to demand children from the wife-takers (although these demands were not always successful).

There is a remarkable parallel between the contemporary practice of transferring children between origin houses and earlier practices. In the recent past, children were transferred between houses during marriage between *liurai* houses or when members of low-status houses were not able to pay their taxes. It is possible that current exchanges invoke the experiences of past generations, when those unable to pay the head tax had to hand over their children to work for the *liurai*. In Funar, as elsewhere in Portuguese Timor, alliances with the colonial administration enabled some *liurai* to strengthen and consolidate their positions. This exempted them from reciprocal obligations, as they were able to collect taxes or demand children (or buffalo) when those taxes could not be paid.

The problem that Funar's villagers face today, especially those from poor or low-status origin houses, is that they frequently do not have the means necessary to raise a *helin* and thus to assert the status of their house group. Nevertheless, there is an enduring preference for managing marriage by giving a *helin*, and thus incorporating women and their descendants into the wife-taking house group. The way in which separation is experienced and expressed is related to material and status inequalities as well as to historical experiences.

Current exchanges between origin houses present continuities with past practices and these exchanges have undergone some historical transformation. Most notably, people say that, in the past, they used to "follow their female ancestors," whereas today, "it goes back and forth." Exchanges between origin houses in the present day may be motivated by past experiences of poverty, loss, and separation. It is for that reason that these exchanges can bring existing tensions and disputes to the surface. These conflicts are directly related to questions of relative status and rank between origin houses, even though they are frequently couched in the language of kinship.

Whereas at the beginning of my fieldwork many of the women in Funar were preoccupied by the fact that I was so far away from home, toward the end these same people started to comment on our impending separation. On the day of my departure, an elderly widow with whom I had harvested corn swayed sadly as she told everyone how she had hugged me at night while we were sleeping in her field hut. "When Menina is gone," she said, "I will hug my blanket thinking of and crying for Menina." During the weeks before my departure, many of the women whom I knew well commented on the loss that my "Timorese mother" would feel when I had gone. "She will think of you, miss you, and cry for you every day when you are gone," they said. Everyone has experienced a form of separation at some point, yet it seemed to me that these women were particularly preoccupied with this topic. I believe that this must be understood not only in the context of the separation that takes place during marriage exchange, but also in a more general historical context and in relation to people's own personal experiences. A further experience that involves separation is death, a topic that I explore in the next chapter.

CHAPTER FIVE

KEEPING THE DEAD AWAY

The body of the *liurai* arrived in Funar two days after he had passed away at his home in Dili. His sudden death, in April 2012, shocked everyone. Unspecified events in the past were being mooted as the cause, and many of his relatives were scared that they themselves would soon follow suit. A further cause for concern was the fact that the *liurai*'s wife initially refused to release his body to be buried in Funar. When she finally agreed to part with her husband, his relatives in Funar gathered to receive the *liurai*'s body at Manekaoli's "scepter house," in front of which a large marquee had been erected. People came from all over the Laclubar subdistrict to show their respect. They gathered under the tent and waited patiently, while the deceased's close relatives huddled together inside the house. Meanwhile, hectic phone calls were made to trace the whereabouts of the body: had it arrived in Laclubar Town yet? Were the relatives from Dili on their way to Funar?

When the first car's headlights illuminated the dark village, a low wail rippled through the waiting crowd. Starting from the front entrance of the tent, the crying spread backward into the depths of the house. In the pitch-black night, one could not make out any of the buildings, and the only sounds to be heard were the cries echoing through the crisp April sky. A growing number of cars arrived, stopped, and deposited their passengers. As those new arrivals approached the tent, the waiting crowd parted to allow them to pass through. In front of the scepter house, a group of men and women from the *liurai*'s house had gathered to receive their brother's dead body and the incoming guests.

The first person to make her way through the crowd was a young child with a backpack, city clothes, and tightly curled hair. She succeeded in suppressing her tears until the crowd embraced her. Other family members followed and were gently enveloped by the mass of bodies, with almost everyone crying. The sounds of mourning intensified with every new entrant. When the large wooden coffin was carried in, the sobbing reached a nearly unbearable intensity. Some flung their hands behind their heads in pain, bent double by grief.

As the coffin was carried into the house, the people in the crowd started to throw themselves at it, swarming around the heavy casket and desperately trying to grasp it. The coffin was placed on a table that had been lovingly covered with a black cloth and a woven *tais*. Flowers and candles had been placed carefully around the table, and another piece of black cloth hung over the coffin from the ceiling. In the left corner stood a small table featuring a framed photo of the *liurai*, taken at the inauguration of the scepter house. It portrayed him full of life: dancing in traditional clothes, a metal plate around his neck, and enthusiastically waving a sword. The table in the corner was also covered with flowers, candles, and an attractively tacky white tablecloth. To the left of the photo someone had placed a large wooden mirror, and to the right a gigantic wooden rosary hung from the wall. As visitors crowded into the room, they were received with open embraces by those inside. There was a tender urgency to the way that people hugged one another, placing their heads gently onto the other's shoulders without the surface of their bodies touching. Sometimes a third or fourth person joined a crying couple. Like onion skins, mourning bodies were layered one on top of another to contain the pain.

The mourning went on for longer than what I had observed at other mortuary ceremonies. It was as if people could not let go—could not bring themselves to line up beside the coffin to say their prayers. Close relatives had gathered around the *liurai*'s body, but rather than standing in silence, they hugged the coffin in the same way that they had been hugged by the other mourners. The *liurai*'s younger sister affectionately stroked the casket that held her brother's corpse. Bending over it, she cried, "My older brother, my older brother! [*u bouk, u bouk!*]" before falling into a loud lament with no decipherable words.

As the crying abated and people started to line up respectfully beside the coffin to offer their prayers, something happened that I had never seen before. A small, elderly man in traditional dress—a *tais* around his hips and a colorful cloth wrapped around his head—pushed through the crowd, carrying a large sword with goat hair attached at the handle. He stopped at the end of the coffin next to the dead man's feet and waited in patient silence. Then he suddenly raised the sword high above his head and swung the blade down toward the coffin. Just before it hit the wood, he stopped.

• • •

Only two days into my first period of fieldwork, I was invited to attend the mortuary ceremony of an elderly female resident. Such ceremonies were a regular occurrence right up until the end of my research in Funar, with mortuary rituals being the ceremony I attended most frequently.[1] (I participated in several dozen mortuary ceremonies during my fieldwork.) When a person from Funar dies, the other residents are expected to come and pay their respects to the deceased and the deceased's kin. Members of the deceased's origin house are always expected to attend, even if they live far away. Although I participated in many mortuary ceremonies, I witnessed only a few ritually elaborate marriage negotiations.

I was told that, in the past, when members of *liurai* houses married and the *helin* was made in one single transaction, important ceremonies would be held to negotiate the *helin* and to celebrate the bride's arrival at her husband's house. In one such case, it was said, torches had been lit all the way from Funar to the *suco* of Manelima, with members of the bride's origin house accompanying her all the way to the groom's residence. During my fieldwork, however, I observed no such elaborate wedding ceremonies.

To say that there were few elaborate marriage rituals during my fieldwork does not mean, of course, that men and women did not get together and have children. As I discussed in Chapter 4, having children was vitally important to many villagers. However, the deficit of marriage rituals is particularly striking when one considers the emphasis on marriage exchange in the anthropological literature about the region.[2] In the course of my fieldwork, I witnessed just one marriage negotiation. When I asked why marriage rituals were so rare, I was told that, nowadays, villagers did not have the resources to buy buffalo for the marriage payments. Others said that

---

[1] David Hicks, too, observes that death rituals among the Tetum are especially inclusive and well-attended ceremonies; see Hicks, *Tetum Ghosts and Kin*, 113.

[2] See, for example: Fox, *The Flow of Life*; and van Wouden, *Types of Social Structure in Eastern Indonesia*.

the Catholic Church did not support animal sacrifice, and hence couples no longer held these ceremonies. Despite these explanations, however, people were evidently capable of providing buffalo for death rituals, as the creatures were slaughtered in large numbers for that purpose.

Why, then, was there such a focus on death rituals and so little regard for marriage ceremonies? What is the significance of death and ceremonies related to the dead in this region? And how is the sudden death of a person related to unresolved issues from the past? I will address these questions by examining what is involved in the ceremonies known as "black rituals/words."

Whereas exchanges during life between territorially rooted house groups unlock the possibility of human detachment from the ancestral land, death rituals are a way of reunifying the dead with the earth, from which humans are thought to originate. The marked proliferation and elaboration of death rituals since independence thus resonate with the reunification of the ancestral land through the villagers' return migration. At the same time, people are confronted with the possibility that funerary rituals may fail and that the dead or unresolved conflicts from the past may haunt the living. By critically evaluating anthropological ideas about the ways in which exchange is thought to create relations among groups, this chapter illustrates how death rituals sever such relations by addressing past conflicts, settling debts and obligations, and reintegrating humans into distinct plots of ancestral land.

BLACK RITUALS, BLACK WORDS

Mortuary ceremonies are called "black rituals" or "black words" (*haha metan*). Throughout the mourning period, a small piece of black cloth is attached to a stick outside the house of the deceased so that passersby will know that a person has died there. When a child or an unmarried person dies, a white piece of cloth is used instead.

When people die, others immediately begin to refer to them as *mainheri* or *matebian* (T.), which may be translated as "recently deceased ancestor" or "ancestral spirit."[3] The body of the deceased (*jisin lolon*) is taken to the cemetery, but the *matebian* can still return to the village. During black rituals, a large number of buffalo and pigs are slaughtered, and people say that death rituals are so elaborate because relatives want to demonstrate that they loved (*adomi*) and thought about (*anoin*) the deceased.[4] Moreover, the deceased have to be properly commemorated. This is done in several phases (see summary on the next page), and there is a constant risk that if it is not done properly, the dead will return to disturb the living.

When the *liurai* of Funar died in 2012, people traveled from far and wide to attend his funeral. Some relatives even crossed the international border from West Timor to participate in the ceremony. The *liurai* had died suddenly, of a heart condition, while only in his fifties. His death sent shockwaves through the village, because he was the latest among a number of members of his origin house (Manekaoli) to die in recent years. People wondered what could be "wrong inside the house" to cause the rapid death of its members. When the news of the *liurai*'s

---

[3] People frequently used the Tetum term *matebian*, which is why I have used it in this chapter.

[4] Elizabeth Traube observes that Mambai say they "feel for" the spirits of the dead; see Traube, *Cosmology and Social Life*, 202.

Generic overview of the different phases of mortuary ceremonies

Crying for the dead *Sero mate*	In the days after a person dies, groups of people belonging to other origin houses visit the relatives of the deceased to cry and pray together; they bring gifts of candles and money.
Burial *A'oe mate*	Immediately after a death, close relatives bring clothes and woven cloth, which are put inside the coffin to prevent the dead person from coming back to ask for them later. Burial of the deceased is accompanied by prayers and ritual speech. A large number of people usually accompanies the coffin to the cemetery, saying prayers as they walk. These are interwoven with hymns and recitations of the names of Catholic saints. After the coffin is buried and covered with earth, flowers and candles are placed on the grave. Everyone leaves the cemetery as fast as they can, often running back to the village, and then reassemble at the house of the deceased.
Eating with the dead *A nora mate*	After every burial, a meal of boiled meat and rice is prepared and then eaten together by those who attend the ceremony. The *lulik* parts of the slaughtered animal (such as the tongue and the heart) are reserved for the guardian of the *lulik* house.
Guarding the dead *Adeer mate*	Every night for a fortnight after a person dies, people sit together in the house of the deceased to remember him or her. During the first week, this vigil is called "guarding the bitter flowers" (*adeer ai-hunan meluk*). In the second week, it is called "guarding the sweet flowers" (*adeer ai-hunan bear*).
Paying for the dead *Selu mate*	In the weeks after a death, the wife-takers meet the wife-givers and negotiate payments and gifts that need to be exchanged. Once the wife-takers have managed to raise the necessary resources, they have to make a payment of buffalo, money, and horses to the wife-givers. The wife-givers, the "owners of the dead" (*mate nain*), then reciprocate with pigs, rice, and woven cloth. The wife-givers then have to give "one" (i.e., one animal) to their wife-givers so that "the fire does not burn the eyes" (*wai na'luhi mata*)—that is, to maintain good relations with their own wife-givers. The children of the deceased also bring animals: one to pay for the dead, and one to slaughter (*selu jisa, taa jisa*).
Taking off the black *Kore metan*	After a death, close relatives are not allowed to bathe and must wear black clothes or a piece of black cloth. Distant relatives can "take off the black" after three months, but the deceased's children must continue to show their respect for six months. After twelve months, the deceased's spouse can take off the black, and a large celebration is held to commemorate this occasion (*kore metan*).

death arrived in Funar, people tried to make sense of what was happening. In the past, someone must have made a "mistake" that caused members of the *liurai's* house to die within a relatively short time of each other. There were also suspicions that he may have been killed by witchcraft or "traditional medicine" that an envious person from his house administrated. A woman from Ada Soran told me that her house would no longer "give" women in marriage to the *liurai's* house, because they were scared that the bride would die. A girl told me that, on the evening of the *liurai's* death, she had seen a very large black bird ("the size of a car") flying over the village. All this was interpreted as a grave omen—the fear of death was on people's minds.

The days following the news of the *liurai's* death were filled with hushed, fretful exchanges, and there were more heated discussions. First, people had to deal with the news that the *liurai's* wife wanted her husband to be buried in Dili so that he would be close to her. This caused outrage among some of the villagers, while others insisted that the *liurai's* wife had to be persuaded gently and could not be forced to release the body. Once she had agreed to her husband's burial in Funar, the next hurdle was dealing with the *liurai's* wife-givers (i.e., the *liurai's* mother's kin), who had erected a tent in Laclubar Town, where they lived, to receive the dead body there. The members of the *liurai's* mother's origin house, who were considered to be the *mate nain* (the owners of the dead), maintained that, because of the sudden death, it was clear that something was wrong inside his origin house and they would not allow the *liurai* to be buried in Funar—they would not "give" his body to Manekaoli. Again, gentle persuasion and numerous negotiations had to take place before any agreement could be reached.

Selu mate (paying for the dead) permanently resolves house membership, as it is the last in a series of exchanges that integrate a person into an origin house. It is literally a payment for the deceased person to enter the receiving house.[5] The mortuary ceremony cannot be completed until all open debts are settled and all problems or disagreements are resolved. The example of the *liurai* shows how indeterminate house membership can be during one's lifetime and even, to an extent, after one's death, when the wife-giver still has the right to make claims to the body. The wife-givers also made claims when the time came to appoint the new *liurai*. The *liurai's* son was supposed to take on the role, but the wife-givers were initially reluctant to "give" the son, worried that he would also die.

During death rituals, origin house membership becomes much more visible than it is in everyday life. This is not only because the deceased is buried in a specific place alongside other members of the same origin house, but also because people make their visits to the house of the deceased together with others in their house group. There is an emphasis on equality during death rituals: attendees eat together and, when crying for the dead, comfort each other irrespective of their gender or status. In this sense, mortuary ceremonies were among the most inclusive rituals that I witnessed.

When the *liurai* died, a number of people explained to me that *liurai* are buried just the same as everyone else. My own observations, however, were at odds with this assertion. When the man dressed in ritual clothing entered the room and swung his sword at the coffin, this was an exceptional gesture of protection. The man was

---

[5] Compare with Forth, who discusses Nage and Keo mortuary payments as compensation to the wife–givers for the corpse; see Forth, "Separating the Dead," 561–63.

part of the *liurai's formatura,* a military force that was summoned to protect the *liurai.* While "guarding the bitter flower," there was always at least one man armed with a sword guarding the coffin. When the body was brought to the cemetery, it was accompanied by an entire parade of soldiers (*moradores*[6]), who marched up and down the tent and made military gestures while the body was being prepared. Evidently, this was not just a regular person who was being buried—the *liurai's* special status was stressed throughout the mortuary ceremony. It seemed to me that the *formatura's* role was more symbolic than for actual protection, underlining the *liurai's* high status.

CEMENTING DIFFERENCE

In Chapter 3, I mentioned the sudden passing of Marco, the well-respected ritual speaker of Ada Lulin, who died in his field hut after two days of severe fever. When the news of Marco's death reached Funar, everyone fell into a state of shock. Walking to the house of the deceased, Marco's sister cried loudly, "My older brother, my older brother, I am so alone now!" Stiff with grief, her daughter exclaimed again and again, "Where did you go? Where did you go? I am thinking of you so much!" At Marco's house, his (classificatory) son bent over the dead body in pain, crying, "My father, my father! Give me just one more word!" (*U amak, u amak! Tatoli haha huan jisa!*)

In the evening, I went with members of Manehiak to the wake ("guarding the bitter flowers") to keep Marco's relatives company and show affection and respect for the deceased. The multi-room house where the ceremony took place was spacious, and at least thirty-five people were in attendance. The atmosphere was solemn; many of those present appeared confused and even scared. People sat close together, whispering quietly, while Marco's wife crouched in the corner looking tired and dazed. The main participants stayed awake all night praying, talking, and crying, and some of the men passed their time gambling, drinking, and playing cards. At some point, I fell asleep on a bamboo bed, and in the early morning I was taken into a separate room along with some children. The Lord's Prayer was recited in Tetum throughout the night.

Marco's "guarding the bitter flowers" ceremony was quite different from that of Benedita, a member of a low-status side-house of Bamatak. Like Marco, Benedita was in her mid- to late-forties when she died quite suddenly. Unlike Marco, however, she was a relatively poor member of a low-status house. When she died, her body remained in the stilted house where she had lived (the "house of the dead," *mate adan*), which was a single room with a hearth. To guard the dead, about fifteen people climbed up the narrow ladder to her house and squeezed into the room. Throughout the night they sang beautiful, melodic chants called *loli* or *sidoo,* which were explained to me as a form of "singing for the dead" (*kanta ba mate*; T.). These chants were largely wordless, containing only small phrases. One person would sing a short phrase and everyone else would join in, humming or repeating the phrase.

---

[6] The term *moradores* comes from the Portuguese colonial period and refers to "special companies of indigenous irregulars established by the Portuguese in the eighteenth century"; see Ricardo Roque, *Headhunting and Colonialism: Anthropology and the Circulation of Human Skulls in the Portuguese Empire, 1870–1930* (New York: Palgrave Macmillan, 2010), xiii. Today, few people in Funar acknowledged this connection to the Portuguese, using the term *moradores* instead to refer to the warriors of the *liurai.*

Proud of the fact that I had attended this gathering, one of the elder women made up a *loli* for me: *malae butin hori namo arook rama malae metan timor* ("a white foreigner from a faraway land has come to meet the black Timorese foreigner"). I think that the "black foreigner" in question refers to the deceased, who has also traveled to a different land — the land of the dead — and is thus also in a sense a foreigner.

When Marco died, the priest from Laclubar Town came to Funar to hold a small Mass in honor of Marco, whom he liked and had invited on several occasions to give ritual speeches at important events, such as the inauguration of Laclubar Town's hospital. Some of Marco's relatives came from Dili by car and brought a coffin with them, and it was they who pushed to give Marco a Catholic burial. During the priest's moving speech, Marco's relatives cried in a restrained way, quite unlike the loud mourning that I had observed during Benedita's funeral.

After the Mass, the male members of Ada Lulin carried the coffin out of the house, and all those gathered started to cry loudly. They tried to hold onto the coffin, clutching at it and softly touching the table on which the coffin had rested.[7] Those attempting to impede the departure of the coffin were quickly reprimanded by a female relative, who told them that they should restrain themselves because they looked stupid/uneducated (*beik*). After the burial, people ran back to the village through the red mud, some discarding their flip-flops to go faster. In this respect, the burial ended like most others, with an urgent and hasty departure from the cemetery.[8]

Benedita's burial was more dramatic than Marco's because her daughter refused to leave the cemetery after the speeches and prayers were completed. As all the others started to make their way home, she clung to the cross that marked Benedita's grave, crying bitterly. Upon seeing Benedita's daughter's reaction, her (classificatory) siblings went over and admonished her for this behavior.[9] Yet she stubbornly persisted until her relatives, by now beside themselves, forcibly dragged her away by her arms. The cemetery, they explained, was a dangerous place, and one could not simply stay there, especially just after a person had been buried.

The main difference between Marco's and Benedita's burial ceremonies was the inclusion (or not) of various Catholic elements. Emphasizing Catholic elements was a way of being educated (*matenek*) and modern (*modernu*) rather than *beik*. Catholicism in this instance was used to raise the status of Marco's house group and to present its members as being connected with foreign practices, since Catholicism is essentially associated with foreigners.[10] Indeed, there were invariably more Catholic elements in the death rituals of high-status origin houses.

---

[7] Hicks describes how the Tetum would try, ritually, to prevent the departure of the coffin from the hamlet to the cemetery; see Hicks, *Tetum Ghosts and Kin*, 115.

[8] Apart from reburial of those who died away from their ancestral land during the Indonesian occupation, there was no secondary burial in Funar. Given how frequent secondary burial is in the region, this may well be due to the influence of Catholicism.

[9] It is noteworthy that these were Benedita's daughter's *classificatory* siblings, since she had described feeling lonely when her mother died on account of having no brothers and sisters. Similarly, I have noted that Marco's "classificatory" son mourned his death because, as I discuss later in this chapter, Marco complained about not having children, and this would not make sense if I had simply written "his son." Henceforth, I only note the "classificatory" relationship if it is relevant to understanding the specific context.

[10] This association of foreigners with Catholicism sometimes made it hard for me to find out about people's Catholic ideas, because most assumed that I was an expert on these issues.

The graves of *liurai*[11] (All Soul's Day, 2006; author's photo)

The cemetery is another place where an origin house's relative status is apparent. Funar's cemetery is located near the *lulik* mountain of Lawadu, close to where the ancestors of Manehiak and Manekaoli are said to have arrived. Unlike in the past, when the dead were buried in the same grave rolled up in a mat, today the dead are buried in single graves near other members of their origin house, although there is no physical demarcation of the different areas that accommodate different origin houses. At the cemetery the dead could look at you, or so I was told, but you could not see them (something that was also said about spirits). That is why no one was supposed to go to the cemetery alone. Others said there were devils that would peer at you while you were there. [12] All of this might explain the haste with which the deceased is buried and the fact that people approach the cemetery in a tight group, protected by the proximity of others and by the words of prayer that they utter.

Today, all of Funar's house-group members are buried in the same cemetery. This was not the case in the past, I was told, when "heathen cemeteries" (*rate jentio*) were scattered throughout the area. Indeed, it is possible that the concentration of graves in one place has augmented the perception of danger of that particular site, which would also explain why people leave the cemetery in such a hurry. The Catholic practice of assembling the dead in one place may have turned this cemetery into a place of menace, such that it can only be approached in large groups.

---

[11] The two large graves in the background are those of the former *liurai* José do Espirito Santo and Hannibal do Espirito Santo.

[12] Fox similarly explores the opposition between spirits on the inside and wild spirits that are associated with the outside and occasionally conflated with devils or Satan. See James J. Fox, "On Bad Death and the Left Hand: A Study of Rotinese Symbolic Inversions," in *Right and Left: Essays on Dual Symbolic Classification*, ed. Rodney Needham (Chicago: The University of Chicago Press, 1973), 349–40.

The graves in Funar's cemetery are not intentionally oriented with respect to compass directions, but there are clear physical differences between graves for high-status and low-status origin houses. The graves of the *liurai* houses often have a large gravestone next to them, and some are built entirely of stone and tiles (see photos, opposite and below). The majority of *liurai* graves are situated on a small hill and are clearly more elaborate than those of low-status houses. Upon death, then, both house membership and the social status of that house group are cemented and fixed. In this respect, there is a process of deterritorialization, because everyone is now buried at the same cemetery. This does not bring people together in an egalitarian community, however. Instead, it brings the social hierarchy to the fore, since there are clear differences between the monumental graves of the *liurai* and the regular graves of the other house groups.

Funar cemetery (All Soul's Day, 2006; author's photo)

Reflecting on fieldwork carried out in the 1960s, David Hicks notes that Tetum *liurai* funerals were distinctively more elaborate than those of commoners or nobles.[13] Differences in status were expressed in different ways, such as through the use of descriptive terms for the coffins of *liurai,* which were referred to as the "boat of the foreigner" (*ro malae;* T.). Speaking more generally, Maurice Bloch and Jonathan Parry have argued that, at the time of death, the social order is reasserted and reproduced.[14] The tombs of the Merina in Madagascar, for example, are "an idealized map of the social order."[15] During death rituals, Bloch and Parry argue, the dead are transformed into an otherworldly and eternal force that comes to represent a transcendental authority that legitimizes the social hierarchy.

---

[13] Hicks, *Tetum Ghosts and Kin*, 114.

[14] Maurice Bloch and Jonathan Parry, introduction, in *Death & the Regeneration of Life*, ed. Maurice Bloch and Jonathan Parry (Cambridge: Cambridge University Press, 1982), 6.

[15] Ibid., 38.

As can be seen from the cemetery photos taken in Funar in 2006 (see previous pages), the differences among origin houses were clearly visible. In that sense, the cemetery may be viewed as an "idealized map" of the social hierarchy. Cemeteries are key sites for the articulation and reification of status, and it is at the cemetery that the socioeconomic differences between house groups are most visible.

As Katherine Verdery notes, dead bodies can be political symbols. They are sites of struggle over meaning and political influence.[16] This was made clear to me when Marco's relatives told me that they would buy tiles for his grave once they had managed to acquire the appropriate resources. I was also told that, in the past, only the *liurai* were permitted to have stone graves. Now everyone is granted this privilege, though not many can afford it. Today, *liurai* have less power than they are said to have had at some point during the Portuguese colonial period, but they have nonetheless managed to secure a number of economic privileges that shore up their status.

In 2010, I returned to Funar after a two-and-a-half-year absence. As I mentioned in Chapter 4, I was surprised to discover that a member of an autochthonous house had become village chief. This change in the local hierarchy was also reflected at the cemetery. The first thing I noticed when I went to the graveyard was that a significant number of "people of the land" had now built stone graves for their dead. When I asked villagers where the money for this had come from, I was told that the people of the land used the "pensions" that the Timorese government now provided to citizens over the age of sixty. Upon receiving this money, the first thing that members of autochthonous houses did was to build stone graves. Before building themselves better houses, they built themselves better graves. A friend of mine told me that if they did not do this, they would risk sudden death. An acquaintance, he argued, had bought himself a motorbike from his pension money before spending it on improving his ancestors' grave—the next day he died in a traffic accident.

In 2015, when I visited Funar again, another transformation had taken place at the cemetery: the graves for *liurai* members—including the *liurai* who died in 2012—had been built to be even more elaborate than the recently built non-*liurai* stone graves. When non-*liurai* started improving the graves of their ancestors, *liurai* needed to distinguish themselves by building even more elaborate and expensive graves. Status competition was most visible at the cemetery, with Funar villagers racing to build ever more ostentatious graves for the dead once they had the funds available.

PAYING FOR THE DEAD

One day, when my hosts, Maria and Adérito, were in Laclubar Town, a neighbor visited me and told me cheerfully, "Today they are paying us" (*sira selu ami,* T.). She was referring to the recent death of a villager and the fact that the wife-takers were going to be making death payments to her origin house, the wife-givers.

House groups are in a permanent state of indebtedness to origin houses from which they receive women, and these debts need to be settled upon death. Despite the fact that descent is reckoned through the male line (i.e., children become part of the father's origin house if the payment of the *helin* is completed), the mother's origin house is recognized, respected, and repaid for the loss it has incurred. If an

---

[16] Katherine Verdery, *The Political Lives of Dead Bodies: Reburial and Postsocialist Change* (New York: Columbia University Press, 1999), 33.

unmarried person dies, the death payments will be smaller, since this person will not have had any children. Thus, marriage creates debts between origin houses, while *selu mate* resolves them.[17]

Death and marriage payments are part of the same process through which people are separated from one origin house and are integrated into another one, becoming a permanent part of their origin house upon death. This produces relations of dependency and obligation between houses. As described by Gregory Forth for the Nage and Keo, mortuary payments may be seen as the "final installment" of the marriage payments, since they confirm the incorporation of the deceased (and their children) into the wife-taking houses.[18] In Funar, the emphasis on death rituals seems to indicate that severing connections (by resolving house membership) was more important at this particular historical moment than entering into new alliances. If relations of exchange are not maintained with the same house group in the same direction over generations, the connections between origin houses may, indeed, be severed once death payments are completed. Because people today are not particularly invested in maintaining the direction of exchange (see Chapter 4), alliances between house groups are less permanent than before. This tallies with my general observation that Funar's origin houses' hierarchical relations were particularly contested in the period immediately after independence.

The ambiguity of house membership during a person's lifetime stands in stark contrast to the fixity of house membership created upon death. The exchanges between wife-givers and wife-takers that take place after death are believed to be an important part of ensuring the continuity of life. If wife-givers are not paid and respected, infertility and poor health are said to befall the wife-takers.[19]

Other instances when the loss of a person demands compensation include accidents or when a person is killed or dies due to the actions or negligence of others. For example, if a person dies by falling out of a tree while harvesting honey, the owner of the honey tree has to offer compensation, either in the form of another person or a plot of land (in such cases land and people are thought to be equally adequate for the purposes of redress, either being acceptable as reimbursement). Such restitution is a form of conflict resolution.

When I visited the *suco* of Manelima, I was told by one man that the villagers had been unimpressed by the meetings organized by the Commission for Reception, Truth and Reconciliation (Comissão de Acolhimento, Verdade e Reconciliação de Timor Leste, CAVR) about the crimes committed during the Indonesian occupation, since they had been based on "foreign" notions of justice. Local residents decided to arrange their own meeting to "cut justice" (*tesi justisa*) instead. It was decided that a former member of the pro-Indonesian militia should give his son to the origin house of the man whom he had killed. Consequently, the son, by now a grown man, was living in the victim's origin house when I carried out my research. This illustrates how the loss of a person can be reimbursed through the gift of another. In both Funar and the Laclubar subdistrict more generally, there were many stories of children being given to compensate for a person who had been killed. Sometimes the child

---

[17] Compare with Traube, *Cosmology and Social Life*, 201.

[18] Forth, "Separating the Dead," 568.

[19] Compare with: Bloch and Parry, *Death and the Regeneration of Life*, 7; Hicks, *Tetum Ghosts and Kin*, 113, 132; and Traube, *Cosmology and Social Life*, 88, 230.

was given generations later—long after the culprit had died—if, for example, the latter's descendants found themselves suffering poor health.

This form of justice seems to be an alternative to the more confessional models of "truth and reconciliation" instigated by the CAVR. The strategy of compensation instead of confession tallies with people's reluctance to discuss the events of the recent past in any detail, since this would bring past conflicts to the fore. By compensating those who have lost someone, people are able to re-establish a balance in the victim's origin house while remaining silent about the details of the betrayal and pain involved.

The loss of a person is not inevitably recompensed with another individual, however. In Funar, for example, members of Bubai were exonerated for killing members of Berlibu when they gave horses, buffalo, and "black" (fertile) land to Berlibu. The reason the Bubai decided to make these gifts was that many of them had fallen ill and some were dying early deaths. They hoped that by paying for the deaths caused by their ancestors their own lives would be spared.[20]

For the Mambai, Traube notes, "black rituals" are occasions when people argue about the number of animals to be exchanged. She states that conflicts over "goats and pigs" only represent the "tip," whereas she is more interested in the "trunk meanings"—that is, the cosmological significance of the rituals themselves.[21] In both Funar and Laclubar, mortuary rituals were occasions when conflicts surfaced, especially if a previous violent death had yet to be resolved or compensated. In such case, mortuary ceremonies usually could not be completed before the conflicts were resolved. When I first went to Laclubar Town, for example, one of the young women who once lived in the same house I stayed in died unexpectedly. I was told that I would not be able to stay there, as for several weeks members of her origin house would be visiting with the aim of resolving past issues that might have caused her death.

Similarly, when Marco died, some of his Dili relatives spent several months in Funar to resolve conflicts within their origin house. People were suspicious about his sudden death. One of the male participants commented that the *lulik* had imprisoned (*kastigu*) Marco because he had tried to "steal the scepter" (*nauk ua*) and concluded that this was the real reason he had died. There were also accusations of witchcraft leveled against some of the members of his origin house. While trying to resolve these issues, Marco's closest relatives did not leave his house for several weeks. They also went without washing and did not carry out the ritual of the "sweet flowers" until some of the disagreements were settled.

Death, then, may provide an opportunity to reassert status differences, but it also represents the ideal time to modify them slightly. Completing the cycles of exchange provides a means for recalculating and recalibrating certain relationships. Although mortuary rituals can be seen to cement differences between origin houses, they also serve to resolve tensions within and between groups. Debts are paid during the exchanges between wife-givers and wife-takers that take place when a person dies. If

---

[20] Compare with McWilliam, "Fataluku Healing and Cultural Resilience in East Timor," 226–27, where he discusses sacrifices and gifts offered by former Fataluku resistance fighters to their ancestors as thanks for providing their blessing during the Indonesian occupation. The ritual carried out to reciprocate the ancestors resolved neglected obligations and involved renewing the blessing already received.

[21] Traube, *Cosmology and Social Life*, 229.

those debts are not resolved, it is believed that the ancestors may disturb the living through illness, misfortune, and infertility.

KEEPING THE DEAD AWAY

It is crucial to remember the dead and keep them satisfied so that they do not interfere with the living. While "guarding the bitter flowers" of Marco, we repeatedly heard loud banging noises coming from nearby. Some women whispered that it was Marco (the *matebian*), annoyed that his wife had started to doze off and making this commotion to wake her up. It was my impression that Marco and his wife did not have a very good relationship, since he had frequently announced in public that he would like to take another wife (his current one had not borne him any children), but could not do so because he had converted to Catholicism. The estrangement of Marco and his wife was common knowledge and thus was the likely basis of the speculation surrounding the source of the banging.

When we were all sitting together, Maria told the other women that Marco's soul (*sumanar*) had been visiting her house even before he died, playing tricks on everyone and frightening them. She recounted how the day before he died she heard groaning noises emanating from my room. Since I had gone to Laclubar Town, at first she thought that I must have fallen ill there and it was my *sumanar* that had come to the house, moaning and groaning. Maria sat down to cry, because she was worried about me, when all of a sudden Marco's *sumanar* appeared, told the children in the house that he was feeling terribly sick and feverish, and asked them to massage his limbs. While we were "guarding the bitter flowers," people joked that Marco had liked me so much that, during his illness, his soul had gone to the house to look for me. After his death, Marco still had agency. I was asked to take a photo of his body, but at that precise moment my camera's battery ran out of charge. Marco's brother said that was a sign (*signal*) from Marco, that he disabled my camera because his face had already become swollen and he was ashamed to be photographed in that state.

I heard of a number of other cases of the dead interfering in the lives of their loved ones. Around Christmas 2007, the tragic news arrived in Funar that Tanha, a teenage girl who had previously lived with my host family, had died suddenly in Dili. Tanha was staying with relatives there to attend secondary school. At first the cause of her death was not clear. Had she died in the conflict that was still going on in Dili? Was she killed by one of the ritual or martial arts gangs? Finally, it emerged that she drowned in the sea, her body having been found by a rescue boat following an extensive search. Everyone in Funar suspected that there was something suspicious about her death. Why would she bathe in the sea when she was unable to swim? There were rumors that a jealous boyfriend lured her into the sea, or that she may have been killed by witchcraft. Some villagers suggested that she died prematurely because her father, a ritual speaker of a side-house, tried to represent himself as being "bigger" and more influential than he really was.

In the months after her death, Tanha continued to pay visits to her parents, her friends, and other members of her origin house. Sometimes the visits were intended to ensure that they would not forget her, while at other times she appeared through the medium of spirit possession, "falling" into the bodies of some of her origin house members. Since Helena, with whom I lived, had been one of her best friends, the dead Tanha kept visiting our house. Helena told me that Tanha walked around the house at night, keeping everyone awake with the sound of her flip-flops. She also stole things from the house. Once she took tapes from the tape recorder, thereby warning her friend Helena not to play music, a sign that she had forgotten her dead friend, since those in mourning are not supposed to listen to music.

One night, we heard scratching noises coming from all over the house. I attributed this to rats looking for food, while the others assured me that Tanha was back again. Everyone was exhausted in the morning, not having been able to sleep because of the noise. While talking about Tanha's *matebian*, my neighbor Dilma mentioned that when it is day for the *matebian*, it is night for the living, and vice versa.[22] Dilma's son asked, "So is it night for Tanha now?" but Dilma chose not to answer, brushing him off and telling him not to ask so many questions.

Visits from people who had died almost always occurred at night. Many residents of Funar told me that the dead spoke to relatives or friends in dreams, or that people who had died recently would visit them during the night to ensure that they had not been forgotten. However, if a person had suffered a violent death, such visits would be even more frequent and insistent, since the dead person would be seeking to draw attention to the suspicious circumstances surrounding her or his demise. Such deaths are called "red deaths" (*mate meran*) while those from natural causes are known as "black deaths" (*mate metan*).[23] People said that a red death caused the blood to become dirty, polluting the blood of future generations.

When Tanha's body was brought back to Funar, a special ritual had to be carried out to "separate/expel the red" (*eta meran; haketa mean*, T.). For the purposes of this ceremony, a ritual specialist walked seven times around Tanha's body, uttering words of ritual speech. A dog was also beheaded to keep the dangerous "red" away. By separating out the "red," the "black" was reinstalled (*atama metan*), thus allowing the body to be buried. A similar ritual was required if a local resident killed another person. (In the past, I was told, this included cases of headhunting.)

An elderly villager from the *suco* Batara, who had been part of the FALINTIL guerrilla force, told me that he killed many people during the time of the Indonesian occupation. For this reason, he felt it necessary to rid himself of the "pollution" or "dirt" (*ka'hoer*) caused by his acts. To achieve this end, a black dog and a red chicken (in other cases, a bird or duck) had to be beheaded and the fowl put into a river. In these cases, the river took the bird away while the beheaded dog waited on the bank of the river to stop the red from returning. Failure to "separate the red" would result in infertility and infant mortality.

When the guardian of Manekaoli's *lulik* house fell ill, people blamed this on a murder that took place inside the house before the Indonesian occupation. The guardian's dead husband was said to have killed one of his relatives who was also one of his wife-givers. I was told in great detail how the person's blood had spilled onto the floor and subsequently dribbled down the ladder and onto the ground. Although the *lulik* house was later destroyed and was only rebuilt when people returned to Funar, the "dirty blood" (*ran ka'hoer*) still adhered to the building and the earth, and it was this that caused its guardian to become ill. Catherine Allerton

---

[22] Forth similarly notes that the community of the dead is an "inverted world" among the Nage in Flores; see Forth, *Beneath the Volcano*, 253.

[23] The category of "bad death" is well known in Timor and Indonesia and usually refers to deaths that are sudden, violent, and inauspicious. See, for example: Fox, "On Bad Death and the Left Hand," 351–52; Sakti, "'Thinking Too Much;'" and Hans Joachim Sell, *Der schlimme Tod bei den Völkern Indonesiens* (The Hague: 'S Gravenhage, Mouton & Co, 1955).

makes a comparable argument, showing how polluted blood that Manggarai call "green blood" can be transmitted both through the body and through association with a room, thus affecting future generations.[24] Despite all the efforts made by the living to keep the dead away and separate themselves from the "dirty blood" spilled by their relatives or ancestors, the separation from the red was not always successful. The dangers posed by death increase if a person dies a red death, but even a black death can spell trouble for the living.

During a visit to Timor-Leste in September 2012, a number of Funar's residents took part in the reburial of two men who were killed by FRETILIN during the latter's conflicts with UDT in 1975. (The reburials were symbolic, since no remains were ever actually found.) These two men were relatives of the *liurai*, and it is quite possible that the reburial was a response to the *liurai*'s death earlier that same year, since his house members were trying to get to the bottom of the problems "inside the house" that were causing members of Manekaoli to die. The reburial started with the cleaning of the house in Dili where the men had lived. A key aim was to "separate the red," which involved mixing pig's blood and coconut juice (which are "cold," *lamuruk*) and pouring this onto the stairs at the entrance of the house. The men whose remains were to be reburied had been members of UDT, and the ceremony was attended by several party representatives. There was a feeling among those who gathered that the deaths of these men, who had not been part of the independence movement, had been somewhat forgotten on the national stage. Unlike those who died in the struggle against the Indonesian occupation and were buried at the national "hero cemetery" in Metinaro, these two men had received little attention from national leaders.

Reburials not only sacralize the political order in moments of drastic transformation, they also allow people to revise the past and negotiate moral responsibility.[25] The reburial of the two men killed by FRETILIN led to the reconfiguration of political relations, but, furthermore, this reburial was a symbol of the region's exclusion. Although the reburial was attended by a small number of national leaders from the UDT party, most victims of previous conflicts who did not fit into the clear-cut "hero" category received little attention at the national level. As Verdery has shown, reburials often take place in moments of epochal shifts.[26] Dead bodies are potent symbols for nationalist discourses, and burials instantiate these discourses in specific territories. Although the reburials revealed Funar's *exclusion* from the nationalist imaginaries, the connection between dead-body politics and the soil were nonetheless pertinent. By bringing the (symbolic) remains of these two men back to Funar and burying them in the ancestral land, villagers sought not only to re-inscribe themselves in the nationalist narrative, but also hoped to resolve the problems of illness and death that had been troubling members of the ruling house for years.

---

[24] Catherine L. Allerton, "Landscape, Power and Agency in Eastern Indonesia," in *Southeast Asian Perspectives on Power*, ed. Liana Chua, Joanna Cook, Nicholas Long, and Lee Wilson (London: Routledge, 2012), 74.

[25] Verdery, *The Political Lives of Dead Bodies*, 32, 112.

[26] Ibid., 35.

GOING BACK TO THE LAND

A variety of different opinions about what happens after death exist in Funar and Laclubar. A number of villagers told me that the dead return to the earth; some claimed that they go to the land of the dead, while others said that they go to heaven (*lalehan*). Another common account was that the dead go on a journey, traveling from the mountain known as Matebian, in the east of Timor-Leste, to the mountain of Ramelau, in the west. En route, they stop off at a spring called Wer Lakamlai, located near Funar and Fatumakerek, to bathe and wash. Indeed, several local residents told me that, while at the spring, they have encountered friends or relatives who had recently died.

During mortuary ceremonies, I often took the opportunity to ask people what happens to the dead. A common response was, "We come from the land and we go back to the land" (*Ita ta maa usi larek, ta ahilas ti larek*). The term *larek* can mean both "earth" and "land," and hence there is some similarity here with the conceptions of the afterlife among the Mambai, who, according to Traube, say that the bodies of the dead decay and return to Mother Earth.[27] Considering that Funar's autochthonous house groups say that they were born from the land, the idea of "return" is particularly pertinent. Although I never heard people in Funar speak of the earth as a mother, the fact that the land gave birth to ancestral siblings suggests a comparable relationship as that expressed by the Mambai.

When I first heard the expression "returning to the land," I thought that it was a translation of the biblical phrase "For dust you are and to dust you will return," since I had heard a priest use a Tetum version of this phrase (*Ita mai husi rai ita hakfila ba rai*) during a funeral. When I put this idea to an acquaintance, he corrected me, saying that these were the words of the ancestors themselves. He explained that the Catholic Church had introduced the idea that the dead go to heaven or "back to God,"[28] but that, according to the ancestors, they actually go to the land of the dead, which is a separate "world" (*mundu*) from that of the living. I do not have definite information on this, but it may be that, like the Mambai case described by Traube, Idaté speakers propose that the body returns to the earth while the spirit of the deceased goes to the world of the dead. I was told that, after burial, the body (*jisin lolon*) of the dead remains at the cemetery, whereas the *matebian* or *mainheri* may return to the village, suggesting a distinction was made between the body and spirit of the dead.

On other occasions when I asked people what happens after death, I was told that I should ask the Catholic priest in Laclubar Town, since he would know more about such matters. It is possible that Catholicism has introduced an element of uncertainty to understandings of afterlife, or perhaps people have always had diverse ideas about what happens after death and Catholicism has simply added an additional possibility to a range of existing theories.[29] Although Funar's residents

---

[27] Traube, *Cosmology and Social Life*, 232.

[28] See Forth, "Separating the Dead," 565, for comparative findings from Flores about the idea of a "return" to God after death.

[29] Compare this with Traube's observation that the Mambai were vague about what happens to the spirits of the deceased immediately after death, even though they were quite clear that dead bodies decayed and returned to Mother Earth (Traube, *Cosmology and Social Life*, 202). See also Forth's findings about a variety of places being named as locations of the dead among the Nage, Flores (Forth, *Beneath the Volcano*, 254). For a summary of the debates on people's fragmentary understanding of what happens after death and the tendency of anthropologists

hold a variety of opinions concerning the afterlife, the dead were continuously identified with the land/earth during mortuary ceremonies.

During the burial, while participants cover the coffin with earth, a cross is erected featuring the deceased's name and date of birth. On one such occasion, I saw people sprinkling animal blood onto the cross. I asked one of the female participants about this, but she appeared embarrassed and tried to ignore me. A person who had witnessed the incident told me later that, in the past, mourners would kill animals for the *matebian* at the cemetery, but now the Catholic Church discouraged this. A member of the Catholic Church explained to me that he tried to dissuade people from making animal sacrifices because Jesus opposed such practices. This may well explain the woman's embarrassment about the animal blood on the cross, and may also shed light on why the dead frequently return to their relatives. Animals used to be slaughtered near the grave of the deceased, and the final meal with the dead was eaten communally at the cemetery. Since the Catholic Church prohibits this practice, however, the meal is now eaten in the village. This may encourage the dead to return to the house of the living, where they may be a disturbance.

The slaughtering of animals during funerals seems to play an important part in keeping the dead satisfied. When I asked people about this practice, they tended to respond, "The *matebian* wants to eat meat; the land wants to eat meat" (*Matebian hakarak han naan, rai hakarak han naan*, T.). Hence the deceased and the land are integrated into the same hungry entity, both of which have an appetite for meat. In a similar vein, Traube has noted that the purpose of "black rituals" in Mambai is to "repay the fatigue of the dead" and to "repay the fatigue of the earth," which illustrates the merging of the dead and the earth.[30] After burials in Funar, the "owner of words" usually makes a small ritual speech expressing respect for the dead and asking for permission to eat. Before eating commences, he pours palm liquor onto the ground "for the *matebian*," thereby placing the deceased in the land. Although people are often uncertain about the exact destination of the dead, their association with the land is continuously emphasized during mortuary rituals. On one such occasion, however, when the palm wine was poured onto the ground, Adérito bent over and whispered, "What a waste [of palm wine]," a small joke that could also suggest skepticism about the procedure.

Despite people's fearful demeanor in the presence of death, they also display a playful attitude toward the ancestors and the land. Once when I returned from a burial in Funar, a woman with whom I lived called out when I entered the house: "Is it really Menina, or is it the *larek-nain* [land spirit/owner; first ancestor] of Lawadu?" While alluding to the danger of spirits, this was also meant as a joke—and demonstrated, moreover, that, as on many other ritual occasions, ancestors and land spirits were not strictly separated from one another.

Furthermore, I was told that while those left behind are "guarding the bitter flowers," the deceased resides inside the stems of the flowers that are placed on the table or mat at the dead person's house after the body has been taken to the cemetery. As mentioned previously, the living members of an origin house are frequently referred to as the flowers of a tree and the ancestors and ancestral land as

---

to impose coherence on these fragments, see Rita Astuti, "What Happens After Death?" in *Questions of Anthropology*, ed. Rita Astuti, Jonathan Parry, and Charles Stafford (Oxford: Berg, 2007), 235.

[30] Traube, *Cosmology and Social Life*, 216.

the trunk. By inhabiting the stem of the flowers, the dead connect the living with the land of the ancestors.

For people of Funar, it is vital to be buried in the village cemetery. When villagers die someplace other than Funar, their relatives may conduct the death rituals close to where the death occurred, but for the burial, the body is preferably returned to Funar. When the former governor of Timor-Leste and supporter of the Indonesian government, Abilío Osório Soares, died in 2007 in Kupang, in West Timor, many of Funar's residents lamented the fact that his body was not brought back to his ancestral land (which is located in the *suco* of Manelima in the Laclubar subdistrict). Several people suggested that the reason he died was that he had left and forgotten about his ancestral land, and hence the *lulik* had "imprisoned" (*kastigu*) him. Some maintained that he had taken potent *lulik* objects away with him to West Timor, and it was this that had led to his demise. Others said that he died of bowel cancer. Abilío Soares's wife-takers (in Funar) said that they would not make the appropriate mortuary payments unless his body was brought back. As this case illustrates, there is a need for the dead to be returned to the ancestral land, where they can become part of the lasting unity of origin houses, ancestral sites, and ancestors.

ADDRESSING PROBLEMS FROM THE PAST

In "The Political Economy of Death," Gillian Feeley-Harnik describes the "florescence" of mortuary rituals in Sakalava, Madagascar, which she interprets as a response to the intrusion of strangers.[31] People take refuge in death rituals because the realm of the dead is the one zone that cannot be controlled by colonial officials. Death rituals in Funar were similarly prolific and elaborate, especially in comparison with marriage ceremonies. In the absence of historical material about the region, it is difficult to verify whether death rituals have always been more elaborate than marriage rituals. Comparative ethnographic data can be of some assistance, such as Forman's observation that death rituals among the Makassae surpassed bridewealth negotiations in both their size and significance.[32] Funar's villagers describe the elaborate marriage exchanges that took place in the past and agree that these are now something of a rarity. To understand the proliferation of death rituals, we need to consider what mortuary ceremonies accomplish that make people so keen to invest in them.

As described above, death rituals, first and foremost, fix house membership. Second, death rituals cement and reinforce the status differences between origin houses. Third, death rituals resolve problems within origin houses as well as obligations between them. Death and marriage rituals are actually part of the same process through which members become separated and are incorporated into a new origin house.

---

[31] Gillian Feeley-Harnik, "The Political Economy of Death: Communication and Change in Malagasy Colonial History," *American Ethnologist* 11, no. 1 (1984): 1–19.

[32] Forman, "Descent, Alliance and Exchange Ideology among the Makassae of East Timor," 152. Another fact that might support the idea that death rituals have always been more elaborate than marriage rituals in this region of Timor-Leste is that there is not, as far as I know, an Idaté term for the Tetum word *lia moris* ("life ritual"), which refers to ceremonies around marriage.

Although people in Funar say that death rituals are carried out in line with "the ways of the ancestors," it is clear that some aspects of the ceremonies have been amended in recent times. For example, people now bury their dead in coffins rather than rolled up in mats, and in single graves rather than communal pits. They also say the Ave Maria and refrain from slaughtering animals at the cemetery. Despite these changes, however, there is an insistence that things need to be done according to custom (*lisan*) to please the dead and stop them from interfering in the lives of the living. Residents look to the ancestors to ensure the continuity of life while at the same time wanting to distance themselves from the dead. Death ceremonies were occasions when relationships with both the dead and the living were renegotiated.[33] Although there were occasions to fulfill obligations toward wife-givers, the dead also required "payment," especially in the case of a red death.[34] Death ceremonies resolved obligations toward the ancestors and toward other groups—hence these two levels of exchange (amongst the living and between the living and the dead) were inextricably entangled.

In Chapters 3 and 4 I examined the tensions surrounding the reconstruction of origin houses and the conflicts between wife-givers and wife-takers. Compared with those practices, death rituals are less conflicted. It seems that people invest more heavily in those rituals that mitigate the dependencies engendered by marriage. In contradistinction to Feeley-Harnik's thesis on the florescence of mortuary rituals in Madagascar, therefore, I suggest that, in Funar, death rituals are not about resisting the influence of foreign colonizers, but, instead, they are used to create or maintain independence from other houses. Yet this need itself may be related to the presence of outsiders, since it is partly due to the colonial (and neo-colonial) interference in the social hierarchy that relations have become tense.

Moreover, it is possible that some of the practices introduced by the Catholic Church, such as the creation of Christian cemeteries where funeral sacrifices are banned, have increased the perceptions of danger that derive from the dead. In contrast to the quite uncomplicated incorporation of the notion of Catholic potency into the notion of *lulik* (see Chapter 1), the conversion to Catholicism seems to have been more problematic in other areas, especially with regard to the burial of the dead.

---

[33] Compare with Traube, *Cosmology and Social Life*, 201.

[34] Timor-Leste's history is one replete with red deaths and communal violence. This prompts the question, how have people dealt with such killings, given that the spirits of the dead can return to haunt the living? This is one of the key questions that I explore in the next chapter.

CHAPTER SIX

FEAR OF THE LAND

Maria and Adérito's house, where I lived during my fieldwork, was particularly comfortable compared to those of other villagers. One day, Maria's brother Abílio, who was living in Laclubar Town, came to visit. His trip was prompted by his desire to attend the reconstruction of his origin house. When he arrived he was clearly tired from the journey, so Maria and some of the children rushed off to prepare a meal of rice and vegetables for him. After we had eaten, Abílio got up, picked up his bag, and went to the house of another relative to spend the night. I was surprised by his departure, because I knew Maria and Adérito's relatives often slept at their house when they visited Funar, and Abílio was welcome to stay there. It was then that Adérito confided in me that his wife's brother was scared of the land. Indeed, throughout my fieldwork, residents of Funar repeatedly told me that they were "scared of the land" (*maes namo*)—a phrase that became key for understanding people's ambiguous relationship with the ancestral environment.

In the past, when Maria and Adérito had visited their children in Dili, Abílio had sometimes stayed at the house by himself, and it was on one of those occasions that he was attacked by two land spirits. The land spirits had come in the guise of two beautiful women. One had black skin and long black hair, while the other had white skin and red hair. They jumped on top of him while he was sleeping, scratching him with their fingernails, and violently tried to seduce him. They "wanted him," Adérito said, laughing somewhat sheepishly. Abílio had managed to escape their grasp by jumping out of bed, running out of the house, and continuing all the way to his brother's house at the other end of the hamlet. Ever since, he had refused to stay overnight at Maria and Adérito's house. He was scared of the land, that is, worried about possibly encountering land spirits.[1]

When I awoke the next morning and went into the kitchen, a number of neighbor women had already gathered there to prepare coffee and fried bananas for the guests who were coming to help with the reconstruction of the origin house. Everyone looked worried. Margarida, a neighbor in her late twenties who was sitting beside the fire, kept rocking back and forth, holding her two-year-old son close to her chest, and muttering, "I am scared, I am scared that they will make a mistake." Maria was worried, too, explaining that the reconstruction of an origin house could be a very dangerous affair: if you didn't follow the ways of the ancestors, there was always a risk that someone could die. Maria tried to convince Margarida to keep her company that evening, or at least to send some of her children over so that more people would be present. But Margarida refused, so Maria kept inviting other people to stay with her overnight because she, too, was scared of the land. Both women expressed their worries about offending the ancestors in terms of "fear of the land."

---

[1] In Chapter 1, I noted that human landowners and nonhuman landowners are both referred to as *larek-nain* or *namo-nain*. To differentiate between the two, I use the term "land spirit" to refer to the latter.

The ancestral land, a source of life, wealth, and productivity, was the main reason for the return migration to Funar in the 1990s. However, the relationship between the landscape and its inhabitants is not always positive. *Maes namo* was a fear expressed by men, women, and children alike. Land spirits are one source of potential danger associated with the land, but fear of offending the ancestors by not following their ways is also articulated in these terms.

The danger associated with the landscape was much more pronounced in Funar than it was in Laclubar Town, where people rarely spoke of a fear of the land. This raises an obvious question: why do people in Funar perceive the landscape to be more dangerous than do those in Laclubar Town? This chapter investigates why the villagers of Funar are scared of the land and how residents of both Funar and Laclubar manage and appropriate the potency of the land.

Anthropologists and historians alike have drawn attention to the way the material world that surrounds us is marked by history, how the landscape can "soak up" memories and thereby enable us to re-experience events that happened long ago. As Simon Schama aptly observed, "Though lines of imperial power have always flowed along rivers, water courses are not the only landscape to carry the freight of history."[2] The landscape can carry the freight of history; it plays a key role in the transmission of memory. Topography itself is infused with history, enabling one to recall or forget the past.[3] This chapter explores this mnemonic capacity, showing how the spiritual landscape itself can be transformed by historical events.

A DANGEROUS LANDSCAPE

After the death of my neighbor Bento, Adérito refused to let me stay at the dead man's house overnight for the mourning ceremony. I therefore dutifully returned home in time for dinner. Since Bento's house was only a few hundred meters away, we could hear singing and crying throughout the night, part of the ceremony to "guard the bitter flowers" (Chapter 5). Unable to sleep, I went to the teenagers' room, as I described in the introduction. Both Helena and Olívia were scared of the land—scared of the *matebian* (the spirit of the deceased), scared of land spirits, and scared of dancing devils in the land.

On many occasions, people in Funar told me that they were scared of the land. When Tanha died (Chapter 5), her friend Helena became preoccupied with the dangers of the land, so much so that for months after Tanha's death Helena would mention her fear of the land several times a day. Similarly, when walking from one place to another, collecting firewood, or going to the well, people warned each other to beware of the dangers of the land and typically tried to avoid going on these sorts of journeys alone. The fear of the land included a variety of different spiritual agents, such as land spirits and ancestors, as well as *lulik* sites. The term I am translating as "fear" (*maes*) also means "respect," and thus the phrase "I am scared of the land" (*au u maes namo*) refers not only to a fearful attitude, but also to a sense of respect and awe.

There was, of course, individual variation: some people expressed their fear of the land more frequently than did others, and some took more precautions to avoid

---

[2] Simon Schama, *Landscape and Memory* (New York: Vintage Books, 1995), 5.

[3] See: Schama, *Landscape and Memory*; and Bloch, *How We Think They Think*; and Simon Harrison, "Forgetful and Memorious Landscapes," *Social Anthropology* 12, no. 2 (2004): 135–51.

the dangers of the landscape. Generally speaking, women and children were considered to be more at risk from the land than were the men. Thus, women and youngsters were considered vulnerable when going to the toilet at night, collecting firewood, or fetching water.[4] Some young men from Funar were said to go to the cemetery at night to practice martial and ritual arts, but these places were considered to be too dangerous for women to go to so late at night. Chico, one of the teenage boys I lived with, told me how Adérito had, on several occasions, fearlessly handled encounters with land spirits that appeared in the form of snakes. Apparently, his lack of fear was what protected him. Thus it is hard to generalize about people's fears based on their gender, as some men exhibited a fear of the land while others did not, and the same is true of women.

I found that age influenced the way in which people related to the landscape. Older men, especially ritual speakers, were considered to be able to mediate its dangers.[5] They could carry out rituals at *lulik* sites, for example, such as asking for rain or asking the ancestors for advice at the cemetery. Age seemed to transcend gender in this respect, since Avó Bea, who lived with us for some time, always went to her field unaccompanied. As mentioned previously, elders were addressed by the Portuguese terms *avô/avó* (m/f), which was also used to speak about ancestors. The transition between elder and ancestor is not linguistically marked, suggesting that elders are already close to being ancestors, which might explain why older people face less danger from the land than do younger women and men. When people die they are reintegrated into the land, becoming a part of it (Chapter 5). As people age, they are clearly getting closer to this state of reunification than are their young neighbors and relatives. The fear of the land is also a fear of nondifferentiation, of becoming part of the land—as one would upon death, something I will return to later.

In all of these examples, the fear felt toward the land cannot be attributed to a single agent. People expressed their fear in relation to a variety of entities, including ancestors, land spirits, devils, and *lulik* sites. What connected these different spiritual agents was the landscape, and people thus tended to articulate their fear and respect toward the different agents by saying that they were scared of the land. People's inability to explain exactly how these spiritual entities related to one another increased the land's potential peril.

There were several other dangers associated with the landscape, but villagers did not always use the expression "scared of the land" in relation to these. While walking through uninhabited areas during the rainy season, I was repeatedly told to beware of little dwarf-like beings called *dore-hui*, which "walk in the clouds beside you" (*hui* means "wild;" *fuik*, T.). Much of the frequent traveling and walking undertaken along mountain paths involves moving in deep fog, especially during the rainy season, and this creates an eerie atmosphere, particularly when walking alone. It was during these walks that people said that the *dore-hui* walked beside

---

[4] Contrast with Hicks's observation for the Tetum, where women, who are thought to be closer to the land than men, were considered to be less at risk from its spiritual dangers; see Hicks, *Tetum Ghosts and Kin*, 36.

[5] When I use the terms "older men," "older women," "older people," and "elders," I refer to the category of people often described by the widely used Tetum terms *"katuas"* (older man) or *"ferik"* (older woman). There is no absolute age at which an individual becomes "older," but the label connotes a person who has some experience in life, who is well respected in the community, and who may already be a grandparent.

them, hidden in the fog. Some described these beings as small, stocky humans; others, as large monkeys. They were said to kidnap humans, especially children, and to eat their fat. The *dore-hui* talked and whistled in a gibberish-sounding language, sometimes replying to the calls of lost children. Many people told me about their encounters with *dore-hui*, which were commonly used as stories to frighten children and prevent them from going out alone.[6]

Other stories that were used to discipline children concerned the threat of *lakahonik* or *ninjas*.[7] These are human thieves who are thought to use spiritual powers to kidnap and kill people, especially children. People said that the bodies of children were stolen to build bridges, since only through the sacrifice of a child would bridges be strong and long-lasting. Throughout the 1990s, there were similar accounts of *ninja* gangs that were associated with militia activities.[8] Narratives concerning "construction sacrifice," in which human sacrifices are made for building projects, are also found across Indonesia. The perpetrators are often associated with government officials or feared outsiders and the rumors tend to be related to concerns about kidnapping (or headhunting).[9] One common explanation for the persistence of such rumors is that they are a product of the colonial era, stemming from a dislike and suspicion of the Dutch. Even though there is a clear link between narratives about human sacrifices and the fertility of the earth in Timor-Leste, contemporary rumors about kidnapping also seem to be associated with the presence of the Indonesian military and urban militia groups during the occupation.[10]

After the crisis of 2006, whenever we received news about the conflicts taking place in Dili, or saw helicopters from the international peacekeeping troops hovering over the area, the people I lived with would say that they were "scared of the land," before adding, "War—[there will be] a big war." The specific fear that the tense political situation in the country would escalate further was often expressed in connection with the more diffuse fear of the land.[11] Thus, it was not only the fear of *lulik* sites and of offending the ancestors, but also anxieties about the onset of war that were expressed in this way. During and after the 2006 crisis, rumors abounded throughout the country of mass graves and massacres, as did the "dystopian" prophecies (discussed in Chapter 2) that led many to fear that worse was to come. There were rumors of violence and the involvement of unknown forces or outside agents in the conflicts.

---

[6] For a comparative overview of similar narratives of wild human-like creatures in Southeast Asia, see Gregory Forth, *Images of the Wildman in Southeast Asia: An Anthropological Perspective* (London: Routledge, 2008).

[7] Compare with Henri Myrttinen, "Phantom Menaces: The Politics of Rumour, Securitisation and Masculine Identities in the Shadows of the Ninjas," in "Engaging Processes of Sense-Making and Negotiation in Contemporary Timor-Leste," 471–85.

[8] Robinson, *"If You Leave Us Here, We Will Die,"* 74.

[9] Robert H. Barnes, "Construction, Sacrifice, Kidnapping and Head-Hunting Rumors on Flores and Elsewhere in Indonesia," *Oceania* 64 (1993): 146.

[10] On human sacrifice and the fertility of the earth, see: Ibid., 155; Janet Hoskins, *Headhunting and the Social Imagination in Southeast Asia* (Stanford: Stanford University Press, 1996); and Friedberg, "Boiled Woman and Broiled Man," 266.

[11] Compare with Green, *Fear as a Way of Life*, who examines the way in which fear (as a response to state-sponsored political violence and repression) has penetrated social memory, everyday life, and the physical bodies of the women in Guatemala, where it has become a chronic condition. She explores the lived experience of violence through silences, secrecy, and the bodily postures and illnesses of her informants.

Some of these fears are probably rooted in the uncertainties of the Indonesian occupation, which was marked by appalling war crimes and mass killings. During this time, people *did* disappear at night and were killed at certain sites in the landscape. However, these fears and rumors about illicit killings and theft of children may not necessarily be simple byproducts of the experience of colonization and occupation, even though these experiences may well have reinforced them. A lack of historical data makes it impossible to make a firm judgment regarding the historical dimension of this fear. It is interesting to note, however, that the rumors are based on a familiar logic of reciprocity. To build bridges—permanent structures within the landscape—it is necessary to make an offering in the form of a human sacrifice. Moreover, these rumors reflect the more widespread notion that, behind the visible world, there is an invisible, unknown realm that is the source of both wealth and misfortune.

Another perceived threat for people in the Laclubar subdistrict comes in the shape of witches, who are also in some sense associated with the landscape. I once observed a teenage girl warn a three-year-old not to throw her food onto the ground by shouting, "Witch land, witch land!" (*Sabu larek, sabu larek!*). At night, the witches, who can take on the shape of birds, are thought to sneak around the houses of those they envy or who are stingy to attack or poison them.[12] Indeed social jealousy and wealth inequality were keys aspects of witchcraft accusations.[13] Putting water in front of windows or splashing holy water (blessed by a priest) around the house is one way of dealing with witches. They are considered to be humans with spiritual powers. For example, some are said to be able to make others ill by speaking secret words to magic stones; others were said to raise gigantic snakes as pets. Although not associated with specific places, witches are nonetheless thought to appropriate elements of the landscape to assist them in their evil deeds.

MITIGATING THE HAZARDS OF THE LANDSCAPE

Given the variety of dangers associated with the land, how do the inhabitants of this region mitigate them? When groups of people walk through the landscape, the young men and women among them frequently let out loud screams that echo around the mountainous terrain. They say that this is a way to indicate their presence to others who might be nearby. When passing along remote footpaths, men also cut small marks in the tree trunks with their machetes to show that someone has been there. Similarly, during the dry season, young men burn large patches of dried grass when they walk from one place to another. The burning is supposed to increase the fertility of the land, although, given the arbitrary manner in which this is commonly done, it could also be interpreted as a technique that people use to make themselves known to the spirits of the landscape and to create signs of human habitation in an otherwise uninhabited environment. When traveling through such a

---

[12] Witches also attack their victims by putting "bad medicine" in their food. Hence, eating with a person can be taken as a sign of one's trust for them. Compare with Maurice Bloch, "Commensality and Poisoning," in *Essays in Cultural Transmission*, ed. Maurice Bloch (London: Athlone, 2005), 45–60.

[13] From my observations during recent visits, it seems that with a growing market economy and concomitant increase in wealth inequality (partly fuelled by the selective distribution of veteran and other pensions), the number of witchcraft accusations in the Laclubar subdistrict has increased.

setting, people repeatedly assert their presence by creating acoustic and visual marks. Moreover, travelers sometimes carry different potions of "traditional medicine" or blessed water with them as protection from the dangers of the journey—especially when the destination is in an unfamiliar place.

People who encounter land or water spirits risk the danger of going mad or dying; for this reason, inexplicable deaths are frequently blamed on spiritual agents. Similarly, those who wander alone too close to *lulik* sites are reported to disappear or become lost. Again, women and children are thought to be particularly vulnerable to the negative effects of contact with these places. *Lulik* is also said to damage modern machinery and technological devices such as cameras and cars. One way of mitigating this difficult relationship is by making small offerings to the land. For example, on one occasion when the driver of a car was having difficulties driving up a steep hill near Laclubar Town, one of the passengers suggested giving some money to the *lulik* land.

Ancestral spirits have similar powers and are also believed to interfere with modern machines. I witnessed an example of this phenomenon after Marco's funeral. Some relatives of the deceased came from Dili to attend the ceremony and hired a vehicle to make the journey. When they were ready to return home, I joined them in the pickup truck for the ride back to Dili together with a number of other villagers. After we had traveled for several hours, however, the car began to slide on the muddy road. The people inside quickly became nervous, saying that they were scared of the land. Someone suggested that Marco's *matebian* had hijacked the car and was trying to force it to turn back because he did not want the guests to leave the funeral ceremony so early. For this reason, we eventually ended up driving back to Funar—a journey of many miles—just to drop off one of the relatives, whom the driver believed Marco had not wanted to go to Dili.

Another way of coping with the dangers of the landscape is to avoid traveling alone. On one journey near the *suco* of Fatumakerek, which is six to seven hours' walk from the center of Funar, we traveled in a large group. During the arduous trek, which required us to cross three high mountains, people helped each other on the steep slopes, pushing and pulling one another up particularly tricky stretches and laughing playfully at those who lost their balance. Some teenage boys shot mangos off the trees with their slingshots and shared the fruit with the group, and I watched two girls try to flirt their way to receiving an extra helping. At one point we walked along a riverbed—mostly dry, apart from a narrow stream in the middle—beside which large water buffalo were resting. Several of my companions jumped into the river fully dressed to cool off from the midday heat. A boy showed his younger sister how to identify clean sources of drinking water, later telling her off for lagging behind in order to have a private conversation with a potential boyfriend.

The party began searching for sweetwater prawns beneath the rocks in the river, and the catch was grilled over a smoldering log. While searching for the prawns, the women and men teased one another endlessly by pretending that someone had come across an eel in the water. When someone screamed, "Eel! Eel!" everyone jumped out of the river in nervous excitement, splashing each other with water when they realized it was a joke. Eels are the "owners of the water" (*wer-nain*) in much the same way that snakes are the "owners of the land" (*larek-nain*), and as "owners," both are considered to be potentially harmful if you go near them. The best way of warding against them is to travel in large groups.

On another occasion when I was walking along the same river with only Helena for company, she adamantly refused to take a break at the same site, insisting that the water spirit would harm us if we did. Without the protection of a large crowd, she considered the site too dangerous as a rest stop. Thus, one way that people reduce their fear of the land is by approaching it in crowds and inhabiting it; when alone, the land seems more dangerous.

Elizabeth Traube notes the significance of silence and noise among the Mambai, arguing that this is a mythological opposition that, during ritual performances, casts nature as silent and humans as "unique noisemakers."[14] This correlates with my observations from Funar, where noise can both signal danger and serve as a source of protection. Similarly, in Dili, a common way of warning others of impending danger was to bang on pieces of metal. The first time I became aware of this was during an earthquake in 2005, just after I had arrived in Timor-Leste for the first time. When the first tremors started during the night, people banged loudly on pieces of metal and everyone came out of their houses. Later, I was told that the noise was intended not only to wake people up, but also "to tell God that we are still here," drawing his attention to the presence of human beings on the earth.[15] When I visited Dili after the 2006 crisis, people warned each other about violent clashes in the streets by banging on metal—the sound of which was often heard for hours at night, its volume reflecting the intensity of the violence. Hence, noise seems to be significant in two ways. First, as a means of alerting the spiritual realm to a human presence; and, second, as a mode of communicating with other humans (e.g., to warn them of impending danger).

I observed several other ways in which the dangers of the land are mitigated. For people to be able to enjoy the benefits of the landscape, they have to cultivate a refined and respectful relationship with it. For instance, it is necessary to be "introduced" to the land when traveling to areas that one has not visited before. This introduction can be made by drawing a cross of mud or earth on a newcomer's forehead, as was done to me when I first traveled outside Funar, thus protecting me from the *lulik* present there.

One day I visited Mount Maubere with a man called Gilberto, who wanted to show me the place where his brother had been killed. Mount Maubere is a large, circular mountain about an hour's walk from the town center. When we reached the top, he pointed to a fenced mound of stones considered to be *lulik* and told me that there was plenty of gold underneath. He regretted not having brought any money or cigarettes to offer to the *lulik* land, as this oversight meant that we might get lost on our way home. It was at this point that he decided to introduce this land to the children who were accompanying us on our journey, since they had never visited the place before. Gilberto tried to warn them about the dangers of the *lulik* land, but the boys were much too busy play-fighting (pretending to be Indonesian soldiers shooting at one another) to pay him much attention—they were in the large ditches that the Indonesians had dug when fighting against the guerrilla forces. Gilberto positioned himself beside the fenced mound of stones and summoned the boys, who lined up in a row and stepped forward one after the other so that Gilberto could

---

[14] Traube, *Cosmology and Social Life*, 17.

[15] Webb Keane states that people in Sumba say they respond to earth tremors by making noise to signal their human presence; see Keane, *Signs of Recognition*, 236.

draw a cross of earth on their foreheads. This respectful introduction to the land was intended to protect the children from the danger it posed.

Gilberto lived in Laclubar Town and was not exposed to the dangers of the land very often. Yet the fact that he thought it necessary to protect the children from the *lulik* land of Maubere indicates that, like many other residents, he was no less worried about the dangers of the land.[16] So when he left town to visit Mount Maubere, he took the necessary precautions to protect himself and his party.

LAND OF WAR AND NEGLECT

As mentioned earlier, people in Funar tend to be more concerned with the dangers of the land than are those who live in Laclubar Town. The former have to avoid the dangers of *lulik* land and land spirits whenever they find themselves away from inhabited areas, such as while fetching water, washing, collecting firewood, working in the fields, and traveling from one place to another. People in Laclubar, by contrast, do not have to take the same precautions in their everyday lives. These residents are not unaware of the dangers or less scared of the land, but they know that the dangers are less acute in densely populated settlements. For example, Pedro, with whom I normally stayed when I was in Laclubar Town, understood the risks and always accompanied me back to Funar when I could not find anyone else to travel with to ensure that I was not be attacked by land spirits during the journey.

Exploring this difference can help to explain why people in Funar are scared of the land in the first place. When they were forcibly resettled by the Indonesian military, they had to abandon their homes and were unable to maintain a respectful and reciprocal relationship with the land of their ancestors. As we have seen, to mitigate the dangers of the landscape, people must inhabit it—where there are no people, the land is considered to be more dangerous. Leaving the land of Funar uninhabited during the Indonesian occupation led to an increased presence of dangerous spiritual agents, such as land spirits. People in Funar told me that they did not like being alone and wanted to live in "crowded" or "lively" (*rame; ramai*, In.) places. Hence, when the villagers returned, they built their houses closer together than they had in the past.

At the beginning of this chapter, I cited the example of Abílio, who refused to sleep at our house because he feared being attacked by land spirits. One of the reasons people gave for land spirits entering the house was because it was built on what had once been *lulik* land. The *lulik* potency had supposedly been removed by means of a small ritual conducted when the couple built their house.[17] In spite of this, however, many villagers still feared the land on which the house was built.

Another reason people gave for the concentration of land spirits around our house was the fact that so many people had been killed there during the war. I was

---

[16] Mount Maubere is strongly associated with death because the ancestors are said to have taken the heads of their fallen enemies to the mountaintop for the *lulik* land to consume. In the more recent past, the Indonesian military took people they considered to be part of the resistance to Mount Maubere to kill them (so that others would not witness the killings and might therefore have less cause to turn against the Indonesian government). Lastly, I was told that family members of the well-known resistance fighter Nicolau Lobato were gunned down at this spot.

[17] This ritual involved the beheading of a dog to keep the *lulik* away. As discussed in Chapter 5, this was the same practice adopted to expel the "red" when a person dies a "red death."

told that because these deaths included East Timorese, Indonesians, and Portuguese, the land spirits were variously described as having white and black skin. Some teenagers joked that I would never feel lonely living at the house, since I would be surrounded by land spirits. They also teased me by referring to my apparent resemblance to the land spirits, these being said to look like foreigners with their white skin and red hair.

When people talked about the dangers associated with the land on which the house was built, they frequently mentioned another story concerning a man named Rama Hana. This man died on the hill above the house during the Indonesian occupation. He was a member of the guerrilla forces and was shot dead by the Indonesian military in the late 1970s. My neighbor recounted how, during the war, he found Rama Hana's body and tried to bury him. However, because he was afraid that the Indonesians would return, he was unable to bury Rama Hana properly, and his arm was left sticking out of the grave. This fact contributed to the danger of the place years later. Indeed, during the villagers' absence because of the occupation, the land had been littered with the bodies and spirits of those who died during the conflict, thus intensifying the dangers of the land for today's living.[18]

The reburial of human remains after the Indonesians left Timor-Leste was a widespread practice, one in which many inhabitants of Laclubar subdistrict invested a considerable amount of time after independence. They located the remains by consulting a person "who can see far" (*matan dook*), who told them where they would find the bones of the deceased. The reburials included not only those who were killed in unsettled and deserted areas, but also those who had been buried far from their home during the Indonesian occupation, when their relatives had not been allowed to take them back to their ancestral land. A sense of uncertainty seems to remain about how "successful" and complete these reburials were, since tales of restless spirits and spirit soldiers were mentioned on several occasions during my stay. Apparently, the inability to resolve all of the past deaths has turned the landscape into a source of danger, and unresolved issues from the past are also considered to have consequences reaching far beyond just this particular region, as I discuss next.

CLOSING THE LAND

In January 2007 I was taking a morning stroll around Laclubar Town when a member of the police, Tiago, called me over and said in a hushed and urgent tone, "Menina, something really important is happening today at Mount Maubere. The elders have gathered there to 'close the land.'" Because Tiago was busy working, he was unable to accompany me to Mount Maubere, about an hour away, so he gave me directions to the nearby hamlet to find the gathering myself. Because people did not like me to walk alone through the countryside, I went to the house of my friends Luciano and Paula, who live near the mountain, to see if I could find a travel companion. When I arrived, Paula, who was making doughnuts to sell to her neighbors, told me that Luciano had already left with the other men to attend the ceremony. She promptly halted her cooking and led me by the hand to where the ceremony was held.

---

[18] Compare with Kwon's discussion of the ghosts of improperly buried war dead inhabiting the environment in Vietnam in *Ghosts of War in Vietnam*.

We proceeded along a narrow footpath, passing through small patches of undergrowth until we came to a large ditch surrounded by lush forest and palm trees and located right at the foot of the mountain. This place was known as Susuk and represented one of several "doors" (*lalamatak*) through which humans could access the potency of the land. We stood at a distance to watch what the dozen men who had gathered at the site were doing. They had already killed a large pig and were now standing around a small stone on which they had sprinkled blood from the pig along with some betel juice. Coins, which had been cut into small pieces, had also been placed on the stone. A man whom I identified as a member of the *liurai* house of Laclubar had come from Dili and was leading the ceremony. He uttered quiet but forceful words of ritual speech directed toward the stone platform. We were standing a good ten meters away from the gathering when Luciano saw us, and it became clear that he wanted us to join them. However, just as he started to beckon us to come over, the ritual speaker had a quiet word with him, informing him that women were not allowed to attend the ritual and that we would have to leave.

I spent the rest of the day by the fire in Paula's kitchen, waiting for Luciano to come home. When he finally arrived, smelling of palm liquor, he told us what happened earlier in the day. First, he gave us some background details, explaining how, during the "war with Indonesia," some elders from the Laclubar subdistrict had mobilized the *lulik* potency of the land to fight the occupiers, a procedure known as "opening the land" (*lo'e larek*). After this "opening," though, the land had never been properly closed. The failure to return the potency back to the land, Luciano said, was the cause of the conflict that erupted across Timor-Leste in 2006.

At the end of 2006, Xanana Gusmão, Timor-Leste's president at the time, launched a national program to "return sharp and pointed weapons" (*halot meit ho kroat*, T.) as a response to the "crisis." The aim of the program was to initiate a series of small, ritualized "amnesties" all over the country and return the weapons used to fight the Indonesians to their proper places.[19] Gusmão's program was based on the premise that, during the resistance struggle, weapons containing spiritual potency had been taken from people's *lulik* houses and never returned. The failure to restore those to their proper places was cited as a reason why conflicts had erupted in 2006. Thus, the ceremonies aimed to return these weapons to their appropriate *lulik* houses in order to create peace and stability throughout the country.

Luciano and the other participants made a direct connection between the small ceremony that took place at the bottom of Mount Maubere and Gusmão's program to return sharp weapons to their rightful places. In their case, however, the "weapon" to be returned was the *lulik* potency of the landscape used to fight the Indonesian occupiers. Once this potency had been mobilized through the "opening of the land" and the Indonesians had been expelled, all that remained was to "close the land." The ceremony near Mount Maubere represented part of this process of "closing the land" (*douk larek*), returning its potency to the ground so that it would not cause any more harm. Women are not allowed to be present during any ceremonies related to warfare, Luciano explained, and this was why we were ushered away. The fact that I was an outsider may also have played a part in the decision.

---

[19] José Trinidade and Bryant Castro, *Rethinking Timorese Identity as a Peacebuilding Strategy: The Lorosa'e-Loromonu Conflict from a Traditional Perspective*, report funded by the European Union and implemented by the Deutsche Gesellschaft für Technische Zusammenarbeit (GTZ), Dili, Timor-Leste, 2007, 43.

Mount Maubere (the "warrior," *asuwa'in*) (2007; author's photo)

The *lulik* potency of Mount Maubere is considered to be an effective weapon for warfare. Indeed, the mountain is often referred to as the "warrior" (*asuwa'in*) or the "head land" (*larek ulun*). It is said to house an army of land spirits (*tropa espiritu*) that can be raised up from the ground whenever the inhabitants of Laclubar face an external threat. These spirit troops are described as the security forces (*seguransa*) or police (*polisi*) of the land and can be mobilized through ritual speech, performed by elders through a ceremony at a *lulik* site. Opening the land requires the sacrifice of a "hot" animal, such as a buffalo, while closing it calls for the death of a "cold" animal, such as a pig.

A resident of Laclubar told me how his ancestors fought a war against the neighboring domain of Samoro by raising spirit troops from the ground. When warriors from Samoro attacked Laclubar, they found the mountains full of armed land spirits, their screams echoing through the valley. The warriors became frightened and ran away. After this incident, however, the *lulik* land killed the wife of the local ruler, Dom Geraldo. He had raised the spirit troops from the ground, and the land required something from him in return for the help he had received.[20]

Along similar lines, the conflicts that erupted in 2006 were interpreted as stemming from the fact that people had neglected their reciprocal obligations toward the ancestral land. Looking after the land means showing gratitude for the beneficial effects that it provides. For the people of this region, the 2006 conflicts illustrated that failing to look after the land can have fatal consequences and may even lead to war. Looking after the land does not only involve inhabiting it and treating it respectfully. Once its potency has been mobilized to provide protection, it is also necessary to show gratitude by "feeding" the land and thereby "closing" it again.

---

[20] See also Judith Bovensiepen, "Opening and Closing the Land: Land and Power in the Idaté Highlands," in *Land and Life in Timor-Leste*, 47–60.

One day over coffee, the police commander of Laclubar Town told me—his eyes glistening with excitement—that he could earn thousands of dollars from the *lulik* land if he wanted to, but that if he did so, the land would kill his children in return. Despite the productive potential of the land, there are limits to the amount people can ask from it. Relations with the ancestral land are thus not only reciprocal in a practical sense; they are also moral, since the land punishes those who are greedy.[21]

In an article analyzing narratives about the Christ-like figure of Tat Felis, Traube examines Mambai ideas about suffering and reciprocity, which are strikingly similar to those found in the Laclubar region. The most important of these concerns the "ideology of reciprocity," according to which those who suffered during the Indonesian occupation need to be "repaid" today.[22] In Traube's example, the relationship between "the people" and the state is modeled on that of other pairs of life-givers and life-receivers, invoking the common principle that those who suffer to give life (in her case, by contributing to the birth of the nation), must be recompensed. Similarly, residents in Funar and Laclubar sought to recompense the land for its support. The "cultural revival" of the post-occupation years was also informed by preexisting dynamics based on obligations between life-givers and life-takers and the debts that the gift of life bestows on the recipients.

ANCESTRAL LAND AND THE FREIGHT OF HISTORY

When Jennifer Cole started her fieldwork among the Betsimisaraka of Madagascar, she was confronted with an apparent lack of memories about the colonial period.[23] However, her exploration of sacrifice rituals shows that colonial memories are present in an implicit form and are integrated with, and subordinated to, the ancestral order. According to Cole, people gain access to the past in rituals via the world of the ancestors, thus co-constituting individual and social memories. In Funar, peoples' relationship with the past is similarly subordinated to the ancestral order that is mediated through the ancestral land. Villagers rarely spoke about the Indonesian occupation, yet they continuously expressed a strong fear toward the land. This fear is key to understanding the ways in which colonialism, violence, and forced resettlement have deeply affected people in this region.

To benefit from the positive aspects of the landscape, the land needs to be looked after. Yet during the Indonesian occupation, people were unable to sustain this reciprocal relationship. The historical loss of political autonomy combined with forced resettlement meant that the people's former spiritual relationship with the landscape was no longer generating the protective effect that it was once thought to produce. Today, this deficiency contributes to the sense of awe and fear felt toward the land. The conflict of 2006 was also interpreted as the result of a failure to maintain reciprocal relations with the land after people called upon its potency in "the war against Indonesia." Once more, then, we see how *lulik* land is thought to take on an agency that is beyond the control of the living.

Anthropological studies of violence and subjectivity have explored how conflict and suffering can reshape social relations, experiences, and systems of meaning.[24] So

---

[21] See Basso, *Wisdom Sits in Places*.

[22] Traube, "Unpaid Wages," 24.

[23] Cole, *Forget Colonialism?*

[24] See, for example, Das et al., *Social Suffering*.

far, however, little attention has been paid to the ways in which the nonhuman environment is affected and transformed by war and violence. Notable exceptions include Christopher Taylor's study of how rivers were conscripted into the Rwandan genocide and Jens Meierhenrich's examination of the ways in which the Rwandan genocide transformed places of memory.[25]

There is a particular understanding of personhood that underlies the ways in which people in Funar relate to the land. As argued in Chapter 1, human beings are considered to emerge from the land; in their primordial state, humans and the land are part of the same substance. The ancestral land is seen as the "trunk," "origin," or "source" of life (*mori ni uun*). The mythical separation from the land—when the ancestors emerged from different sites in the landscape—is reproduced upon birth. Humans become separated from the land when they are born: at birth, the placenta ("the younger sibling," *walin*) is returned to the land and buried under the parental house. Throughout life, then, there is a differentiation between people and place. When humans die, however, they "return to the land" (*ahilas no larek*). Thus, personhood is constituted in a dialectical relationship with the land that involves both processes of differentiation and nondifferentiation or reintegration.

It is my contention that the "fear of the land" must be understood against the background of this particular understanding of personhood. The ancestral landscape is an effective resource, one with which people ensure the continuity of life. It reflects the permanence of the ancestral past and fosters future prosperity. People strive to establish reciprocal relations with the land in a way that mirrors relations of the past, yet there is a subtle awareness that historical events have been transforming this landscape.

The fearful and respectful attitude toward the land exhibited by Funar's residents is probably not a new development, but it does appear that the experience of war and dislocation has intensified such sentiments. Fear and respect mediate the ways in which people relate to the ancestral land and how they relate to the past via the land. There is a fear not only of having neglected the ancestral land, but also of being too close to the land—of coming close to a state of nondifferentiation during life. Devils grabbing your legs, bones sticking out of a makeshift grave, and seductive land spirits are all expressions of nondifferentiation between people and place—a unity that usually occurs only upon death. The fear of the land is hence also a fear of death, a fear of becoming part of the land and thus relinquishing one's human form.[26]

The villagers, then, face a Goldilocks-type dilemma of finding *just* the right balance with regard to the ancestral land. They need to be close to it, which is achieved by carrying out the appropriate rituals to ensure its productivity, but must also continuously distance themselves from certain spiritual dangers associated with it. The fear of the land is thus not simply a fear that an external agency has become threatening. Since humans and the land are considered to be consubstantial in primordial times, it is also a fear of something that is part of the self.

In a context where humans and the land are considered to share a primordial unity, violence and conflict necessarily transfigure the relationship between the

---

[25] See: Meierhenrich, "The Transformation of Lieux de Mémoire"; and Taylor, *Sacrifice as Terror*.

[26] For a more detailed analysis of the dangers of nondifferentiation between people and place, see Bovensiepen, "Lulik: Taboo, Animism, or Transgressive Sacred?"

two—in this case, by turning the land into an increased source of danger and fear. This is important for two reasons. First, it illustrates how the return and reinvigoration of people's relations with the land entails not just the reproduction of past relations, but also how those relationships were transformed and reconstituted by people's absence. Second, the fear and respect felt toward the landscape influence the ways in which people engage with it. Refusing to sleep at someone's house, avoiding certain places, and making sure one is not alone are all forms of behavior that illustrate how being scared of the land affects people's interactions with the world around them.

NOT ANCESTOR,
NOT NOT-ANCESTOR

"I can't stop looking at it," said Helena. "I can't." She paused. "[It's a film] about *sembilan-sembilan*." The term *sembilan-sembilan* is Indonesian for "ninety-nine" and refers to the post-referendum violence of 1999. Helena was holding a flashy new mobile phone in her hand and playing adroitly with the buttons, scanning through the photos and films stored on her memory card. She had been showing me photos of herself and her friends posing in front of cars and buildings, imitating scenes from American or Indonesian music videos.

When I completed my doctoral fieldwork in 2007, I gave Helena a mobile phone as a goodbye present. It was something she had really wanted, such devices being a rare commodity in Funar at that time. She was proud of it, and for her it expressed the special friendship we had. Five years later, nearly everyone in Funar owned a mobile phone or had access to one through friends and family. Nonetheless, charging phones and adding credit was a constant struggle. People used phones not only to communicate, but also to listen to music and take photos. On my visit to Funar in 2010, when I walked with Helena and other friends to Mount Lawadu, sexually explicit rap songs in English could be heard blaring from Helena's mobile phone without interruption.

In July 2012, when Helena and I were once again sitting together, she showed me a new use for her mobile device. Helena had saved a video about the 1999 massacres on her phone that she said a friend sent to her. She said it was one of a series of political clips that were circulated widely across the country. I had known Helena for seven years by then, and this was first time that I ever heard her mention *sembilan-sembilan*. That is to say, it was the first time she commented to me about the atrocities committed during the Indonesian occupation.

Loud metallic sounds started to blast from Helena's phone again, and her hands began to shake. Theo, a ten-year-old boy she was looking after, leaned on her leg and tried to play with her phone. Helena pushed him away gently, pressed pause, and quietly passed the phone over to me so that I could watch the film.

Dramatic and hyper-sentimental music in Tetum accompanied the clip. In the past my friend's taste for kitsch made me laugh, but there was nothing amusing about this video. It was one of the most violent film clips I have ever seen. It showed brutal killings and contained close-up footage of butchered corpses and body parts piled on top of each other. I felt sick. There were detailed images of gaping wounds, split skulls, and disemboweled bodies. There were shots of crying relatives covered in blood, running in panic from the terror or embracing the mutilated bodies of their loved ones.

When I watched the film, I did not doubt that these were, indeed, images from the 1999 massacres. If I had not known that these events had actually occurred, I would have switched off the film. But knowing that they did happen, turning it off would have felt like denying the cruel reality of these events. So I watched the clip to the end.[1]

Helena, who usually didn't let a minute pass without talking, was silent for a long time. She watched me carefully as I held her mobile; her eyes were watery, and her thin hands continued to shake.

"When I first saw it, I could not stop crying," she said softly, adding, "I had to look at it again and again." I had never seen Helena so serious. "When I feel alone, I watch it," she sighed.

Theo crawled onto my lap, reaching for the phone. "I want to see," he moaned.

"You should not let him watch this," I said to Helena, holding the phone up so Theo could not grab it. "This is not for children." She smiled and replied, "Oh, he has seen it already … he really wanted to. I told him he would not be able to sleep, but he wanted to see it."

I passed the mobile back to Helena. Theo, still trying to get his hands on the phone, followed and nestled back into Helena's lap. "It's about what Indonesia did to Timor-Leste," Theo said proudly. "I learned about it in school; many, many people died."

· · ·

Can the language of suffering be learned? It seems that both Theo and Helena were becoming versed in the national language of victimhood and trauma. It is a language used to communicate with NGO workers, and it is a language of collective solidarity—one that lends itself particularly well to the grand project of building a nation. People in Timor-Leste have come to frame their experiences during the Indonesian occupation in this language of suffering and trauma, as it allows them to make claims to the condition of victimhood. This is true not just in Timor-Leste. As Fassin and Rechtman have pointed out, suffering in contemporary society is no longer expressed in terms of inequality or redistribution, but through the notion of trauma and associated moral and political assumptions.[2]

When I first visited Timor-Leste in 2005, only a few people in Laclubar subdistrict knew how to speak this particular language of suffering. The situation was clearly different in other areas, where people recounted the suffering they experienced during the occupation with a sense of dignity and pride. In 2012 and, more significantly, in 2015, when I returned, many Funar villagers had started to frame previous experiences in terms of the Indonesian occupation and the struggle for independence. By comparison, in 2005–07, they hardly ever did so. Moreover, in 2015, veteran pensions were a significant part of the incomes of quite a few of the people whom I met during my fieldwork, which meant that these individuals had successfully claimed the status of victim or resistance fighter (or relative thereof), which qualified a person for this pension. A cynical view, articulated by friends in Dili, is that the government's veterans' pension program accelerated the framing of individuals' past experiences in terms of victimhood and repression.

---

[1] I now have doubts about whether all the images were, indeed, from the 1999 massacres, since I could not obtain any evidence for the existence of such footage. Nevertheless, a number of Timorese friends and acquaintances asserted that they had seen footage of the 1999 massacres.

[2] Fassin and Rechtman, *The Empire of Trauma*, 19.

Yet for the large part I would say that the fact that Funar's residents were slow to adopt the language of national victimhood and suffering does not mean that it was any less authentic for them, or that when it was finally used it did not express genuine suffering or pain. Helena's life, for example, had been shaped strongly by the poverty and dislocation that her parents experienced due to the Indonesian occupation. However, it took her some time to connect her own personal trajectory to the national discourses of suffering that was circulating in the country. Once she tuned into these narratives, the emotions attached to them mingled with other feelings, like loneliness: "When I feel alone, I watch [the video clip]." Ten-year-old Theo learned to speak the language of national suffering when he was still young, in history classes at school. The circulation of violent video clips reinvigorates the pain, sustains the suffering, and, perhaps, allows people to relive some of the traumatic experiences. The watching of such videos, and the sometimes clichéd retelling of Timor-Leste's national history, allows individuals to stake a claim to this nation.

My initial research objective was to study people's memories of the Indonesian occupation, yet, in the years immediately after independence, residents of Funar spoke little about this period unless I prompted them to do so. By the end of my initial fieldwork in 2007, I was still unable to reconstruct in any meaningful way what life had been like during the Indonesian military occupation for those communities that later resettled in Laclubar Town. Only a few residents openly declared that they had been supporters of "self-rule" (*ukun rasik aan*), and fewer still framed their political thinking, past experiences, and hopes about the future in nationalistic terms. What they discussed with me in great detail was their relationship with the ancestral land and their investment in "following ancestral ways."

Since the end of my doctoral fieldwork in 2007, much has changed. Whenever I return, new buildings have popped up in Funar. Today, the road is in better condition and there are more cars and motorbikes. Many houses have access to electricity, either through a generator or solar panels. The dirt floors of the houses are slowly being covered with cement. Since 2007, Timor-Leste's state budget has been growing rapidly, relying heavily on the country's Petroleum Fund. Development projects are making their mark, money is gradually finding its way to the countryside, and pensions are handed out to every adult over sixty. In Funar, residents have more money than they did immediately after independence, and thus people can afford mobile phones, motorbikes, and increased numbers of livestock. They are not rich, but their lives are changing; more than that, they are slowly becoming part of the East Timorese nation.

I started this book by asking why people in Funar seemed so unconcerned by the recent occupation and conflict, yet so attached to their ancestral land and customs. When I first carried out fieldwork, only a few people in this region had access to the language of trauma and to any post-conflict development apparatus (including NGOs and government agencies providing funds for post-conflict reconstruction — very few of these agencies were active in Laclubar in the years after the country regained independence). It was a transitional phase, and the inhabitants of Laclubar subdistrict were in an awkward position. Few people in this region were active independence or FRETILIN supporters; most members of the elite had chosen either the UDT party or the pro-Indonesian APODETI.[3] Moreover, the last governor of occupied Timor, Abílio José Osório Soares, was from Laclubar, and while under Indonesian rule inhabitants of the Laclubar subdistrict may have benefited from this political connection. Yet despite this connection, many inhabitants decided to stay in Timor-Leste when their relatives fled across the border to Indonesia in 1999. They were certainly not all collaborators, but neither were they all guerrilla fighters or war heroes. In the post-occupation period, which was characterized by bipolar thinking—a conceptual division between opportunists and oppressed, collaborators and heroes—there was no place in the collective nationalist imagination for the ambiguity characteristic of inhabitants of the Laclubar subdistrict. This does not mean that they did not experience suffering; rather, it means that following independence their suffering could not be so easily matched with nationalist discourses of resistance.

It took residents of the Laclubar subdistrict quite some time to integrate their experiences into nationalist discourses, which shows the limitations of nationalist rhetoric in capturing the diverse choices and sacrifices people made during the occupation. It may well be—and the *krise* of 2006 seems to support this—that even in regions where residents embraced nationalist discourses more swiftly, some groups and individuals were left feeling excluded from nation-building processes and as a result experienced the sense that they did not get the recognition they deserved.

In this book, I have sought to capture another dimension of post-conflict recovery, one that was perhaps accentuated during the period of transition. I have teased out people's non-narrative engagement with the past via the land that not only embodies the ancestors, but has also absorbed their actions. Funar's inhabitants dealt with the past via the ancestral landscape, since their sense of self and personhood is closely interwoven with their place of origin. The return to the ancestral land, the revival of ancestral traditions, and the reinvigoration of potent sites were all ways of responding to the experiences of conflict, loss, and displacement. This reunification with the land and the revival of ancestral ways were forms of recovering from the past, but they also generated new tensions and fears.

This emphasis on the revitalization of ancestral practices and customs is not unique to Funar, as ethnographic studies from elsewhere in the country make apparent. In the introduction, I outlined two different ways in which scholars describe such practices: either in terms of their continuity and its restorative effects, or by paying attention to the ambiguities and paradoxes that characterized the post-occupation years. This book adds to the first approach by arguing that the reinvigoration of ancestral practices immediately after independence was a way of dealing with past conflicts, including the Indonesian occupation. The past is addressed by settling unfulfilled obligations toward life-giving entities, including the ancestors, other social groups (such as wife-givers), and the ancestral land. This study also highlights how the recovery process was fragile, and how the practices that were being revived were perennially subject to dispute and contestation.

My argument is that continuity and contestation are, in fact, interdependent. Funar residents evoked the notion of a golden and unchanging ancestral past to

---

[3] FRETILIN (Frente Revolucionária de Timor-Leste Independente, Revolutionary Front for an Independent East Timor); UDT, (União Democrática Timorense, Timorese Democratic Union), and APODETI (Associacão Popular Democratica Timorense, Timorese Popular Democratic Association, East Timor).

counterbalance the tensions and ambiguities they encountered in the present. The post-occupation period was a time of uncertainty, and not knowing what the future would bring increased residents' desire to invest heavily in the image of a permanent golden past. It may well be that with increasing integration into the nation, the influence of discourses of modernity, or growing political stability, identification with other, more transient notions will gain prominence. However, in a time of uncertainty, the unchanging ancestral realm provided a sense of stability. In addition, references to an unchanging ancestral realm were a crucial aspect of negotiating status.

RISKS OF RECOGNITION

When Funar villagers moved back to the land of the ancestors and began rebuilding their origin houses, disagreements about how groups related to one another and to the ancestral landscape began to surface. There were differing interpretations of the origin narratives that recounted the ancestral journeys and the claims to status that could be deduced from them. Rather than providing resolution, ritual interactions rendered these otherwise undisclosed and incongruous claims visible. For example, the inauguration of Berlibu's scepter house involved the public recounting of Berlibu's origin narrative, which led a number of villagers to express doubts about its truthfulness. The reconstruction of Bamatak's scepter house not only brought to the fore contestations about the status of the house vis-à-vis other houses, but also created disagreements amongst its members. The inauguration of Manehiak's *lulik* house and the transfer of José caused tensions between Manehiak's members and their wife-takers from Ada Soran. These events were occasions during which lingering tensions and unresolved differences frequently came to the surface.

This book has demonstrated how house groups' status differences were asserted and reconfigured during ritual encounters. By invoking a fixed ancestral order, residents sought to make claims regarding the status of their own house groups authoritative and unassailable. The members of Lawadu (Manehiak and Manekaoli), for example, maintained that their high status as *liurai* was determined during the time of the ancestors, when their ancestors won a contest against Bamatak thanks to the superiority of their customs for burying the dead. Bamatak's members asserted that their *lulik* objects were so potent that they caused other origin houses to go up in flames. Autochthonous house groups (i.e., Berlibu, Bubai, and Fahelihun) emphasized their status as "people of the land," although some (e.g., Berlibu) also maintained that they had received a scepter from the Portuguese so as to highlight their entitlement to political power, whereas in other contexts Manehiak and Manekaoli also claimed an autochthonous origin in Funar.

The reconstruction of Funar was characterized by continuous contestations over authority. One of the key points of contention was the power of the *liurai*, in particular, the question of whether they were entitled to "give orders" to other villagers. Some stressed the independence and autonomy of their house group, while others emphasized the overarching authority of the *liurai*. This competition over status shows that social relations were not simply reproduced during the revival of ancestral practices, but were transformed and recalibrated. The effects of these contestations were readily apparent in the election of 2009, when a non-*liurai* person was elected to the office of village chief. Sacred sites in the landscape served as the *matériel* for people's challenges to status and rank and for their contradictory claims over the "true" nature of the supposedly unchanging hierarchical order.

When renegotiating social and hierarchical relations between house groups, local residents concealed their own intentions and apportioned agency to an external source. This was the case, for example, when Manehiak's members maintained that they did not *choose* José to become the guardian of their *lulik* house, but were simply following the preferences of the ancestors. References to a primordial and predetermined ancestral realm were used to legitimize these types of claims. As Keane has argued, material and linguistic signs of authority must appear "natural" to be effective; they must conceal human intention.[4] Similarly, for ritual interactions (or "scenes of encounter") to be authoritative, they need to appeal to an agency that is assumed to transcend that of those present. This was readily apparent in Funar, where people tapped into the agency of the ancestors to make their status claims more authoritative than otherwise possible.

The encounters among house groups during ritual performances, when origin narratives are publicly recounted, thus present a challenge: will those who witness the claims to status accept them? In other words, to legitimize their status, house groups depend upon one another for recognition and acknowledgement. The need to be recognized by others creates mutual dependence.[5] This is the contradiction I have in mind when I say that the post-conflict situation has made inherent contradictions in people's cultural logics visible. This tension between autonomy and interdependence characterized many aspects of the cultural revival in Funar, including knowledge practices, the rebuilding of origin houses, and exchange relations among house groups. As Keane points out, it is not enough to assert that ritual perpetuates domination or the distribution of political authority within a given context.[6] Rather, it is essential to explore the inherent hazards and risks involved in these encounters. Keane holds that for signs to be representations of authority, they must be prone to failure. Ritual may perpetuate domination of some groups over others, but it is an inherently risky venture.

In line with Keane's argument, ritual practices in Funar, such as the inauguration of origin houses or agricultural sites, pose as much risk as they enable assertions of status and domination. Local residents recognize that rituals might fail, and I have given examples of such instances, including the near-failure of the *lulik* possession when Manehiak's *ada lelo* was inaugurated, and the aborted inauguration of Bamatak's scepter house. The main risk, it seems, stems from the possibility that house groups will not be recognized by others. In Funar, too, then, the authoritative nature of ritual action is dependent on the very real possibility that it might fail. Nonetheless, in some of the cases I described, it seems as if the participants *expected* the failure of rituals. The anticipation of failure may not only be due to the inherent hazards of ritual encounters, but may also have been accentuated by a history of inequalities, past obligations, and ongoing disputes. These made it hard for villagers to overcome or control the hazards of social and ritual interaction.

This became particularly clear in my discussion of the transfer of José from the wife-taking Ada Soran to the wife-giving Manehiak (Chapter 4). Members of Manehiak expressed their worries about the dangers of the inauguration of

---

[4] Keane, *Signs of Recognition*, 20.

[5] Ibid., 16.

[6] Ibid., xiv, 6, 23.

Manehiak's *lulik* house well in advance. Their worries were well founded, since the event did, indeed, lead to conflict when the members of Ada Soran resisted Manehiak's claims to José. The tensions surrounding José's transfer must be understood in their historical context, in the sense that the obligations toward Manehiak (as wife-givers) today are structurally similar to past obligations toward the *liurai*, when commoners could not pay their taxes and had to pass children to *liurai* as domestic servants or slaves.

There is a further dimension to the hazards of ritual encounters: they are associated not only with the possibility of failed recognition by other house groups or with long-standing conflicts among groups, but also with the dangers posed by the ancestors and by *lulik* land. The former, who are embodied in the landscape and are objectified in territorially rooted origin houses, are a source of well-being and prosperity. The reconstruction of Funar involved the reestablishment of appropriate relations with these emplaced ancestors, who had been neglected during the time of the villagers' forced resettlement. As I mentioned in Chapter 1, local residents frequently spoke about the powerful qualities of the ancestors and the landscape; they idealized ancestral times by nostalgically claiming that, in the past, golden discs used to fly to Funar and gold used to hover over *lulik* mountains. This was a time of well-being and prosperity, because the ancestors knew the "customs" of "receiving" the gold.

PRIMARY RELATIONS

How can we make sense of the discrepancy between people's ideal of fixity and their actual experience of conflict and contestation over ancestral words, house membership, and status? In the comparative regional literature, we find an emphasis both on the fluidity of social identity and on notions of permanence and rootedness. An example of the former is the idea that, in Southeast Asia, personhood is malleable and not given at birth, but rather constituted throughout life through practices such as commensality.[7] An example of the latter can be found in scholarship that focuses on the importance of the notion of origins amongst Austronesian peoples.[8] Both elements, the malleability as well as the permanence of personhood, were present in Funar, where people responded to experiences of rupture, dislocation, and historical uncertainty by taking the opportunity to refashion the social hierarchy. The most legitimate way of doing so was to invoke a never-changing ancestral order. It is this emphasis on fixity that allowed people to make claims to status in the first place. The paradox is that apparently permanent ancestral identities must be constantly reworked and sustained.

This paradox characterizes ritual interactions not just in Funar,[9] but, as I have demonstrated in several chapters, it has become particularly accentuated there due to the physical destruction of origin houses and people's forced dislocation. When they returned to their ancestral land, Funar residents were confronted with a kind of tabula rasa, where the challenge was to rebuild the village, the social hierarchy, and

---

[7] See: Carsten, "The Substance of Kinship and the Heat of the Hearth," 224; and Fox, "The House as a Type of Social Organisation on the Island of Roti," 174.

[8] See: Errington, "Recasting Sex, Gender, and Power," 47–49; and Fox, introduction to *Origins, Ancestry and Alliance.*

[9] Keane, *Signs of Recognition,* 18, 27.

signs of authority more or less from scratch, while having to sustain the notion that nothing much had changed, since this notion was key to the way claims to authority could be made in the first place.

By seeking to reconnect with the ancestral land, the residents of Funar were not just reconstituting existing hierarchies, they were also reinvigorating a primary relationship with the life-giving land. Hence, this book speaks to phenomenological approaches to place that emphasize the primacy of dwelling. It does so by showing how much effort and work need to be invested in sustaining primordial relations with the land and with the ancestors. In Funar, this effort included looking after the land and ensuring that the connection with it was fully recovered. Another contribution of this book is my exploration of how the maintenance of primordial relations with place can also be risky. This is because absolute unification with the land only occurs upon death. Hence, reconnecting with the land involved the danger of becoming part of the land in a nondifferentiated state, which would mean collapsing into a primordial unity where humans and the nonhuman environment are no longer differentiated.

Having moved back to the land of the ancestors, which they call the "trunk of life," Funar residents aimed to revive relations with the ancestral realm in an effort to mobilize its life-giving properties. In this sense, the return to Funar can be understood as a direct response to past ruptures, as well as a way of recovering from these ruptures. However, this process was not simply a form of psychological reconstruction; rather, it entailed reconstituting a unity with the land, between ancestors and descendants, trunk and tips. In moving back, inhabitants were not just seeking recognition from other house groups and from the ancestors, they were also trying to negate their previous separation from the land.

Although people strive to "follow the ancestors," the ancestors are a constantly threatening presence. If people do not adhere to their ways, they risk illness, infertility, war, and death. The relationship of the living to the ancestors has probably always been one of fear, awe, and respect. However, as I argue in Chapter 6, the fact that Funar's inhabitants neglected the ancestral land during their forced exodus meant that their relationship with the land became particularly strained. The revival of ancestral traditions is about satisfying the ancestors that inhabit the land, thereby making up for the years of neglect by fulfilling obligations toward life-giving entities while also establishing a healthy distance from them. Moreover, the notion that the land is part of human existence before life and after death also indicates that fear of the land is equally a fear of a part of the self that has become externalized.

When viewed in the additional context of post-occupation poverty, the need to attend to the land and to the ancestors that were neglected may explain the comparative lack of attention paid to ritualized marriage exchanges (Chapter 5). It may be that Funar's inhabitants partly retreated from marriage ceremonies to avoid obligations and dependency in the context of general mistrust and political division. It is equally possible that villagers were so concerned with the wrath of their neglected ancestors that most of the ritual attention was focused on restoring relationships with the dead as opposed to the living.[10] In analyzing the origin narratives of the "people of the land," it seems that the primary debt is toward the land that gave birth to humans. Perhaps it is only after that primary relationship is

---

[10] Compare with Sakti, "'Thinking Too Much.'"

attended to that people feel able to risk investing more fully in alliances with other house groups.

LIFE AS SACRIFICE

Origin narratives in Funar involve two related presuppositions. First, there is an a priori distinction between types of people, apparent in the fact that different house groups are thought to have independent origins; and second, there is a strong notion of nondifferentiation, evident in the suggestion that there is an original consubstantial unity between people and the land. Human ancestors are the extensions or offspring of the landscape; they are part of it, yet have been separated from it. To create life, something needs to be given up or sacrificed, and thus the unity between land and people is relinquished so that human beings can come into existence and establish their house groups. This is reminiscent of Bruce Lincoln's conceptualization of sacrifice as transformative negation, according to which "one entity [...] is given up for the benefit of some other species, group, god, or principle that is understood to be 'higher' or more deserving in one fashion or another."[11] What is significant about this definition for the case discussed here is that through the original sacrifice, which produced life, the very entities involved in this process are transformed.

In his analysis of sacrifice, Lincoln interprets certain Indo-European practices—such as the debreasting of the Amazons or other forms of surgical intervention—as ritual reenactments of origin myths, in which sacrifice results in transformative negation. This has a parallel in Funar. When returning to the ancestral land, Funar's inhabitants emphasized their wish to live just like the ancestors, paying little attention to recent historical episodes of occupation and dislocation. The latter reproduced the mythic separation of humans from the landscape, yet, during the occupation, the result of this separation was not the genesis of human groups, but rather death and suffering. The separation from the land was so extreme that no fruitful connection could be maintained therewith. This explains why moving back to the ancestral land was such a central concern for the people of Funar, because their return involved a reconnection with the source of life and thus a reenactment of people's mythic unification with the land. This reconnection with the "trunk of life" involved negating the previous separation (when resettled) and reestablishing the primordial unity between people and place.

In some instances, however, humans can become part of the land while they are still alive, and this is another cause for anxiety and dread. During my fieldwork, I was told on a number of occasions that the land had imprisoned a particular person's soul (see Chapter 5). This meant that the body of the person was still amongst the living, but the soul (*sumanar*) had become part of the land. One symptom of this condition was severe illness, which was interpreted as the body wanting to follow the soul back into the earth. Another way in which people could identify that the unification of a person's soul with the land had taken place was if they heard human cries from the cemetery, where the land had imprisoned human souls. People tried to counteract this by making animal sacrifices to the land, but these sacrifices were not always successful. Some people suffered for years and experienced severe health

---

[11] Bruce Lincoln, *Death, War, and Sacrifice: Studies in Ideology and Practice* (Chicago: The University of Chicago Press, 1991), 204.

problems until eventually they died, while their *sumanar* remained "imprisoned" (*kastigu*) by *lulik* land at the cemetery.[12]

Moving back following their resettlement, Funar's inhabitants faced the challenge of finding a balanced relationship with the ancestral land. When the villagers were forcibly dislocated, they were disconnected from the source of life and prosperity. The balance between the differentiation and unification of people and land was pushed too far toward separation, so that people were entirely disconnected from their most significant source of life. Upon their return, the villagers sought to reestablish a relationship with the land without reverting to the original unity of consubstantiality.

The forced displacement of Funar's inhabitants at the onset of the Indonesian occupation involved the total separation of people from the land, echoing the original mythic separation of the two when the ancestors emerged from the land and were hence separated from it, albeit in a much more tumultuous and violent fashion. When the villagers moved back, they had to negate this separation to reconnect themselves to the source of life. In returning to Funar, the villagers reestablished the mythic unity between land and people, a unity that had to be negated to reproduce life. In that sense, the return migration may be understood as a negation of the original negation.

In his study of Yukaghirs in northeastern Siberia, Rane Willerslev analyzes ideas about how humans and animals can turn into each other temporarily during hunting, while also emphasizing the dangers this process is thought to entail. He captures this tension between the need to imitate animals and the dangers this poses by arguing, following Schechner, that during the mimetic practices employed during a hunt, Yukaghirs become "not animal, and not not-animal."[13] One may describe Funar villagers' relationship with the ancestral land—what I framed in terms of the Goldilocks principle in Chapter 6—in a similar way: when returning to their ancestral lands, Funar residents were confronted with the need to become just like the ancestors, while needing to make sure they never became fully identified with them. They had to be not ancestors (as this would imply death) and not not-ancestors.

The main argument of this monograph is that the inhabitants of Funar responded to being uprooted by connecting themselves to a mythic ancestral past. Their unification with the ancestral land was itself a way of responding to past events. Human beings are considered to be constituted from the nonhuman environment and to share a primordial unity with its ancestral form. The revival of ancestral customs and the reunification with the ancestral land represents an attempt to "escape" history and to reproduce the original unity. Yet such attempts are frequently unsuccessful, as the past inevitably imprints itself onto social existence. Rather than interpreting people's reluctance to speak about the traumatic events of colonization, occupation, and dislocation as a form of psychological repression or post-traumatic stress, I have shown how these experiences are implicit in people's

---

[12] For a more detailed analysis of this argument, see Bovensiepen, "Lulik: Taboo, Animism, or Transgressive Sacred?"

[13] Rane Willerslev, "Not Animal, Not Not-Animal: Hunting, Imitation and Empathetic Knowledge among the Siberian Yukaghirs," *The Journal of the Royal Anthropological Institute* 10, no. 3 (2004), 649.

daily practices, in their engagement with the landscape, and in the ritualized reconstruction of ancestral houses.

Despite the emphasis on the value of the ancestral land as a source of wealth, morality, and prosperity, there is an equally strong sense that the neglected ancestral land has increasingly become a source of threat and danger due to the bloodshed it has absorbed and the neglected reciprocal relations towards it. The key to grasping this apparent paradox lies in a particular understanding of place and personhood that has shaped the experience of recent historical events. Exploring the burdens that the primordial unity of people and place imposes on people's daily lives provides the basis for understanding the return to the ancestral land as a mythical reenactment of a primordial state. This emerges not just in their mode of being in place and history, but also in the ways that they approach knowledge, exchange, and death. Dealing with the emotional and moral dilemmas and the political conflicts that the unification with the ancestral land provokes is central to understanding post-conflict recovery.

A GOLDEN PAST

Nunuk Lawadu	A Lawadu banyan tree
Nunuk huan kaek	A banyan tree with small/ green fruits
Natehe no larek	Casts its shadow over the land[14]
Nunuk huan bear	With sweet fruits

Members of the origin house Lawadu told me these verses to illustrate what the ancestral land and the ancestral houses meant to them. The ancestors are like the trunk of a tree—the banyan tree that once stood on top of Mount Lawadu—and the ancestors' protection allows their descendants to prosper (become "sweet").

We can use the image of the banyan tree and its fruits/tip to conceptualize social and historical transformations. The recent historical and political events can be seen as the "tip"—impermanent and constantly changing—whereas the ancestral realm is akin to the fixed and rooted ancestral trunk. This way of thinking is exemplified by the suggestion that the Portuguese only gave a scepter to the *liurai* because the *liurai*'s entitlement to rule had been predetermined during ancestral times. In this way, the ancestral trunk both produces and encompasses the impermanent events of the present. Thus, recent historical developments are dependent on and contained by a fixed, predetermined ancestral past. Social relations may be contested and changeable, but transformations only occur within the limits of what has been decided by the ancestors. This means that people can dare to take risks in everyday life (at the level of the tip) as long as they stay anchored at the base (the trunk). The botanical metaphor of the banyan tree that is so frequently evoked in the region provides a dynamic model of social change, since it entails a sense of encompassment, growth, and diversification.[15]

---

[14] Several people have translated the third line as "puts its shadow over all people." I have chosen a more literal translation ("casts its shadow over the land"), but here the term "land" (*larek*) also stands for the people who inhabit it. Moreover, people use both *nunuk* and *hali* to refer to a banyan tree, *hali* being the same as its Tetum equivalent.

[15] Compare with: McKinnon, *From a Shattered Sun*, 133; and Fox, introduction to *Origins, Ancestry and Alliance*, 8.

As I mentioned above, the paradox lies in the fact that while people see their political hierarchy as encompassed by the ancestral past (the trunk), they nonetheless have to engage in a collective effort to maintain the image of permanence. Although descendants (fruits and flowers, the impermanent tip) are produced and encompassed by the ancestral world, much of the work of reviving the ancestral traditions involves sustaining the ancestors as an external source of life and potency. While the ancestral land (the trunk of life) is thought to have given rise to its human offspring, it is the latter who need to sustain the former, creating permanence out of the impermanent flow of life. This involves making the invisible world of the ancestors visible by creating enduring material signs that index ancestral presence and authority, including origin houses, *lulik* objects, stone graves, and fenced mounds of stones to protect subterranean gold. This process entails transforming the invisible potency of the ancestors, who have the ability to affect the world of the living, into visible signs of authority.

In the narratives I discussed in the first two chapters, the potency of the ancestral land is associated with gold. Gold epitomizes potency not only because it symbolizes wealth, but also because of its enduring material qualities. The simultaneous durability and malleability of gold make it a particularly pertinent emblem for the ancestral world. As for Lio of Flores,[16] gold is life-giving; it is a sign of a fused identity when the material world (objects, houses, places) is imbued with a spiritual (human or nonhuman) presence. I chose to call this book *The Land of Gold* because the revival of the potent ancestral realm was one of the foremost concerns for the highlanders in the years after Timor-Leste regained independence. The notion of "the land of gold" embodies residents' hopes concerning fertility and agricultural productivity, which depend on the establishment of an appropriate relationship with the ancestors and the landscape. It also stands for some of the utopian hopes associated with gold, such as the idea that subterranean riches can bring wealth, enduring prosperity, well-being, and quite possibly sudden societal transformation.

Assertions about the abundance of gold in Funar were accompanied by fears that foreigners would steal it. This anxiety resonates with concerns that the prosperous world of the ancestors may not be completely recaptured, as well as with fears about the colonial or neocolonial theft and exploitation of local resources. These fears are rooted in history, not only because the search for gold was a motivating factor in Portuguese colonial expansion, but also because other natural resources (especially oil and gas) played a part in Indonesia's occupation and continue to attract foreign interest and claims today.

For anyone familiar with the history of Timor-Leste and its long struggle for independence, it may seem absurd to speak about a "land of gold"—after all, one's immediate associations with this country are likely to be mass violence and political conflict. However, I employ this phrase to draw attention to both the destructive and productive potential associated with gold, and all the things that gold implies. For many residents of the Laclubar subdistrict, gold stands for *lulik*, a characteristically indigenous ancestral potency. Gold signifies the potency of their objects, origin houses, and the life-giving properties of the ancestral landscape. I also use the phrase "land of gold" figuratively—first, to refer to people's utopian ideas surrounding this potency and, second, to allude to the colonial history of Timor-Leste, in which the quest for wealth was a significant motivating factor that drove colonial exploitation.

---

[16] Howell, "Of Persons and Things," 422. See also Chapter 1.

Even though people in Funar strove to recapture the "golden" ancestral past, there were often moments during which they disengaged from the ancestors and defied the past instead. This was frequently the case at events that were described as "busy" or "lively" (*rame*), such as festivities that involved dancing or singing.[17] Recall the ritual chanting (*loli*) during funerals or the singing of harvest songs, which gave rise to an animated sense of sociability and vitality. On other occasions, villagers, especially young adults, invested a lot of effort into organizing festive events where they could dance and be in a crowded and busy space—*rame rame*, as they would say. For this purpose, tents were erected to create a dance floor. There, in a crowded space, people danced in couples, by the light of candles and to the sound of songs in Portuguese or Tetum played on a small tape recorder, until dawn.

Once I was sensitive to the frictions and risks that characterized everyday life in Funar, I realized that people could detach themselves from the ancestors by organizing "crowded" events. These were times when people effectively allowed themselves to live in the moment and were temporarily disengaged from the burden of the past. What villagers said they liked about these events was the noise and the vitality of human bodies—the very sense of "crowdedness" and "liveliness." It was during these moments of heightened sociality and sociability that people were most distant from the dead and from obligations toward ancestors and the land. At times, there was an atmosphere of defiance as people separated themselves from the fear and tension that were so commonplace at other times. This was apparent, for example, in the sheer enjoyment of the present moment, and in *rame* activities, such as playing music or dancing, which are entirely opposed to the sincerity and heaviness that can be associated with the dead. Following the ancestors in every aspect meant pursuing death, because it is upon death that one becomes an ancestor. There may be an enduring ancestral order that people refer to and become part of when they die, but as humans they live in the ever-changing present. A certain element of impermanence and fluidity is necessary to distance oneself from the permanent realm of the dead. Through the dancing, the noise, and the crowdedness, Funar residents recognized that the living cannot be exactly like the ancestors—that tips cannot be trunks.

---

[17] *Rame*, or *ramai* in Indonesian, is a term that is often associated with crowded or noisy events; see Catherine L. Allerton, "Making Guests, Making 'Liveliness': the Transformative Substances and Sounds of Manggarai Hospitality," in "The Return to Hospitality: Strangers, Guests, and Ambiguous Encounters," ed. Matei Candea and Giovanni da Col, special issue, *Journal of the Royal Anthropological Institute* 18, no. S1 (2012): S49–S62.

GLOSSARY

Selected Idaté Words[1]

ada — house

ada lelo — lit. "house of the sun"; house of spiritual potency opposed to the house of the scepter (*ada ua*) representing political power

ada lisan — "customary house"; a generic, umbrella term used for different kinds of origin houses; used interchangeably with *ada lulin* and *ada ulun*

ada lulin — *lulik* house (also referred to as *ada lulik*)

(1) named ancestral origin house comprising a number of smaller side houses; used interchangeably with *ada lisan* and *ada ulun*
(2) sacred house, house of spiritual potency or ritual authority; used interchangeably with *ada lelo* and opposed to *ada ua*[2]
(3) proper name (written Ada Lulin) to refer to the *lulik* house of Bamatak

ada soran — houses that are comprised within a named origin house; lit. "side houses" (also the proper name of one such house when written with capital letters as Ada Soran)

ada ua — house of political power; lit. "house of the scepter"

ada ulun — lit. "head house"; generic term for an origin house that encompasses a number of smaller houses, also referred to as *ada lisan* (customary house) and *ada lulik*

aldeia — hamlet; basic territorial division below the *suco* level

anamahinak — wife-takers; lit. "female children"

---

[1] Several of the terms listed here are the same in Tetum, others derive from Portuguese.

[2] The term *ada lulin* is used as an umbrella term for origin houses in general *and* it is used for one element in a complementary pair, *ada lulik* opposed to *ada ua* (sacred house opposed to scepter house). Hence, one term of the binary opposition also represents the whole, which is a common feature of categorical asymmetry, according to James J. Fox, "Category and Complement: Binary Ideologies and the Organization of Dualism in Eastern Indonesia," in *The Attraction of Opposites*, eds. David Maybury-Lewis and Uri Almagor (Ann Arbor: The University of Michigan Press, 1989), 47.

anan kiak	"poor child," often given as translation for the Tetum term *oan hakiak*, foster child
arisa	complete payment of *helin* leading to integration of a woman into her husband's origin house
asuwa'in	warrior
atan	slave
avô/avó	grandparent, ancestor; way of addressing elders—*avó* for women, *avô* for men, per the Portuguese spelling
banas	hot
dato	(1) ritual authority or guardian of a *lulik* house (2) "aristocracy," nobles
haha	words, language, speech, ritual
haha metan	death ritual when a person has died of natural causes
haha meran	death ritual when a person has died a "bad death"
hali/halik	banyan tree, also *nunuk*
helin	marriage payment/compensation
lamuruk	cold
larek	land (*namo* refers to specific plots)
larek-nain	lit. "person/master/owner of the land" (1) autochthonous people, i.e., human land owners (2) land spirits (also *namo-nain*), i.e., nonhuman land owners
lisan	custom, tradition; also referred to as *adat* (Indonesian), *kultura*, and *tradisaun*
liurai	ruler, king, "native chief"
lulik/luli	potent and proscribed; frequently translated as "sacred," "taboo," "holy," and "prohibited"; can be used as noun, verb, or adjective
luliwai	ancestor (*avô* is more commonly used)
maes	fear, respect, awe
mainheri	spirit of the dead (*matebian* in Tetum, which is frequently used)

malae	foreigner
matebian	spirit of the dead (Tetum); also *mainheri* (Idaté)
nain	person, master, owner, custodian
naiuun	wife-givers; lit. "my mother's trunk"
namo	specific plots of land (*larek*); field
namo-nain	nonhuman land owners, land spirits (also *larek-nain*)
nunuk	banyan tree, also *hali/halik*
osa meran	gold
reino	kingdom, domain, chieftaincy
selu mate	mortuary payments
suco	"village"; administrative unit below the subdistrict level
sumanar	soul
ua	scepter; refers to other objects that are emblems of political power; other translations include cane, staff, or rattan stick (*bastão* in Portuguese)
ukun	political power, rule
usar	navel
uun	trunk, base, source, origin
wai matan	(1) hearth (2) "household" (people living together sharing a fireplace)
walin	younger sibling (m/f); placenta

Acronyms

APODETI   Associação Popular Democrática Timorense, Popular Democratic Association of East Timor. Political party founded in 1974 that supported East Timor's integration with Indonesia.

ASDT   Associação Social Democrática Timorense, Social Democratic Association of East Timor. Founded in 1974 in favor of independence, later became FRETILIN. In 2001, it was revived by Francisco Xavier do Amaral as a party independent from FRETILIN.

CAVR   Comissão de Acolhimento, Verdade e Reconciliação de Timor-Leste, Commission for Reception, Truth, and Reconciliation. An independent statutory authority established in 2001 to document and record information about violence and crimes committed between 1974–99.

FALINTIL   Forças Armadas de Libertação Nacional de Timor-Leste, National Liberation Forces of East Timor. Formed in August 1975, dissolved in January 2001.

FRETILIN   Frente Revolucionária de Timor-Leste Independente, Revolutionary Front for an Independent East Timor. Political party with a socialist agenda that was in favor of independence and played an essential part in the resistance struggle. In September 1974, ASDT changed its name to FRETILIN.

UDT   União Democrática Timorense, Democratic Timorese Union. Political party founded in 1974 in favor of independence after a period of federation with Portugal.

BIBLIOGRAPHY

Acciaioli, Greg. "Culture as Art: From Practice to Spectacle in Indonesia." *Canberra Anthropology* 8, no. 1–2 (1985): 148–72.

Allerton, Catherine L. *Potent Landscapes: Place and Mobility in Eastern Indonesia.* Honolulu: University of Hawai'i Press, 2013.

———. "Landscape, Power and Agency in Eastern Indonesia." In *Southeast Asian Perspectives on Power*, ed. Liana Chua, Joanna Cook, Nicholas Long, and Lee Wilson. London: Routledge, 2012, 67–80.

———. "Making Guests, Making 'Liveliness': The Transformative Substances and Sounds of Manggarai Hospitality." In "The Return to Hospitality: Strangers, Guests, and Ambiguous Encounters," ed. Matei Candea and Giovanni da Col, special issue, *Journal of the Royal Anthropological Institute* 18, no. s1 (2012): S49–S62.

———. "Introduction: Spiritual Landscapes of Southeast Asia." In "Spiritual Landscapes in Southeast Asia: Changing Geographies of Potency and the Sacred," ed. Catherine L. Allerton, special issue, *Anthropological Forum* 19, no. 3 (2009): 235–51.

———. "The Path of Marriage: Journeys and Transformation in Manggarai, Eastern Indonesia." *Bijdragen tot de Taal-, Land- en Volkenkunde* 160, no. 2/3 (2004): 339–62.

Amnesty International. *East Timor Violations of Human Rights: Extrajudicial Executions, "Disappearances," Torture and Political Imprisonment, 1975–1984.* London: Amnesty International Publications, 1985.

Archer, Robert. "The Catholic Church in East Timor." In *East Timor at the Crossroads: The Forging of a Nation*, ed. Peter Carey and G. Carter Bentley. Honolulu: University of Hawai'i Press, 1995, 120–33.

Anderson, Benedict R. *Language and Power: Exploring Political Cultures in Indonesia.* The Wilder House Series in Politics, History, and Culture. Ithaca, NY: Cornell University Press, 1990.

Astuti, Rita. "What Happens after Death?" In *Questions of Anthropology*, ed. Rita Astuti, Jonathan Parry, and Charles Stafford. Oxford: Berg, 2007, 227–48.

————. *People of the Sea: Identity and Descent among the Vezo of Madagascar.* Cambridge: Cambridge University Press, 1995.

Atkinson, Jane M. "How Gender Makes a Difference in Wana Society." In *Power and Difference: Gender in Island Southeast Asia*, ed. Jane M. Atkinson and Shelly Errington. Stanford: Stanford University Press, 1990, 59–94.

Barnes, Robert H. "Construction, Sacrifice, Kidnapping and Head-Hunting Rumors on Flores and Elsewhere in Indonesia." *Oceania* 64 (1993): 146–58.

Barnes, Susana. "Origins, Precedence and Social Order in the Domain of Ina Ama Beli Darlari." In McWilliam and Traube, *Land and Life in Timor-Leste*, 23–46.

————. "Gift Giving and Gift Obligations: Strategies of Incorporation and Accommodation in the Customary Domain." Paper presented at the Seventh Euroseas Conference, Lisbon, July 2–5, 2013.

Basso, Keith H. *Wisdom Sits in Places: Landscape and Language among the Western Apache.* Albuquerque: University of New Mexico Press, 1996.

Bellwood, Peter. "Hierarchy, Founder Ideology and Austronesian Expansion." In Fox and Sather, *Origins, Ancestry and Alliance,* 18–40.

Belo, Carlos Filipe Ximenes. *Os Antigos Reinos de Timor-Leste. (Reys de Lorosay e Reys de Lorothoba, Coronéis e Datos).* [The old kingdoms of Timor-Leste. Kings of Lorosay and Kings of Lorothoba, Coronels and Datos.] Baucau: Tipografia Diocesana Baucau, 2011.

Bexley, Angie, and Maj Nygaard-Christensen. Introduction to "Engaging Processes of Sense-Making and Negotiation in Contemporary Timor-Leste," ed. Angie Bexley and Maj Nygaard-Christensen, special issue, *The Asia Pacific Journal of Anthropology* 14, no. 5 (2013): 399–404.

Bexley, Angie, and Nuno Rodrigues Tchailoro. "Consuming Youth: Timorese in the Resistance against Indonesian Occupation." In "Engaging Processes of Sense-Making and Negotiation in Contemporary Timor-Leste," ed. Angie Bexley and Maj Nygaard-Christensen, special issue, *The Asia Pacific Journal of Anthropology* 14, no. 5 (2013): 405–22.

Bloch, Maurice. "Commensality and Poisoning." In *Essays in Cultural Transmission,* ed. Maurice Bloch. London: Athlone, 2005, 45–60.

————. *How We Think They Think: Anthropological Approaches to Cognition, Memory and Literacy.* Oxford: Westview, 1998.

———. *From Blessing to Violence: History and Ideology in the Circumcision Ritual of the Merina of Madagascar*. Cambridge: Cambridge University Press, 1986.

———. "The Past and the Present in the Present." *Man* 12, no. 2 (1977): 278–92.

———. "Symbols, Song, Dance and Features of Articulation: Or Is Religion an Extreme Form of Traditional Authority?" *Archives Européennes de Sociologie* 15 (1974): 497–514.

Bloch, Maurice, and Jonathan Parry. Introduction to *Death and the Regeneration of Life*, ed. Maurice Bloch and Jonathan Parry. Cambridge: Cambridge University Press, 1982, 1–44.

Bourchier, David. "The Romance of Adat in the Indonesian Political Imagination and the Current Revival." In *The Revival of Tradition in Indonesian Politics: The Deployment of Adat from Colonialism to Indigenism*, ed. Jamie S. Davidson and David Henley. London: Routledge, 2007, 113–29.

Bourdieu, Pierre. *The Logic of Practice*. London: Polity Press, 1990.

Bovensiepen, Judith. "Entanglements of Power, Kinship and Time in Laclubar." In *Doing Fieldwork in Timor-Leste*, ed. Maj Nygaard-Christensen and Angie Bexley. Copenhagen: Nias Press, forthcoming.

———. "Diferentes Perspectivas Sobre o Passado: os Portugueses e a Destruição e Vitória de Funar." In *Timor-Leste: Colonialismo, Descolonização, Lusotopia*, ed. Rui Feijó. Porto, Portugal: Afrontamento, forthcoming.

———. "Installing the Outsider 'Inside': House-Reconstruction and the Transformation of Binary Ideologies in Independent Timor-Leste." *American Ethnologist* 41, no. 2 (2014): 290–304.

———. "Lulik: Taboo, Animism or Transgressive Sacred? An Exploration of Identity, Morality and Power in Timor-Leste." *Oceania* 84, no. 2 (2014): 121–37.

———. "Opening and Closing the Land: Land and Power in the Idaté Highlands." In McWilliam and Traube, *Land and Life in Timor-Leste*, 47–60.

———. "Paying for the Dead: On the Politics of Death in Independent Timor-Leste." *The Asia Pacific Journal of Anthropology* 15, no. 2 (2014): 103–22.

———. "Words of the Ancestors: Disembodied Knowledge and Secrecy in East Timor." *Journal of the Royal Anthropological Institute* 20, no. 1 (2014): 56–73.

———. "Ich gebe dir mein Kind: Verwandtschaftsbeziehungen und Pflegschaften in Osttimor." In *Verwandtschaft Heute,* ed. Erdmute Alber, Bettina Beer, Julia Pauli, and Michael Schnegg. Berlin: Reimer, 2010, 73–92.

Boxer, Charles R. *The Portuguese Seaborne Empire 1415–1825.* London: Hutchinson & Co., 1969.

———. *The Topasses of Timor.* Mededeling no. 73. Amsterdam: Koninklijk Vereeniging Indisch Instituut, 1947.

Bubandt, Nils. "Violence and Millenarian Modernity in Eastern Indonesia." In *Cargo, Cult and Culture Critique,* ed. Holger Jebens. Honolulu: University of Hawai'i Press, 2004, 92–116.

Caldwell, Ian, and David Henley, eds. "Stranger Kings in Indonesia and Beyond," special issue, *Indonesia and the Malay World* 36, no. 105 (2008).

Cannell, Fenella. *The Anthropology of Christianity.* Durham: Duke University Press, 2006.

———. *Power and Intimacy in the Christian Philippines.* Cambridge: Cambridge University Press, 1999.

Carsten, Janet. "The Substance of Kinship and the Heat of the Hearth: Feeding, Personhood, and Relatedness among Malays in Pulau Langkawi." *American Ethnologist* 22, no. 2 (1995): 223–41.

Carsten, Janet, and Stephen Hugh-Jones, eds. *About the House: Lévi-Strauss and Beyond.* Cambridge: Cambridge University Press, 1995.

Casey, Edward S. *Getting Back into Place: Toward a Renewed Understanding of the Place-World.* Bloomington: Indiana University Press, 1993.

Certeau, de, Michel. *The Practice of Everyday Life.* Berkeley: University of California Press, 1988.

Commission for Reception, Truth and Reconciliation (CAVR). *Chega! Final Report of the Commission for Reception, Truth and Reconciliation in East Timor (Comissão de Acolhimento, Verdade e Reconciliação de Timor Leste).* Dili: CAVR, 2006.

———. *Report, Inauguration Ceremony and 2nd National Public Hearing.* Balide, Dili, Timor-Leste, February 17–18, 2003; report February 19, 2003.

Clamagirand, Brigitte. "The Social Organization of the Ema of Timor." In Fox, *The Flow of Life,* 134–51.

Cleary, Paul. *Shakedown: Australia's Grab for Timor Oil*. Crows Nest, Australia: Allen & Unwin, 2007.

Cole, Jennifer. *Forget Colonialism? Sacrifice and the Art of Memory in Madagascar*. Berkeley: University of California Press, 2001.

Cotton, James. *East Timor, Australia and the Regional Order: Intervention and Its Aftermath in Southeast Asia*. London: Routledge Curzon, 2004.

Crick, Malcolm R. "Anthropology of Knowledge." *Annual Review of Anthropology* 11 (1982): 287–313.

Cristalis, Irena, and Catherine Scott. *Independent Women: The Story of Women's Activism in East Timor*. London: CIIR (Catholic Institute for International Relations), 2005.

Crook, Tony. *Anthropological Knowledge, Secrecy and Bolivip, Papua New Guinea: Exchanging Skin*. Oxford: Oxford University Press, 2007.

Cunningham, Clark E. "Order in the Atoni House." *Bijdragen tot de Taal-, Land- en Volkenkunde* 120 (1964): 34–68.

Cruz da Silva, Jorge da. *Hanessan Hatohar (Aliança) Maklouk entre Lulik no Religião Católica: Comemoração Igreja Soibada Halo Tinan Atus Ida, 1904–2004*. Baucau, Timor-Leste: Diocese of Baucau, 2004.

Das, Veena, Arthur Kleinman, Margaret Lock, Mamphela Ramphele, and Pamela Reynolds, eds. *Remaking a World: Violence, Social Suffering, and Recovery*. Berkeley: University of California Press, 2001.

Das, Veena, Arthur Kleinman, Mamphela Ramphele, and Pamela Reynolds, eds. *Violence and Subjectivity*. Berkeley: University of California Press, 2000.

Descola, Philippe. "Human Natures." *Social Anthropology/Anthropologie Sociale* 17, no. 2 (2009): 145–57.

———. *Par-delà Nature et Culture*. Paris: Gallimard, 2005.

Dunn, James. *East Timor: A Rough Passage to Independence*, 3rd ed. Double Bay, Australia: Longueville Books, 2003.

Durand, Frédéric. *East Timor: A Country at the Crossroads of Asia and the Pacific: A Geo-Historical Atlas*. Chiang Mai: Silkworm Books; Bangkok: IRASEC, 2006.

———. *Catholicisme et Protestantisme dans l'Ile de Timor 1556–2003: Construction d'une Identité Chrétienne et Engagement Politique Contemporain*. Toulouse: Editions Arkuiris; Bangkok: IRASEC, 2004.

Ellen, Roy. *Nuaulu Ritual Practices: The Frequency and Reproduction of Rituals in a Moluccan Society*. Leiden: KITLV Press, 2012.

Eltringham, Nigel. *Accounting for Horror: Post-Genocide Debates in Rwanda*. London: Pluto Press, 2004.

Errington, Shelly. "Recasting Sex, Gender, and Power: A Theoretical and Regional Overview." In *Power and Difference: Gender in Island Southeast Asia*, ed. Jane M. Atkinson and Shelly Errington. Stanford: Stanford University Press, 1990, 1–58.

Farmer, Paul. *Pathologies of Power: Health, Human Rights, and the New War on the Poor*. Berkeley: University of California Press, 2003.

Fassin, Didier. "The Humanitarian Politics of Testimony: Subjectification through Trauma in the Israeli–Palestinian Conflict." *Cultural Anthropology* 23, no. 3 (2008): 531–58.

Fassin, Didier, and Richard Rechtman. *The Empire of Trauma: An Inquiry Into the Condition of Victimhood*. Trans. Rachel Gomme. Princeton: Princeton University Press, 2009.

Feeley-Harnik, Gillian. "The Political Economy of Death: Communication and Change in Malagasy Colonial History." *American Ethnologist* 11, no. 1 (1984): 1–19.

Ferguson, James. *Expectations of Modernity: Myths and Meanings of Urban Life on the Zambian Copperbelt*. Berkeley: University of California Press, 1999.

Feuchtwang, Stephan. "Theorising Place." In *Making Place: State Projects, Globalisation and Social Responses in China*, ed. Stephan Feuchtwang. London: UCL Press, 2004, 3–30.

Field, Annette Marie. "Places of Suffering and Pathways to Healing: Post-Conflict Life in Bidau, East Timor." PhD thesis, James Cook University, 2004.

Firoz, Bahar F., Haq Nawaz, James F. Jekel, and Ramin Ahmadi. "Psychiatric Morbidity Associated with Human Rights Abuses in East Timor." Report, Yale Genocide Studies Program: Yale East Timor Project, 2001. http://elsinore.cis.yale.edu/gsp/east_timor/index.html, accessed June 12, 2015.

Fitzpatrick, Daniel, Andrew McWilliam, and Susana Barnes. *Property and Social Resilience in Times of Conflict: Land, Custom and Law in East Timor*. Farnham and Burlington: Ashgate Publishing Company, 2012.

Forman, Shepard. "Descent, Alliance and Exchange Ideology among the Makassae of East Timor." In Fox, *The Flow of Life*, 152–77.

———. "East Timor: Exchange and Political Hierarchy at the Time of the European Discoveries." In *Economic Exchange and Social Interaction in Southeast Asia*, ed. Karl L. Hutterer. Ann Arbor: Center for South and Southeast Studies, University of Michigan, 1978, 97–111.

Forth, Gregory. "Separating the Dead: The Ritual Transformation of Affinal Exchange in Central Flores." *Journal of the Royal Anthropological Institute* 15 (2009): 557–74.

———. *Images of the Wildman in Southeast Asia: An Anthropological Perspective.* London: Routledge, 2008.

———. *Beneath the Volcano: Religion, Cosmology and Spirit Classification among the Nage of Eastern Indonesia.* Leiden: KITLV Press, 1998.

———. *Rindi: An Ethnographic Study of a Traditional Domain in Eastern Sumba.* The Hague: Martinus Nijhoff, Verhandelingen van het Koninklijk Institut voor Taal-, Land- en Volkenkunde, 1981.

Fox, James J. "Installing the 'Outsider' Inside: The Exploration of an Epistemic Austronesian Cultural Theme and Its Social Significance." In "Stranger Kings in Indonesia and Beyond," ed. Ian Caldwell and David Henley, special issue, *Indonesia and the Malay World* 36, no. 105 (2008): 201–18.

———. "Place and Landscape in Comparative Austronesian Perspective." In Fox, *The Poetic Power of Place*, 1–21.

———. "Genealogy and Topogeny: Towards an Ethnography of Rotinese Ritual Place Name." In Fox, *The Poetic Power of Place*, 91–102.

———. Introduction to Fox and Sather, *Origins, Ancestry and Alliance*, 1–17.

———. "The Transformation of Progenitor Lines of Origin: Patterns of Precedence in Eastern Indonesia." In Fox and Sather, *Origins, Ancestry and Alliance*, 130–53.

———. "Comparative Perspectives on Austronesian Houses: An Introductory Essay." In *Inside Austronesian Houses: Perspectives on Domestic Designs for Living*, ed. James J. Fox. Canberra: Australian National University, 1993, 1–28.

———. "Category and Complement: Binary Ideologies and the Organization of Dualism in Eastern Indonesia." In *The Attraction of Opposites*, ed. Maybury-Lewis and Almagor, 33–56.

———. Introduction to *To Speak in Pairs: Essays on the Ritual Languages of Eastern Indonesia*, ed. James J. Fox. Cambridge: Cambridge University Press, 1988, 1–28.

———. "The House as a Type of Social Organisation on the Island of Roti." In *De la Hutte au Palais: Société "A Maison" en Asie du Sud-est Insulaire*, ed. Charles Macdonald and members of the ECASE. Paris: Edition du CNRS, 1987, 171–79.

———. "Adam and Eve on the Island of Roti: A Conflation of Oral and Written Traditions." *Indonesia* 36 (October 1983): 15–23.

———. "On Bad Death and the Left Hand: A Study of Rotinese Symbolic Inversions." In *Right and Left: Essays on Dual Symbolic Classification,* ed. Rodney Needham. Chicago: The University of Chicago Press, 1973, 342–68.

Fox, James J., ed. *The Poetic Power of Place: Comparative Perspectives on Austronesian Ideas of Locality*. Canberra: Australian National University, 1997.

———., ed. *The Flow of Life: Essays on Eastern Indonesia*. Cambridge: Harvard University Press, 1980.

Fox, James J., and Clifford A. Sather, eds. *Origins, Ancestry and Alliance: Explorations in Austronesian Ethnography*. Canberra: Department of Anthropology, Australian National University, 1996.

Francillon, Gérard. "Incursions upon Wehali: A Modern History of an Ancient Empire." In Fox, *The Flow of Life*, 248–65.

Friedberg, Claudine. "Boiled Woman and Broiled Man: Myths and Agricultural Rituals of the Bunaq of Central Timor." In Fox, *The Flow of Life*, 266–89.

Grainger, Alex. "Alternative Forms of Power in East Timor 1999–2009: A Historical Perspective." PhD thesis, London School of Economics and Political Science, 2014.

Green, Linda. *Fear as a Way of Life: Mayan Widows in Rural Guatemala*. New York: Columbia University Press, 1999.

Greenhouse, Carol J., Elizabeth Mertz, and Kay B. Warren, eds. *Ethnography in Unstable Places: Everyday Lives in Contexts of Dramatic Political Change*. Durham: Duke University Press, 2002.

Gunn, Geoffrey. *Timor Loro Sae: 500 Years*. Macau: Livros do Oriente, 1999.

Gunter, Janet. "Kabita-Kaburai, De Cada Dia: Indigenous Hierarchies and the Portuguese in Timor." In "Parts of Asia," ed. Christiana Bastos, special issue, *Portuguese Literary & Cultural Studies* 17/18 (2010): 281–301.

Hägerdal, Hans. *Lords of the Land, Lords of the Sea: Conflict and Adaptation in Early Colonial Timor, 1600–1800*. Leiden: KITLV Press, 2012.

———. "Colonial Rivalry and the Partition of Timor." *IIAS (International Institute for Asian Studies) Newsletter* 40 (2006): 16.

Halbwachs, Maurice, *On Collective Memory*. Chicago: University of Chicago Press, 1992.

Harrison, Simon. "Forgetful and Memorious Landscapes." *Social Anthropology* 12, no. 2 (2004): 135–51.

Henley, David. "Conflict, Justice, and the Stranger-King Indigenous Roots of Colonial Rule in Indonesia and Elsewhere." *Modern Asian Studies* 38, no. 1 (2004): 85–144.

Henley, David, and Jamie S. Davidson. "In the Name of Adat: Regional Perspectives on Reform, Tradition, and Democracy in Indonesia." *Modern Asian Studies* 42, no. 4 (2008): 815–52.

Hicks, David. *Rhetoric and the Decolonization and Recolonization of East Timor*. London: Routledge, 2014.

———. *A Maternal Religion: The Role of Women in Tetum Myth and Ritual*. Special report, no. 22, Monograph Series on Southeast Asia. DeKalb: Northern Illinois University Center for Southeast Asian Studies, 1984.

———. *Tetum Ghosts and Kin: Fertility and Gender in East Timor*, 2nd ed. Long Grove: Waveland, 2004, first published 1976.

Hill, Helen. *Stirrings of Nationalism in East Timor: FRETILIN 1974–1978. The Origins, Ideologies and Strategies of a Nationalist Movement*. Otford: The Contemporary Otford Press, 2002.

Hirsch, Eric. "Introduction—Landscape: Between Place and Space." In *The Anthropology of Landscape: Perspectives on Place and Space*, ed. Eric Hirsch and Michael O'Hanlon. Oxford: Clarendon Press, 1995, 1–30.

Højer, Lars. "Absent Powers: Magic and Loss in Post-Socialist Mongolia." *Journal of the Royal Anthropological Institute* 15, no. 3 (2009): 575–91.

Hoskins, Janet. "Slaves, Brides and Other 'Gifts': Resistance, Marriage and Rank in Eastern Indonesia." *Slavery and Abolition* 25, no. 2 (2004): 90–107.

———. *Biographical Objects: How Things Tell the Stories of People's Lives*. New York: Routledge, 1998.

———. *Headhunting and the Social Imagination in Southeast Asia*. Stanford: Stanford University Press, 1996.

———. *The Play of Time: Kodi Perspectives on Calendars, History, and Exchange*. Berkeley: University of California Press, 1993.

———. "Doubling Deities, Descent, and Personhood: An Exploration of Kodi Gender Categories." In *Power and Difference: Gender in Island Southeast Asia*, ed. Jane M. Atkinson and Shelly Errington. Stanford: Stanford University Press, 1990, 273–306.

Howell, Signe. "Many Contexts, Many Meanings? Gendered Values among the Northern Lio of Flores Indonesia." *Journal of the Royal Anthropological Institute* 2, no. 2 (1996): 253–69.

———. "The Lio House: Building, Category, Idea, Value." In Carsten and Hugh-Jones, *About the House: Lévi-Strauss and Beyond*, 149–69.

———. "Of Persons and Things: Exchange and Valuables Among the Lio of Eastern Indonesia." *Man* 24, no. 3 (1989): 419–38.

Howell, Signe, and Stephen Sparkes, eds. *The House in Southeast Asia: A Changing Social, Economic and Political Domain*. London: Routledge, 2013.

Hull, Geoffrey. *Standard Tetum-English Dictionary*. 3rd ed. Winston Hills, Australia: Sebastiao Aparicio da Silva Project in association with Instituto Nacional de Linguistica (INL), Timor-Leste, 1999.

Ingold, Timothy. "Rethinking the Animate, Re-animating Thought." *Ethnos* 71, no. 1 (2006): 9–20.

———. *The Perception of the Environment: Essays in Livelihood, Dwelling and Skill*. London: Routledge, 2000.

———. "The Temporality of the Landscape." *World Archaeology* 25, no. 2 (1993): 152–74.

International Crisis Group (ICG). "Resolving Timor-Leste's Crisis." *Asia Report*, no. 120 (2006).

Irvine, Judith. "Ideologies of Honorific Language." *Pragmatics* 2, no. 3 (1992): 251–62.

Jolliffe, Jill. *East Timor: Nationalism and Colonialism*. Queensland: University of Queensland Press, 1978.

Kahn, Joel S. *Southeast Asian Identities: Culture and Politics of Representation in Indonesia, Malaysia, Singapore and Thailand*. Singapore: Institute of Southeast Asian Studies, 1995.

Kammen, Douglas. "Fragments of Utopia: Popular Yearnings in East Timor." *Journal of Southeast Asian Studies* 40, no. 2 (2009): 385–408.

———. "Master-Slave, Traitor-Nationalist, Opportunist-Oppressed: Political Metaphors in East Timor." *Indonesia* 76 (October 2003): 69–85.

Keane, Webb. *Christian Moderns: Freedom and Fetish in the Mission Encounter*. Berkeley: University of California Press, 2007.

———. *Signs of Recognition: Powers and Hazards of Representation in an Indonesian Society*. Berkeley: University of California Press, 1997.

Kiernan, Ben. "The Demography of Genocide in Southeast Asia: The Death Tolls in Cambodia, 1975–79, and East Timor, 1975–80." *Critical Asian Studies* 35, no. 4 (2003): 585–97.

Kingsbury, Damien, and Michael Leach. *East Timor: Beyond Independence*. Melbourne: Monash University Press, 2007.

Kipp, Rita Smith, and Susan Rodgers, eds. *Indonesian Religions in Transition*. Tucson: University of Arizona Press, 1987.

Kirksey, Eben. *Freedom in Entangled Worlds: West Papua and the Architecture of Global Power*. Durham: Duke University Press, 2012.

Kirsch, Stuart. *Reverse Anthropology: Indigenous Analysis of Social and Environmental Relations in New Guinea*. Stanford: Stanford University Press, 2006.

Kleinman, Arthur, Veena Das, and Margaret Lock, eds. *Social Suffering: Essays*. Berkeley: University of California Press, 1997.

Kuipers, Joël C. *Language, Identity and Marginality in Indonesia: The Changing Nature of Ritual Speech on the Island of Sumba*. Cambridge: Cambridge University Press, 1998.

———. *Power in Performance: The Creation of Textual Authority in Weyewa Ritual Speech*. Philadelphia: University of Pennsylvania Press, 1990.

———. "Talking About Troubles: Gender Differences in Weyewa Ritual Speech Use." In *Power and Difference: Gender in Island Southeast Asia*, ed. Jane M.

Atkinson and Shelly Errington. Stanford: Stanford University Press, 1990, 153–75.

Kwon, Heonik. *Ghosts of War in Vietnam*. Studies in the Social and Cultural History of Modern Warfare, No. 27. Cambridge: Cambridge University Press, 2008.

———. *After the Massacre: Commemoration and Consolation in Ha My and My Lai*. Berkeley: University of California Press, 2006.

Latour, Bruno. *We Have Never Been Modern*. London: Harvester Wheatsheaf, 1993.

Leach, James. "Leaving the Magic Out: Knowledge and Effect in Different Places." In "Recognising and Translating Knowledge," ed. James Leach and Richard Davis, special issue, *Anthropological Forum* 22, no. 3 (2012): 251–70.

Lévi-Strauss, Claude. *The Way of the Masks*. Trans. Sylvia Modelski. Seattle: University of Washington Press, 1982.

Lincoln, Bruce. *Death, War, and Sacrifice: Studies in Ideology and Practice*. Chicago: The University of Chicago Press, 1991.

Loch, Alexander. *Haus, Handy & Halleluja. Psychosoziale Rekonstruktion in Osttimor. Eine Ethnopsychologische Studie zur Postkonfliktuösen Dynamik im Spannungsfeld von Identität, Trauma, Kultur und Entwicklung*. Frankfurt: IKO, Verlag für Interkulturelle Kommunikation, 2007.

Martinkus, John. *A Dirty Little War*. Sydney: Random House Australia, 2001.

Mamdani, Mahmood. *When Victims Become Killers: Colonialism, Nativism, and the Genocide in Rwanda*. Princeton: Princeton University Press, 2001.

Marchand, Trevor H. J. Preface and introduction to "Making Knowledge," ed. Trevor H. J. Marchand, special issue, *Journal of the Royal Anthropological Institute* 16, no. 1 (2010): iii–v, 1–21.

Mauss, Marcel. "Body Techniques." In *Sociology and Psychology*, ed. Marcel Mauss. London: Routledge and Kegan Paul, 1979, 79–123.

Maybury-Lewis, David, and Uri Almagor, eds. *The Attraction of Opposites: Thought and Society in a Dualistic Mode*. Ann Arbor: University of Michigan Press, 1989.

McKinnon, Susan. *From a Shattered Sun: Hierarchy, Gender, and Alliance in the Tanimbar Islands*. Madison: University of Wisconsin Press, 1991.

McWilliam, Andrew. "Diasporas: New Fataluku Diasporas and Landscapes of Remittance and Return." *Local-Global: Identity, Security, Community* 11 (2012): 72–85.

———. "Exchange and Resilience in Timor-Leste." *Journal of the Royal Anthropological Institute* 17, no. 4 (2011): 745–63.

———. "Fataluku Living Landscapes." In McWilliam and Traube, *Land and Life in Timor-Leste*, 61–82.

———. "Fataluku Healing and Cultural Resilience in East Timor." *Ethnos* 73, no. 2 (2008): 217–40.

———. "Houses of Resistance in East Timor: Structuring Sociality in the New Nation 1." *Anthropological Forum* 15, no. 1 (2005): 27–44.

———. *Paths of Origin, Gates of Life: A Study of Place and Precedence in Southwest Timor*. Verhandelingen van het Koninklijk Instituut voor Taal-, Land- en Volkenkunde, vol. 202. Leiden: KITLV Press, 2002.

McWilliam, Andrew, and Elizabeth G. Traube, eds. *Land and Life in Timor-Leste: Ethnographic Essays*. Canberra: ANU E-Press, 2011.

Meierhenrich, Jens. "The Transformation of Lieux de Mémoire: The Nyabarongo River in Rwanda, 1992–2009." *Anthropology Today* 25, no. 5 (2009): 13–19.

Meitzner Yoder, Laura S. "Tensions of Tradition: Making and Remaking Claims to Land in the Oecusse Enclave." In McWilliam and Traube, *Land and Life in Timor-Leste*, 187–216.

Myrttinen, Henri. "Phantom Menaces: The Politics of Rumour, Securitisation and Masculine Identities in the Shadows of the Ninjas." In "Engaging Processes of Sense-Making and Negotiation in Contemporary Timor-Leste," ed. Angie Bexley and Maj Nygaard-Christensen, special issue, *The Asia Pacific Journal of Anthropology* 14, no. 5 (2013): 471–85.

Navaro-Yashin, Yael. *The Make-Believe Space: Affective Geography in a Postwar Polity*. Durham: Duke University Press, 2012.

Neves, Guteriano Nicolao S. "The Paradox of Aid in Timor-Leste." Paper presented at Cooperação Internacional e a Construção do Estado no Timor-Leste, University of Brasilia, Brazil, July 25–28, 2006.

Nevins, Joseph. *A Not-So-Distant Horror: Mass Violence in East Timor*. Ithaca: Cornell University Press, 2005.

National Statistics Directorate (NSD) and United Nations Population Fund (UNFPA). *Population and Housing Census of Timor-Leste 2010*. Dili: NSD and UNFPA, 2011.

———. *Timor-Leste Census of Population and Housing 2004*. Dili: NSD and UNFPA, 2006.

Nygaard-Christensen, Maj. "Negotiating Indonesia: Political Genealogies of Timorese Democracy." In "Engaging Processes of Sense-Making and Negotiation in Contemporary Timor-Leste," ed. Angie Bexley and Maj Nygaard-Christensen, special issue, *The Asia Pacific Journal of Anthropology* 14, no. 5 (2013): 423–37.

———. "The Rebel and the Diplomat: Revolutionary Spirits, Sacred Legitimation and Democracy in Timor–Leste." In *Varieties of Secularism in Southeast Asia: Anthropological Explorations of Religion, Politics and the Spiritual*, ed. Nils Bubandt and Martjn van Beek. London: Routledge, 2012, 209–29.

Nygaard-Christensen, Maj, and Angie Bexley. Introduction to *Doing Fieldwork in Timor-Leste*. Copenhagen: Nias Press, forthcoming.

Palmer, Lisa, and Demetrio do Amaral de Carvalho. "Nation Building and Resource Management: The Politics of 'Nature' in Timor–Leste." *Geoforum* 39 (2008): 1321–32.

Pannell, Sandra. "Welcome to the Hotel Tutuala: Fataluku Accounts of Going Places in an Immobile World." *The Asia Pacific Journal of Anthropology* 7, no. 3 (2006): 203–19.

Pedersen, Morten A. "Totemism, Animism and North Asian Indigenous Ontologies." *Journal of the Royal Anthropological Institute* 7, no. 3 (2001): 411–27.

Pélissier, René. *Timor en Guerre: Le Crocodile et les Portugais, 1847–1913*. Orgeval: René Pélissier, 1996.

Pemberton, John. *On the Subject of "Java."* Ithaca: Cornell University Press, 1994.

Pietsch, Samuel. "The Deputy-Sheriff Warns his Apurs: Australia's Military Intervention in East Timor, 1999." PhD thesis, Australian National University, 2009.

Pinto, Constancio, and Matthew Jardine. *East Timor's Unfinished Struggle: Inside the Timorese Resistance*. Boston: South End Press, 1997.

Población, Enrique Alonso, and Alberto Fidalgo Castro. "Webs of Legitimacy and Discredit: Narrative Capital and Politics of Ritual in a Timor-Leste Community." *Anthropological Forum* 24, no. 3 (2014): 245–66.

Povinelli, Elizabeth. *The Cunning of Recognition: Indigenous Alterities in the Making of Multiculturalism*. Durham: Duke University Press, 2002.

Rees, Edward. *Under Pressure: Falintil-Forças de Defesa de Timor Leste, Three Decades of Defence Force Development in Timor Leste: 1975–2004*. Geneva: Geneva Centre for the Democratic Control of Armed Forces (DCAF), 2004.

Reuter, Thomas. "Land and Territory in the Austronesian World." In *Sharing the Earth, Dividing the Land: Land and Territory in the Austronesian World*, ed. Thomas Reuter. Canberra: ANU E-Press, 2006, 11–38.

Ricoeur, Paul. *Histoire et Vérité*. Paris: Le Seuil, 1955.

Robinson, Geoffrey. *"If You Leave Us Here, We Will Die": How Genocide Was Stopped in East Timor*. Princeton: Princeton University Press, 2009.

———. *East Timor 1999: Crimes against Humanity*. Report commissioned by the United Nations Office of the High Commissioner for Human Rights (OHCHR), July 2003. Jakarta, Indonesia, and Dili: HAK Association & Institute for Policy Research and Advocacy, 2006.

Roque, Ricardo. *Headhunting and Colonialism: Anthropology and the Circulation of Human Skulls in the Portuguese Empire, 1870–1930*. New York: Palgrave Macmillan, 2010.

Ross, Fiona. *Bearing Witness: Women and the Truth and Reconciliation Commission in South Africa*. London: Pluto Press, 2003.

Rutherford, Danilyn. *Raiding the Land of the Foreigners: The Limits of the Nation on an Indonesian Frontier*. Princeton: Princeton University Press, 2003.

Sahlins, Marshall. "The Stranger-King or, Elementary Forms of the Politics of Life." In "Stranger Kings in Indonesia and Beyond," ed. Ian Caldwell and David Henley, special issue, *Indonesia and the Malay World* 36, no. 105 (2008): 177–99.

Sakti, Victoria K. "'Thinking Too Much': Tracing Local Patterns of Emotional Distress after Mass Violence in Timor-Leste." In "Engaging Processes of Sense-Making and Negotiation in Contemporary Timor-Leste," ed. Angie Bexley and Maj Nygaard-Christensen, special issue, *The Asia Pacific Journal of Anthropology* 14, no. 5 (2013): 438–545.

Schama, Simon. *Landscape and Memory*. New York: Vintage Books, 1995.

Schlicher, Monika. *Portugal in Ost-Timor: Eine Kritische Untersuchung zur Portugiesischen Kolonialgeschichte in Ost-Timor: 1850 bis 1912*. Hamburg: Abera-Verlag Meyer, 1996.

Schramm, Katharina. Introduction to "Landscapes of Violence: Memory and Sacred Space," ed. Katharina Schramm, special issue, *History & Memory* 23, no. 1 (2011): 5–22.

Schrauwers, Albert. "Through a Glass Darkly: Charity, Conspiracy, and Power in New Order Indonesia." In *Transparency and Conspiracy: Ethnographies of Suspicion in the New World Order*, ed. Harry G. West and Todd Sanders, 125–47. Durham: Duke University Press, 2003.

Schrempp, Gregory A. *Magical Arrows: the Maori, the Greeks, and the Folklore of the Universe*. Madison: University of Wisconsin Press, 1992.

Schulte Nordholt, Herman G. *The Political System of the Atoni of Timor*. Trans. Maria J. L. van Yperen. Verhandelingen van het Koninklijk Instituut voor Taal-, Land- en Volkenkunde, vol. 60. The Hague: Martinus Nijhoff, 1971.

Scott, Michael W. "Proto-People and Precedence: Encompassing Euroamericans through Narratives of 'First Contact' in Solomon Islands." In Stewart and Strathern, *Exchange and Sacrifice*, 141–76.

———. *The Severed Snake: Matrilineages, Making Place, and a Melanesian Christianity in Southeast Solomon Islands*. Durham: Carolina Academic Press, 2007.

Sell, Hans Joachim. *Der schlimme Tod bei den Völkern Indonesiens*. The Hague: 'S Gravenhage, Mouton & Co., 1955.

Silva, Kelly da. "Negotiating Tradition and Nation: Mediations and Mediators in the Making of Urban Timor-Leste." In "Engaging Processes of Sense-Making and Negotiation in Contemporary Timor-Leste," ed. Angie Bexley and Maj Nygaard-Christensen, special issue, *The Asia Pacific Journal of Anthropology* 14, no. 5 (2013): 455–70.

Spyer, Patricia. "Diversity with a Difference: Adat and the New Order in Aru (Eastern Indonesia)." *Cultural Anthropology* 11, no. 1 (1996): 25–50.

Stewart, Pamela J., and Andrew Strathern, eds. *Exchange and Sacrifice*. Durham: Carolina Academic Press, 2008.

Strathern, Andrew, and Pamela J. Stewart. "Introduction: Aligning Words, Aligning Worlds." In Stewart and Strathern, *Exchange and Sacrifice*, xi–xxxvi.

———. *The Python's Back: Pathways of Comparison between Indonesia and Melanesia.* Westport, CT: Greenwood Publishing Group, 2000.

Strathern, Marilyn. *The Gender of the Gift: Problems with Women and Problems with Society in Melanesia.* Los Angeles: University of California Press, 1988.

Taylor, Christopher C. *Sacrifice as Terror: The Rwandan Genocide of 1994.* Oxford: Berg, 2001.

Taylor, John G. *East Timor: The Price of Freedom.* London: Zed Books, 1999.

Therik, Tom. *Wehali: The Female Land: Traditions of a Timorese Ritual Centre.* Canberra: Australian National University / Pandanus Books, 2004.

Traube, Elizabeth G. "Planting the Flag." In McWilliam and Traube, *Land and Life in Timor-Leste,* 117–40.

———. "Unpaid Wages: Local Narratives and the Imagination of the Nation." *The Asia Pacific Journal of Anthropology* 8, no. 1 (2007): 9–25.

———. "Obligations to the Source." In Maybury-Lewis and Almagor, *The Attraction of Opposites,* 321–44.

———. *Cosmology and Social Life: Ritual Exchange among the Mambai of East Timor.* Chicago: University of Chicago Press, 1986.

Trinidade, José, and Bryant Castro. *Rethinking Timorese Identity as a Peacebuilding Strategy: The Lorosa'e-Loromonu Conflict from a Traditional Perspective.* Report funded by the European Union and implemented by the Deutsche Gesellschaft für Technische Zusammenarbeit (GTZ). Dili, Timor-Leste, 2007.

Trinidade, José "Josh." "*Lulik*: The Core of Timorese Values." Paper presented at 3rd Timor-Leste Study Association (TLSA) Conference, Dili, June 30, 2011.

Tsing, Anna Lowenhaupt. *In the Realm of the Diamond Queen: Marginality in an Out-of-the-Way Place.* Princeton: Princeton University Press, 1993.

Tyson, Adam D. *Decentralization and Adat Revivalism in Indonesia: The Politics of Becoming Indigenous.* Abingdon: Routledge, 2010.

United Nations Development Programme (UNDP). *Timor-Leste Human Development Report 2006: The Path out of Poverty, Integrated Rural Development.* Darwin and Dili: United Nations Development Programme, 2006.

Valeri, Valerio. "Buying Women But Not Selling Them: Gift and Commodity Exchange in Huaulu Alliance." *Man* 29, no. 1 (1994): 1–26.

———. "Reciprocal Centres: The Siwa-Lima System in the Central Moluccas." In Maybury-Lewis and Almagor, *The Attraction of Opposites*, 117–41.

Verdery, Katherine. *The Political Lives of Dead Bodies: Reburial and Postsocialist Change.* New York: Columbia University Press, 1999.

Vischer, Michael P, ed. *Precedence: Social Differentiation in the Austronesian World.* Canberra: ANU E-Press, 2009.

Viveiros de Castro, Eduardo. "Cosmological Deixis and Amerindian Perspectivism." *Journal of the Royal Anthropological Institute* 4 (1998): 469–88.

Waterson, Roxana. "Houses and Hierarchies in Island Southeast Asia." In Carsten and Hugh-Jones, *About the House: Lévi-Strauss and Beyond*, 47–68.

West, Harry G., and Todd Sanders. "Introduction: Power Revealed and Concealed in the New World Order." In *Transparency and Conspiracy: Ethnographies of Suspicion in the New World Order*, ed. Harry G. West and Todd Sanders. Durham: Duke University Press, 2003, 1–38.

Willerslev, Rane. *Soul Hunters: Hunting, Animism, and Personhood among the Siberian Yukaghirs.* Berkeley: University of California Press, 2007.

———. "Not Animal, Not *Not*-Animal: Hunting, Imitation and Empathetic Knowledge among the Siberian Yukaghirs," *Journal of the Royal Anthropological Institute* 10, no. 3 (2004), 629–52.

Wilson, Richard A. *The Politics of Truth and Reconciliation in South Africa: Legitimizing the Post–Apartheid State.* Cambridge: Cambridge University Press, 2001.

van Wouden, Franciscus A. E. *Types of Social Structure in Eastern Indonesia.* Trans. Rodney Needham. The Hague: Martinus Nijhoff, 1968. First published 1935 by Universiteitsboekhandel en Antiquariaat J. Ginsberg.

Wurm, Stephen A., and Shirô Hattori. *Language Atlas of the Pacific Area.* Canberra: Australian Academy of the Humanities in collaboration with the Japan Academy, 1981.

Yoder, Laura Meitzner. "Custom, Codification and Collaboration: Integrating the Legacies of Land and Forest Authorities in Oecusse Enclave, East Timor." PhD thesis, Yale University, 2005.

Zola [Antonio Pádua Correia]. *Quatorze Annos de Timor.* Dili: [self-published], 1909.

Zur, Judith. *Violent Memories: Mayan War Widows in Guatemala.* Boulder: Westview Press, 1998.

INDEX

SOUTHEAST ASIA PROGRAM PUBLICATIONS
Cornell University

Selected Titles on Indonesia

Cornell Modern Indonesia Project Publications

Number 77   *Beyond Oligarchy: Wealth, Power, and Contemporary Indonesian Politics,*
             ed. Michele Ford and Thomas B. Pepinsky. 2014. ISBN 978-0-87727-
             303-5 (pb.)

Number 76   *Producing Indonesia: The State of the Field of Indonesian Studies,* ed. Eric
             Tagliacozzo. 2014. ISBN 978-0-87727-302-8 (pb.)

Studies on Southeast Asia

Number 59   *The Politics of Timor-Leste: Democratic Consolidation after Intervention,*
             ed. Michael Leach and Damien Kingsbury. 2013.
             ISBN 978-0-87727-759-0 (pb.)

Number 50   *State of Authority: The State in Society in Indonesia,* ed. Gerry van
             Klinken and Joshua Barker. 2009. ISBN 978-0-87727-750-7 (pb.)

Number 48   *Dependent Communities: Aid and Politics in Cambodia and East Timor,*
             Caroline Hughes. 2009. ISBN 978-0-87727-748-4 (pb.)

Number 45   *Conflict, Violence, and Displacement in Indonesia,* ed. Eva-Lotta E.
             Hedman. 2008. ISBN 978-0-87727-745-3 (pb).

Number 44   *Friends and Exiles: A Memoir of the Nutmeg Isles and the Indonesian
             Nationalist Movement,* Des Alwi, ed. Barbara S. Harvey. 2008.
             ISBN 978-0-877277-44-6 (pb).

Number 40   *Laskar Jihad: Islam, Militancy, and the Quest for Identity in Post-New Order
             Indonesia,* Noorhaidi Hasan. 2006. 266 pp. ISBN 0-877277-40-0 (pb).

Number 39   *The Indonesian Supreme Court: A Study of Institutional Collapse,*
             Sebastiaan Pompe. 2005. 494 pp. ISBN 0-877277-38-9 (pb).

Number 35   *Nationalism and Revolution in Indonesia,* George McTurnan Kahin, intro.
             Benedict R. O'G. Anderson (reprinted from 1952 edition, Cornell
             University Press, with permission). 2003. 530 pp. ISBN 0-87727-734-6.

Number 34   *Golddiggers, Farmers, and Traders in the "Chinese Districts" of West
             Kalimantan, Indonesia,* Mary Somers Heidhues. 2003. 316 pp.
             ISBN 0-87727-733-8.

Number 30   *Violence and the State in Suharto's Indonesia,* ed. Benedict R. O'G.
             Anderson. 2001. Second printing, 2002. 247 pp. ISBN 0-87727-729-X.

Number 28   *The Hadrami Awakening: Community and Identity in the Netherlands East
             Indies, 1900-1942,* Natalie Mobini-Kesheh. 1999. 174 pp.
             ISBN 0-87727-727-3.

Number 27   *Tales from Djakarta: Caricatures of Circumstances and their Human Beings,*
             Pramoedya Ananta Toer. 1999. 145 pp. ISBN 0-87727-726-5.

Number 25   *Figures of Criminality in Indonesia, the Philippines, and Colonial Vietnam,* ed. Vicente L. Rafael. 1999. 259 pp. ISBN 0-87727-724-9.

Number 22   *Young Heroes: The Indonesian Family in Politics,* Saya S. Shiraishi. 1997. 183 pp. ISBN 0-87727-721-4.

Number 20   *Making Indonesia,* ed. Daniel S. Lev, Ruth McVey. 1996. 201 pp. ISBN 0-87727-719-2.

Number 17   *The Vernacular Press and the Emergence of Modern Indonesian Consciousness,* Ahmat Adam. 1995. 220 pp. ISBN 0-87727-716-8.

Number 14   *Sjahrir: Politics and Exile in Indonesia,* Rudolf Mrázek. 1994. 536 pp. ISBN 0-87727-713-3.

Number 13   *Fair Land Sarawak: Some Recollections of an Expatriate Officer,* Alastair Morrison. 1993. 196 pp. ISBN 0-87727-712-5.

Number 8   *The Politics of Colonial Exploitation: Java, the Dutch, and the Cultivation System,* Cornelis Fasseur, ed. R. E. Elson, trans. R. E. Elson, Ary Kraal. 1992. 2nd printing 1994. 266 pp. ISBN 0-87727-707-9.

Number 7   *A Malay Frontier: Unity and Duality in a Sumatran Kingdom,* Jane Drakard. 1990. 2nd printing 2003. 215 pp. ISBN 0-87727-706-0.

SEAP Series

Number 21   *Securing a Place: Small-Scale Artisans in Modern Indonesia,* Elizabeth Morrell. 2005. 220 pp. ISBN 0-877271-39-9.

Number 16   *Cutting across the Lands: An Annotated Bibliography on Natural Resource Management and Community Development in Indonesia, the Philippines, and Malaysia,* ed. Eveline Ferretti. 1997. 329 pp. ISBN 0-87727-133-X.

Number 7   *Intellectual Property and US Relations with Indonesia, Malaysia, Singapore, and Thailand,* Elisabeth Uphoff. 1991. 67 pp. ISBN 0-87727-124-0.

Language Texts

INDONESIAN

Beginning Indonesian through Self-Instruction, John U. Wolff, Dédé Oetomo, Daniel Fietkiewicz. 3rd revised edition 1992. Vol. 1. 115 pp. ISBN 0-87727-529-7. Vol. 2. 434 pp. ISBN 0-87727-530-0. Vol. 3. 473 pp. ISBN 0-87727-531-9.

Indonesian Readings, John U. Wolff. 1978. 4th printing 1992. 480 pp. ISBN 0-87727-517-3

Indonesian Conversations, John U. Wolff. 1978. 3rd printing 1991. 297 pp. ISBN 0-87727-516-5

Formal Indonesian, John U. Wolff. 2nd revised edition 1986. 446 pp. ISBN 0-87727-515-7

To order, please contact:

Cornell University Press Services
750 Cascadilla Street
PO Box 6525
Ithaca, NY 14851 USA

Phone: 607 277 2211 or 800 666 2211 (US, Canada)
Fax: 607 277 6292 or 800 688 2877 (US, Canada)
SEAP.einaudi.cornell.edu/publications

Lightning Source UK Ltd.
Milton Keynes UK
UKHW030727260822
407817UK00009B/666